Is South China Sea a New Flesh Point of 21st Century

Is South China Sea a New Flesh Point of 21st Century

Dr. S. Chandra

PRASHANT PUBLISHING HOUSE
DELHI-110094

Published by :
Prashant Publishing House
C-34, 28 Foota Road, Gali-3,
West Karwal Nagar, Delhi-110094
Phone : 011-22963970, Mob. : 9810396373
e-mail.: prashantpublishinghouse@gmail.com

Is South China Sea a New Flesh Point of 21st Century

First Published 2019

ISBN 978-81-938012-9-1

PRINTED IN INDIA
Published by Mr. R.K. Jha M/s Prashant Publishing House and Published at H.S. Offset House Press, Delhi.

Contents

	Preface	*(vii)*
1.	Introduction	1
2.	The South China Sea: Flashpoint of the Asia	19
3.	South China Sea Conflict and Troubled Waters	60
4.	South China Sea : The 21st Century's Leading Flashpoint	78
5.	South China Sea: The State of Crisis and Setting the Stage for Flashpoint	123
6.	The Real Secret of the South China Sea Conflicts	148
7.	China and Japan: Sea Islands on the Frontline of a New International Flashpoint	168
8.	South China Sea Dispute and China's Window of Opportunity	202
9.	Great Powers, Grand Strategies: The Fresh Game in the South China Sea	228
10.	Dispute and Objectives of the South China Sea	265
	Bibliography	295
	Index	298

Preface

The recent upsurge in tensions in the South China Sea represents a security flashpoint with global consequences. The South China Sea is a strategic maritime link and a vital gateway for shipping in East Asia. While it is economically and strategically an integrated entity and a key region for the emerging economies of the Asia-Pacific, many countries have staked a sovereign claim over its waters and islands. The dispute has the potential to turn into a military conflict that could end up affecting the peace and security of the entire region.

The South China Sea is and will continue to be the ultimate geopolitical flashpoint of the young 21st century – way ahead of the Middle East or Russia's western borderlands. No less than the future of Asia – as well as the East-West balance of power – is at stake.

Furthermore, the United States provides the region with an alternative, and a form of protection, against potential Chinese economic and political domination. This has led to a strengthening of ties between the United States and many of its traditional allies in the region, while helping to promote closer ties with former rivals such as Indonesia, Vietnam and Myanmar. Finally, the US' recent pivot towards Asia is likely to continue as the Pacific region has emerged as the world's most important economic and political region, replacing the North Atlantic in this role.

For China, Southeast Asia is often viewed as a region that is entirely within China's sphere of influence and many Chinese leaders believe that this entitles their country to play the leading role in this region. However, this assumption has led China to take a hard line towards defending and reinforcing its claims to the vast majority of the South China Sea, a body of water in which five Southeast Asian countries also have maritime claims. This Chinese assertiveness, together with China's rising economic power, has led many Southeast Asian countries to determine that it is not in their best interest to allow China to dominate the region. Thus, many countries in the region are looking to outside powers such as the US, India or Japan to play a greater role in Southeast Asia. This is a key reason why Myanmar has moved quickly to expand its political and security ties with these outside powers at the expense of its once close ties with China.

The South China Sea (SCS) issue has now arrived at a critical point. China should take the advantages of this opportunity to adjust its South China Sea approach – to steer from a "unilateral win" formula to "multilateral win" formula, so as to take lead in the problem-solving process. This new approach should drive the South China Sea problem-solving process to a faster track, in the process clearing out major obstacles to building a Southeast Asian hub for the 21st Century Maritime Silk Road (MSR).

Based on different opinions regarding sovereignty over islands and reefs and maritime interests and rights, the claimant parties in the South China Sea can be divided into two groups: mainland China and Taiwan, and the four ASEAN claimants (Vietnam, the Philippines, Malaysia, and Brunei). The majority of the ASEAN non-claimants, along with some outsiders — led by European countries, the United States, Japan and Australia — tend to support the claims made by the ASEAN claimants, whereas a minority of the ASEAN non-claimants, Russia, South Korea, and some other outsiders stand neutral. Although there also are some disputes between the ASEAN claimants themselves, for the moment these disputes are considered "minor" in the face of their mutual confrontation with China.

This is a reference book. All the matter is just compiled and edited in nature, taken from the various sources which are in public domain.

This book will definitely prove to be a boon to teachers, students and research scholars.

—*Editor*

1

Introduction

One of the most dangerous confrontations between the United States and China is heating up. Warships are being deployed, bombers are taking wing and threats are being exchanged — all of it sparked by China's growing mastery of the use of the world's most overlooked natural resource: Sand. The point of contention is a set of man-made islands China has built in a strategic and hotly-disputed patch of the South China Sea. It's one of the world's busiest shipping routes, and home to some 10 per cent of the world's fish. What's more, billions of barrels of oil and trillions of cubic feet of natural gas lie under the sea floor.

So it's no surprise that virtually every country in the region — China, Taiwan, Vietnam, Brunei, Malaysia and the Philippines — lays at least partial claim to a scattering of dozens of rocks and reefs called the Spratly Islands that sit strategically in that area.

But China has expanded its claims in the sea for decades, including some Spratly outcrops that it seized from Vietnam in a 1988 clash that left dozens of soldiers dead. And, particularly since 2014, it has used its industrial might to create facts in the water.

Two years have passed since the Permanent Court of Arbitration (PCA) gave its landmark ruling on the South China Sea dispute that could have been the template for a rule-based maritime order and a basis for determining a country's claim to the Exclusive Economic Zone (EEZ) and territorial waters.

FACTS IN THE WATER

In recent years, China has built up an armada of oceangoing dredging ships, among the most technologically advanced in the world. The country's annual dredging capacity — the volume of sand and muck it can haul up from underwater — has more than tripled since 2000, to more than one billion cubic meters. That's more than any other nation.

Starting in late 2013, Beijing set a fleet of these dredgers to work raising millions of tonnes of sand from the sea floor and using it to firm its pieces of territory in the Spratly Islands. Within 18 months, these ships built nearly 3,000 acres of new land.

This type of megascale land reclamation is increasingly common. In recent decades, advancing technology has made it easier and cheaper to move ever greater quantities of sand from ever greater depths and deliver it with ever greater accuracy onto predetermined places. The biggest dredges today are more than 700 feet long. Stood on end, they would top a 60-storey apartment building.

They carry pipes that can pull up sand from 500 feet below the water's surface. Countries from Singapore to the Netherlands are using them to expand their coastlines and even build new islands from scratch. China has done the same. In 2015 alone it created the equivalent of two Manhattans of new real estate. All told, according to a Dutch research group, human beings since 1985 have added 5,237 square miles (8,428 square km) of artificial land to the world's coasts — an area about as big as Connecticut or the nation of Jamaica.

MILITARY AMBITIONS

But of even greater concern is how China's island-building is serving its military ambitions. Almost as soon as the sand was dry on the Spratlys, China began building military bases. Beijing's armed forces have installed anti-missile weaponry, runways capable of handling military aircraft, structures that US officials believe are designed to house long-range missile launchers, and port facilities that may be capable of accommodating nuclear submarines.

This expansion of China's military power in the Pacific is an intensifying flash point between China, the US and its Pacific allies. At his confirmation hearings to become US secretary of state, Rex Tillerson compared China's Spratly build-up to Russia's invasion of Crimea.

In recent weeks, the US has flown B-52s over, and sailed two warships past, the disputed archipelago. For its part, China landed a long-range bomber on one of the newly-made islands. In June, US Defence Secretary Jim Mattis denounced China's build-up as "intimidation and coercion".

Chinese President Xi Jinping responded that "we cannot lose even one inch of (our) territory". All of which shows that in the 21st century, geopolitical power goes beyond who controls the territory.

CHINA'S COMPREHENSIVE POLICY IN THE SOUTH CHINA SEA

To seize the right to the actual control over the South China Sea in accordance with the U-shaped claim, China has enhanced its considerable presence inside this line with the comprehensive access by expanding not only its military operation, but paramilitary and civilian activities in the region as well.

Militarily, China is intensifying its army building, particularly the modernization of its naval force with the construction of the naval base in Sanya (Hainan) that plays the role as a door to advance towards the South China Sea. To send a deterrence message to other claimants in the South China Sea, China has intensified the frequency and the degree of coordination by launching its naval exercises in the South China Sea. The most important event happened in July 2010 when the navy of the People's Liberation Army (PLA) for the first time mobilized at least 12 modern warships from three fleets (the North Sea Fleet, the East Sea Fleet and the South Sea Fleet) to launch the large-scale joint naval exercises in the

South China Sea. In terms of the paramilitary force, China has deployed in the South China Sea the patrol boats from different law enforcement forces. In certain period of time, this country has unilaterally banned the fishing activities from May to August (imposed every year since 1999); the maritime law enforcement of China have many times seized the Vietnamese fishermen, confiscated their fishing boats and demanded the fines from USD 8,000 to USD 10,000 for the release of the Vietnamese fishermen. In early April 2010, China even announced its sending big fishing vessels to the (Sprealy) Archipellago to protect its fishing boats and it is increasing the number and advancing far to the South. This is the first time, China has done it, apart from its unilateral banning of fishing. On June 23, 2010, the fishing vessel 311 of China had aimed its big machine gun at a vessel of Indonesia and threatened to attack this vessel when a Chinese fishing boat was seized by the Indonesian force in the area inside Indonesia's exclusive economic zone in the Natuna Archipellago.

On the diplomatic front, China's consistent strategy of the South China Sea is to have only the bilateral negotiation with the smaller claimant countries and obstructed the efforts of multi-lateralizing and internationalizing the issue, especially any effort of interference on the US part. The Chinese Foreign Minister once warned that the multi-lateralization and internationalization of the South China Sea issue "will only worsen and make the settlement of the issue more difficult."

In terms of the energy exploitation in the South China Sea, in early summer of 2007, China threatened that a number of foreign oil and gas companies should stop their exploratory activities in the sea with their Vietnamese partner or they had to face the unpredictable consequences in their doing business with China.

On the one hand, China lodged its protest against the energy exploiting activities in the areas inside the U-shaped line; on the other hand, it supported the idea of joint exploitation of the energy resources inside this line in the South China Sea. In principle, other claimants did not protest against the concept of joint exploitation; however, how to determine clearly the acceptable area for the joint exploitation project remained one of the hardest nuts to crack in putting the idea into reality. ASEAN claimant States will surely not accept any suggestions from China concerning the agreement to the joint exploitation inside the exclusive economic zones and continental shelves they had declared, the areas 500 nautical miles or even 700 nautical miles from Hainan Island. The ASEAN claimant countries were ready to cooperate with foreign partners, including Chinese partners, with one condition that their right to sovereignty must be respected. As it is proved in the 2005 Agreement on the Joint Marine Seismic Survey in the South China Sea between the National Oil and Gas Groups of China, the Philippines and Vietnam, the Philippines had to postpone the extension of the agreement because of the domestic protest against the government's concession of the Philippine sovereignty by allowing the area of the joint exploitation project to overlap the country's exclusive economic zone.

A number of reasons help explain why China returns to its decisive access in the South China Sea in recent years. First of all, with its impressive economic growth in consecutive decades, China has accumulated its economic and military strength to a degree that allows this country to become more decisive in its treatment to the foreign parties, especially in and after the 2008-2009 global financial crises. Secondly, the relative stability in the relations between China and Taiwan in recent years has allowed China to shift its priorities, potentials and resources to other external issues, particularly the South China Sea issue. Thirdly, the rise of nationalism together with the ever bigger activities and role of the PLA as well as the ever constantly increasing competition between different interests groups within the internal affairs of China (the competition between the legal executive agencies, the energy groups and the coastal provinces) have complicated the process of planning and implementation of China's policy on the South China Sea. Fourthly, the move of the other claimants in the South China Sea has also forced China to have its reaction; however, its reaction is very excessive. Fifthly, the shortage of an effective mechanism to control the dispute in the South China Sea, especially the adjustment of the parties' treatment (including China) has created conditions for China to follow its decisive standpoint.

The Way of Getting Suppler Access after the ARF-17

China's ever more decisiveness in the South China Sea in recent years has caused worries to the ASEAN States, thus creating opportunities to the US "to return" Asia. In 2010, for the first time in an informal meeting of the ASEAN Regional Forum (ARF), US Secretary of State Hillary Clinton made a long speech, high lighting the US standpoint in the South China Sea issue. The speech declares that the US has it national interests, among other things, to the free navigation and the right to get access to the common sea space in Asia and the respect of international law in the South China Sea.

The US ever more increasing involvement in the South China Sea and the intensified cooperation between the US and the ASEAN States after the ARF-17 in July 2010 in Hanoi seem making influence on China's calculations. Especially, Ms Clinton's eloquent speech together with the response from a lot of other States at the ARF-17 had caused an internal debate in China about China's wisdom of elevating the "South China Sea" to be "core interest". Some military strategists and scholars held that the inclusion of the South China Sea into the national core interest group of China, at least in this stage, "is not a wise step". They judged that this claim would "cause a nuisance and annoyance to the US" and possibly "cause the tension with China's neighbouring State."

They argued that being the biggest State in East Asia, China should be held responsible for reducing the differences and building the consensus in the region. The result is that on October 4, 2010, Assistant Foreign Minister Hu Zheng Yao declared that China was making its efforts to build a new security concept, in which China remained committed to playing "a constructive role" in addressing the regional and international issues, and at the same time, China would make efforts to resolve the existing maritime and territorial disputes by peaceful means through friendly negotiations with the neighbouring countries.

China's supple tone in the diplomatic arena seems being correlative with this country's moves in the South China Sea in a few year-end months of 2010. Before the ADMM+ meeting held in Hanoi in October 2010 and after a number of diplomatic protests from the Vietnamese side, China kept Vietnam informed that it would release the fishing boat and 9 fishermen held near the Hoàng Sa (Paracel) Archipelago over one month before. On August 17, US Deputy Assistant Defence Minister Mr. Robert Scher also mentioned in a press conference in Hanoi that the Pentagon did not see any of China's "recent" intimidation to the international oil and gas companies operating in the South China Sea.

A Series of New Tensions in the first Half of 2011

However, China's supple tone after the ARF-17 in Hanoi only reflects its tactical changes in the South China Sea issue. In the first half of 2011, China once again got tough access with its more decisive attitude.

The Incidents on the Sea

A number of incidents during this period of time highlighted China's way of getting access by continuing its decisiveness in the South China Sea. The Aquino administration had lodged its protest against at least 6 of China's provocative incidents during the year, including the Reed Bank incident, in which China infringed the waters inside the 200-nautical-mile exclusive economic zone of the Philippines. Some other serious incidents reported by the Philippine army in June 2011, including a Chinese marine surveillance ship and a naval ship that were discovered having unloaded the building materials and erected the pillars in the adjacent areas of the Iroquois Bank and the Amy Douglas Bank – a Philippine-claimed submerged stone bank and inhabitation area which lies 230km to the Southwest of Palawan province. If the report of the Philippine army is precise, it is clear that China has violated seriously the DOC 2002, particularly Article 5 of the DOC, in which it is clearly stated that "the Parties undertake to exercise self-restraint in the conduct of activities that would complicate or escalate disputes and affect peace and stability including, among others, refraining from action inhabiting on the presently uninhabited islands, reefs, shoals, cays and other features and to handle their differences in a constructive manner."

As far as the energy exploiting activities of the Philippines are concerned, on March 2, 2011, two Chinese patrol boats came and harassed aggressively a seismic survey ship working for the Forum Energy Company contracted with the Philippine government to conduct the exploration of a gas mine in the Reed Bank, 80 km west of Palawan. Earlier, China had sent a number of diplomatic protests when the Philippines had awarded a service contract to the Forum Energy Company in the area that was included in the already expired Tripartite Agreement on the Joint Seismic Survey already signed by the national oil and gas companies of China, Vietnam and the Philippines in 2015. The Forum Energy Company regarded the area in the contract stretching over 880,000 hectares inside the Reed Bank as lying outside the (Spratly) Archipellago. After that Philippine Minister of Energy Angelo. T. Reyes explained that area lay inside the Philippines' 200 nautical mile exclusive economic zone and "if it lies inside the EEZ, the Philippine government has the right to conduct the exploration, exploitation and use of the natural resources and sign the agreement."

On May 26, 2011, another incident happened in the area only 80 nautical miles from the coast of the southern part of Central Vietnam, inside the exclusive economic zone of Vietnam. This time, three Chinese marine surveillance ships had approached closely and harassed Binh Minh 02 ship of Vietnam when the ship was conducting the oil and gas exploratory and survey activities in the South China Sea. These Chinese ships had after that cut the seismic survey cables of the Binh Minh 02 ship and warned the ship on encroaching the territory of

China. However, the Foreign Ministry Spokesman of Vietnam declared in a press conference on May 29, 2010 that the area the Binh Minh 02 ship conducted its survey activities lay completely inside the exclusive economic zone and the 200 nautical mile continental shelf of Vietnam and 622 nautical miles away from Hainan Island of China. Foreign Minister Spokeswoman of Vietnam, declared "the actions have been planned in a very systematic way from the Chinese side with the efforts of turning the undisputed areas into the disputed areas."

It is not clear whether these cable cutting incidents had been carried out in accordance with a premeditate plan in Beijing or it is only the actions started by the marine law enforcement forces at the local level of China. In a sideline meeting on June 3, 2011 of the Shangri-La Dialogue in Singapore, Chinese Defence Minister Liang Guanglie committed again with his neighbour that China would not create any threat and Vietnamese Defence Minister Phùng Quang Thanh also stressed that such a cable cutting incident on May 26, 2011 should not be repeated. Based on the development of the incident, it seems that possibly the Defence Ministry of China had nothing to do with the process of making a decision on the aforesaid incident.

On the part of the Chinese Foreign Ministry, during this time, it had reserved a lot of time and efforts to prepare for the ARF-18 and other meetings with its ASEAN counterparts in Indonesia in July 2011. That is why, logically, the Chinese Foreign Ministry should have avoided making any incidents that could have led to the scenario of the ARF-17 in Hanoi in 2010, where China had been completely isolated as far as the diplomatic aspect is concerned"

SOUTH CHINA SEA: BUILDING UP TROUBLE

Whoever replaces Barack Obama will face many difficult choices but few are likely to be as stark as those in the Asia Pacific region. In a 497-page, densely argued ruling this week, an international tribunal in The Hague blew away the legal ambiguity that has long surrounded China's claim to control the bulk of the South China Sea — one of the busiest trading routes in the world.

How the White House responds to the verdict in the coming months will help define Washington's relationship with Beijing for years, and dramatically influence the geopolitics of the region.

Washington sees the ruling, issued by the Permanent Court of Arbitration, after a complaint from the Philippines, as a victory for what some US officials describe as a 21st century rules-based order over China's 19th-century plans for its own sphere of influence.

By rejecting so many of the assumptions that underpinned Beijing's claims in the South China Sea, the tribunal has put it on the spot. If China continues occupying reefs and developing them into potential military bases — a process that has accelerated since 2014 — it will be acting outside the bounds of international law. The US would then have to decide its next steps and how much military force it is prepared to deploy.

"China has to make a decision — is it going to adhere to the rule of law and act like a world leader with responsibilities, or is it going to go its own course," says Ben Cardin, the senior Democrat on the Senate foreign relations committee. However, he adds: "They will probably assert their sovereignty by additional island building or military activity."

In an interview before the court ruling was announced, Max Baucus, US ambassador to China, said one of his messages to government officials in Beijing was that "we're in a whole new chapter here... The old chapter was talk for the sake of talk, agree to disagree," he added. "We're past that. The new chapter is [about] actions".

Competing rivalries

There are multiple rivalries in the South China Sea and they operate on two levels. A host of islands, rocks and reefs are claimed by China, Vietnam, the Philippines, Malaysia,

Brunei and Taiwan, and the disputes combine fishing rights, potential natural resources and national pride.

For the US and China, the South China Sea is more a matter of the geopolitics of sea control. The US Navy has policed the crucial maritime waterway for most of the past 70 years, and believes that China wants to slowly nudge it out of crucial parts of the western Pacific. A dominant position in the South China Sea would give Beijing a platform to exert greater influence over the foreign policies of its neighbours and the terms of economic engagement in east Asia.

The Hague ruling has delivered a significant blow to that project. The five-judge panel ruled unanimously that China does not have "historic rights" to the resources within its infamous "nine-dash line", which delineates its claim to about 85 per cent of the waterway.

The tribunal also said that none of the land features in the Spratlys archipelago — in the centre of the South China Sea — could be considered as islands, which under international law would give them a 200-mile "exclusive economic zone". The result — which Beijing contests — sharply curtails its legal claim to control.

For the US, the ruling gives it the chance to demonstrate that the channel is an international waterway where any navy can sail legally — and raises the potential cost for China should it expand its military footprint through further land reclamation. But officials hope the verdict could also provide the basis for a new round of regional diplomacy about the disputes.

Over the past four years, the Obama administration has tried to beef up its presence in the region in order to deter China — a policy known as the "pivot". Michael McDevitt, a retired rear admiral, says that since 2013 there have been two US destroyers in the South China Sea at any one time.

"The US presence has dramatically increased," he says. The US has also revamped its military relationships in the region. Having kicked out US armed forces at the end of the cold war, this year the Philippines opened five bases to US aircraft. Washington is also discussing positioning military equipment for the first time in 40 years in Vietnam, at a base in Da Nang.

Ambiguous environment

At times, Beijing's island-building has confused the US. It has found it difficult to respond to Chinese "salami-slicing", where its moves to change the facts on the ground are too small to attract a backlash, in contrast to Russia's 2014 annexation of Crimea.

The Obama administration has also found itself divided over how strongly it should push back against China, with the Pentagon — and especially Pacific Command — advocating tougher military action to deter further land reclamation. Yet at times, this has been in conflict with other goals, such as securing Chinese support for last year's climate change agreement.

Before the ruling, China operated in an environment of much greater legal ambiguity. When the US Navy began a series of "freedom of navigation operations", designed to challenge excessive claims, a senior official said Ashton Carter, the defence secretary, held "dozens of hours of meetings with lawyers, poring over maps". Yet even then, some US officials believe that the resulting patrols by US ships sent signals that were often confusing in legal terms.

Backed by the ruling, the Pentagon has a much clearer view of the legal status of most of the features in the South China Sea to guide its patrols. "The ruling puts wind in the sails of what the US has already been doing," says Timothy Heath, a China expert at the Rand Corporation. But he does not anticipate any drastic changes. "China is not going to leave voluntarily anytime soon and the US does not want a war over this issue," he says.

The US is likely to encourage allies in the region, such as Australia and Japan, to conduct similar operations in order to emphasise the claim that these are international waters.

European allies may also get involved. The UK and France have expressed an interest in conducting South China Sea missions, which they can justify in terms of defending international law.

The Hague's decision coincided with a Beijing summit between the EU and China. In his formal opening remarks hours ahead of its release, Donald Tusk, the president of the European Council, referred to the "important ruling" that was coming and told China's premier, Li Keqiang, that "the rule-based international order is in our common interest... both China and the EU have to protect it".

"They were very upset that Tusk raised the matter publicly," says one person briefed on the talks. "The Europeans have never seen the Chinese side so angry." A scheduled press briefing featuring Mr Li and Mr Tusk was cancelled at short notice, when the EU insisted that journalists be allowed to ask questions that Beijing officials knew would be dominated by the territorial dispute.

US commitment

The ruling comes during a US presidential campaign that is creating nervousness among Asian allies about the reliability of American commitments, especially with regard to the pending Trans-Pacific Partnership trade pact. For many in the region, the TPP is a once-in-a-generation commitment by the US — a reassurance that Washington genuinely see its future tied to Asia. It is for that reason that Mr Carter has said that the agreement would be "worth another aircraft carrier".

However, TPP is opposed by both the presumptive Democratic and Republican nominees, Hillary Clinton and Donald Trump . Mr Trump has also raised the prospect of pulling US troops out of Japan and South Korea and encouraging both countries to develop their own nuclear deterrent against North Korea — which would substantially undercut the US military position if implemented.

There is also the awkward irony that the US Senate has yet to ratify the UN Law of the Sea Treaty, the basis for The

Hague ruling. When it was debated two years ago, some Republican senators warned it could be used to overrule American sovereignty claims — precisely the complaint China is making. As a result, Beijing is refusing to accept the ruling based on an agreement it has fully signed up to, while the US is calling for the enforcement of a treaty it has declined to back.

In the short term, top of the list of potential Sino-US flashpoints is Scarborough Shoal, 140 miles from the Philippines' coast where China took control three years ago. Earlier this year, the Obama administration delivered private warnings to Beijing not to begin a new exercise in land reclamation. Although US officials refuse to say if Scarborough Shoal is covered by the mutual defence treaty between the countries, some in Washington would like to see a formal declaration in order to deter Beijing.

"I think we should be prepared to take military action in Scarborough Shoal" if China tries to build a new artificial island, says Admiral Dennis Blair, former head of US Pacific Command. "Draw the line there."

SOUTH CHINA SEA BECOMING A POTENTIAL FLASHPOINT

Cautioning that the current situation in South China Sea is worsening due to the dangerous activities of China that have serious implications for security and development of many countries in the Indo-Pacific region, including India, he said that all parties should exercise self-restraint to avoid any escalation in the situation in the region. He also favoured strict and full implementation of the Declaration on the Conduct of Parties (DOC) and early adoption of the Code of Conduct on the South China Sea.

Asserting that Vietnam has historical evidence and legal foundation to confirm its sovereignty over both Paracel and Spratly Islands in the South China Sea, the Vietnamese Ambassador said that his country has since 17th century owned and peacefully controlled these islands. However, the envoy said that Vietnam was ready to work with other claimants to settle the territorial disputes over Paracel and Spratly Islands by means of multilateral and also bilateral negotiations in a peaceful manner in accordance with international laws.

Painting a grim scenario, he said that China's activities were threatening peace, security, stability and cooperation in South China Sea. Before 1947, all geographical maps printed by China showed their territory stopped at Hainan Island only. In 1974, China forcibly occupied Paracel Islands which were under Vietnanam's administration. In 1988, China again used force to occupy some reefs in the Spratly Islands, the envoy said. In 2009, he pointed out, China officially claimed an area within a nine-dot lines as their historic waters which cover 80 per cent of South China Sea and overlap in a large scale with the EEZs of all other countries surrounding the South China Sea, including Vietnam, the Philippines, Malaysia, Indonesia and Brunei.

Over the past 20 months, more than 2,900 acres of land has been reclaimed by China, accounting for 95 per cent of all land reclaimed by others in the Spratly Islands over the past 40 years, he claimed. China has also built airstrips on three artificial islands and began conducting flights to the airstrip it had built at Fiery Cross Reef of Spratly Archipelago. Most recently, China has built a helicopter base on Duncan island and deployed HQ-9 long-range surface-to-air missiles on Woody island of Paracel Archipelgo which indicate China's firm intention to militarize the South China Sea, the envoy said. Appreciating India's position on resolving the South China Sea disputes peacefully, the Vietnamese Ambassador cited as a “”good example””, the settlement of the maritime disputes between India and Bangladesh in the Bay of Bengal by using the UN's Arbitration Tribunal.

Spread over 3.7 million square kilometer surface area, the South China Sea not only provides the surrounding countries with oil and gas, seafood and other natural resources, but also serves as the most critical shipping route between the Pacific and Indian Ocean. Nearly 30 per cent of world's cargo passes through the South China Sea. With China's aggressive campaign in the region, it is clear that this complicated 21st century dispute where half a dozen nations are making competing claims and tension has escalated in recent years is not heading towards an early and peaceful settlement. Concerns are not misplaced about the South China sea becoming yet another flashpoint with serious global consequences.

WHY IS THE SOUTH CHINA SEA CONTENTIOUS?

China, Vietnam, the Philippines, Taiwan, Malaysia and Brunei all have competing claims. China has backed its expansive claims with island-building and naval patrols. The US says it does not take sides in territorial disputes, but has sent military ships and planes near disputed islands, calling them "freedom of navigation" operations to ensure access to key shipping and air routes. Both sides have accused each other of "militarising" the South China Sea. There are fears that the area is becoming a flashpoint, with potentially serious global consequences.

What is the argument about?

It is a dispute over territory and sovereignty over ocean areas, and the Paracels and the Spratlys - two island chains claimed in whole or in part by a number of countries. Alongside the fully fledged islands, there are dozens of rocky outcrops, atolls, sandbanks and reefs, such as the Scarborough Shoal.

Why are they worth arguing over?

Although largely uninhabited, the Paracels and the Spratlys may have reserves of natural resources around them. There has been little detailed exploration of the area, so estimates are largely extrapolated from the mineral wealth of neighbouring areas. The sea is also a major shipping route and home to fishing grounds that supply the livelihoods of people across the region.

Who claims what?

China claims by far the largest portion of territory - an area defined by the "nine-dash line" which stretches hundreds of miles south and east from its most southerly province of Hainan. Beijing says its right to the area goes back centuries to when the Paracel and Spratly island chains were regarded as integral parts of the Chinese nation, and in 1947 it issued a map detailing its claims. It showed the two island groups falling entirely within its territory. Those claims are mirrored by Taiwan. However, critics say China has not clarified its claims sufficiently - and that the nine-dash line that appears on Chinese maps encompassing almost the entirety of the South China Sea includes no coordinates. It is also not clear whether China claims only land territory within the nine-dash line, or all the territorial waters within the line as well.

Vietnam hotly disputes China's historical account, saying China had never claimed sovereignty over the islands before the 1940s. Vietnam says it has actively ruled over both the Paracels and the Spratlys since the 17th Century - and has the documents to prove it. The other major claimant in the area is the Philippines, which invokes its geographical proximity to the Spratly Islands as the main basis of its claim for part of the grouping. Both the Philippines and China lay claim to the Scarborough Shoal (known as Huangyan Island in China) - a little more than 100 miles (160km) from the Philippines and 500 miles from China. Malaysia and Brunei also lay claim to territory in the South China Sea that they say falls within their economic exclusion zones, as defined by UNCLOS - the United Nations Convention on the Law of the Sea. Brunei does not claim any of the disputed islands, but Malaysia claims a small number of islands in the Spratlys.

RECENT FLASHPOINTS

The most serious trouble in recent decades has flared between Vietnam and China, and there have also been stand-offs between the Philippines and China. Some of the incidents include:

- In 1974 the Chinese seized the Paracels from Vietnam, killing more than 70 Vietnamese troops.

- In 1988 the two sides clashed in the Spratlys, with Vietnam again coming off worse, losing about 60 sailors.
- In early 2012, China and the Philippines engaged in a lengthy maritime stand-off, accusing each other of intrusions in the Scarborough Shoal.
- Unverified claims that the Chinese navy sabotaged two Vietnamese exploration operations in late 2012 led to large anti-China protests on Vietnam's streets.
- In January 2013, Manila said it was taking China to a UN tribunal under the auspices of the UN Convention on the Laws of the Sea, to challenge its claims.
- In May 2014, the introduction by China of a drilling rig into waters near the Paracel Islands led to multiple collisions between Vietnamese and Chinese ships.

Have they tried to reach a resolution?

China prefers bilateral negotiations with the other parties. But many of its neighbours argue that China's relative size and clout give it an unfair advantage. Some countries have argued that China should negotiate with Asean (the Association of South East Asian Nations), a 10-member regional grouping that consists of Thailand, Indonesia, Malaysia, the Philippines, Singapore, Brunei, Laos, Vietnam, Myanmar and Cambodia. However, China is opposed to this, while Asean is also divided over how to resolve the dispute.

The Philippines has sought international arbitration instead. In 2013, it announced it would take China to an arbitration tribunal under the auspices of the UN Convention on the Laws of the Sea, to challenge its claims. In July 2016, the tribunal backed the Philippines' case, saying China had violated the Philippines' sovereign rights. China had boycotted the proceedings, and called the ruling "ill-founded". It says it will not be bound by it.

2

The South China Sea: Flashpoint of the Asia

At first glance, there is nothing particularly remarkable about this area of the Pacific. Stretching from the southern shores of the People's Republic of China and Taiwan in the north to Malaysia and Indonesia in the south, it covers about 3.5 million square kilometers and contains three archipelagos containing over 250 islands, reefs, shoals, atolls and sandbars, most of them containing no indigenous population, and many of them submerged for part or all of the year.

Upon closer inspection, however, the waters comprising the South China Sea are of central importance to the region. It is the second busiest sea lane in the world, and contains proven oil reserves of over 7 billion barrels, with an estimated 28 billion barrels total and 266 trillion cubic feet of natural gas. As the sea's importance becomes more and more pronounced, and as the region itself sees its major players asserting themselves more aggressively on the world stage, the area has become a flashpoint for disputes between China, Vietnam, and the Philippines. Now, tensions in the areaare threatening to spill over into armed confrontation.

This growing tension is made possible by an increasingly assertive Chinese Navy, bolstered by a number of technological upgrades in recent years that are increasingly transforming it into a world-class naval power.

Founded in 1949 with less than two dozen poorly-equipped ships, the naval force of the fledgling communist Chinese PLA relied for the first two decades of its existence on vessels purchased from the Soviet Union. In the 1970s, the Chinese began designing and building its own surface ships, and currently have assault ships, destroyers, frigates, and nuclear attack submarines in their increasingly sophisticated fleet. China is even set to commission its first aircraft carrier later this year. Purchased from Ukraine and refitted by the Chinese themselves, the ship began sea trials last year and is expected to enter the fleet within the next several months.

All of these developments have given rise to a new era of Chinese naval aggression, and has even led to China asserting itself more forcefully on the world stage. Recently I had a chance to talk to Eric Draitser, the host of the Stop Imperialism podcast and contributor to BoilingFrogsPost.com, about the situation, and the position that China, the US and the other players in the region are taking in this conflict.

From this US-China nationalistic struggle for dominance over the prized sea lane, however, a third way is emerging, one that is being pushed by a corporate, multi-national power elite. In this third way, disputes will not be settled one by one between disputant countries, but through a regional organization that will have increasing power to arbitrate over the region's disputed waters.

The idea comes from the International Crisis Group, a supposedly non-partisan, non-profit, non-governmental organization that is supposedly "committed to preventing and resolving deadly conflict" around the globe. In reality, it is a mouthpiece for the same international "superclass" touted by the likes of David Rothkopf, with funds coming from the Carnegie Corporation, the Rockefeller Brothers Fund, BP, Chevron, Shell, Morgan Stanley, and an assorted who's who of council members, donors and advisors. Representing the same oligarchical interests as the Bilderberg Group, the Trilateral Commission, and other supranational organizations, the

International Crisis Group asserts a post-nationalist philosophy of so-called humanitarian interventions and regional governmental frameworks.

Unsurprisingly, the Crisis Group's white paper on the South China Sea standoff attempts to "resolve" the conflict by saying that everyone is to blame, and only a strengthened and re-invigorated ASEAN or similar organization will be able to act as an effective moderator in the dispute.

Having failed to reach a consensus on a public communique for the first time in its 45 year history at a ministerial meeting last month, ASEAN is now being seen as too weak and ineffective to arbitrate the region's tensions and the Crisis Group is advocating the building up of a stronger regional framework to produce "joint management" of the region's resources.

Left unstated in the report is that these ideas are being promoted by the self-same corporate chieftains and political insiders who have been advocating for the subsumption of national sovereignty in North and South America, Africa, and Europe, in the name of "regional" governments that are bureaucratic in nature, democratically opaque, and open to manipulation and control by the multinational corporations and institutional foundations behind organizations like the Crisis Group.

Now, once again, the people of the Asia-Pacific region are left between a rock and a hard place. Forced to choose between supporting their national interests in aggressive naval squabbles over uninhabited islands or to cede their sovereignty to unelected, unaccountable regional government institutions, it seems that no matter what they do, the people pay with their lives and their freedom for the wars of conquest and geopolitical games of their so-called leaders.

As the tension in the South China Sea continues to rise, it is by no means certain how these disputes will be resolved. However, one thing is for certain: in this Asia-Pacific century, the South China Sea will continue to be a key piece of the chessboard for any would-be regional superpower.

SOUTH CHINA SEA

The Permanent Court of Arbitration (PCA) in The Hague on Tuesday ruled that China has no legal basis to claim "historic rights" to islands in the South China Sea and had violated the Philippines' sovereign rights.

"The Tribunal concluded that there was no legal basis for China to claim historic rights within the sea areas falling within the 'nine-dash line'," the Hague-based Permanent Court of Arbitration said. The nine-dash refers to a demarcation line on a 1947 map of the sea, which is rich in energy, mineral and fishing resources.

The tribunal also found China had violated the Philippines' sovereign rights. "Having found that certain areas are within the exclusive economic zone of the Philippines, the Tribunal found that China had violated the Philippines' sovereign rights in its exclusive economic zone by (a) interfering with Philippine fishing and petroleum exploration, (b) constructing artificial islands and (c) failing to prevent Chinese fishermen from fishing in the zone." In a unanimous, hard-hitting ruling, the Hague tribunal maintained that the disputed Spratly islands "cannot generate maritime zones collectively as unit" as claimed by China.

There are three separate and distinct conflicts in the South China Sea, a fact that is normally confabulated in news coverage:

1. There are dozens and dozens of islands in the South China Sea, subject to conflicting claims by various countries [think of the scene in Braveheart "These Documents Were Lies When You Wrote Them!"]. The United States takes no position in such third party disputes.
2. China claims the entire South China Sea, via the infamous "Nine Dash Line" map. The United States says this claim is silly, since under international law maritime claims must be based on pieces of ground [coasts, rocks, etc], and cannot be based on simple lines on a map [actually, there are several such maps, and

the lines do not line up]. The United States conducts Freedom of Navigation operations to assert US claims. China finds such operations annoying. China only discovered this ownership in 1949. China's claim to the entire South China Sea is unique in maritime law, and contravenes the fundamental principle of the Law of the Sea that requires maritime claims to be based on land features, not arbitrary lines on the water on a map. There is no basis for a "split the difference" compromise.

3. China has dredged coral and sand to form a handful of artificial islands which it is using as unsinkable aircraft carriers. Shina appears to assert that this artificial ojects have territorial waters. These claims violate a fundamental principle of maritime law that such artificial creations cannot acquire territorial waters. Arguing in the alternative, China might claim that since the entire South China Sea constitutes internal waters, the territorial water around the artificial islands is simply an extention of that claim.

The United States called in late 2015 for a halt to China's artificial island-building, and in recent weeks has tried to signal its determination to challenge Beijing over the disputed sea by sending military ships and planes near the islands.

The US said it has no intention of ending patrol missions across international waters and airspace, even as China rebuked it for sending a warship on 27 October 2015 near disputed South China Sea islets and reefs claimed by Beijing. "The United States is going to fly and sail anywhere where international law allows," the White House said in a statement. It added that "we would communicate in private to China what we would say in public. These operations are conducted in accordance with international law and applied evenhandedly around the globe."

Beijing's foreign ministry said 28 October 2015 it summoned U.S. Ambassador Max Baucus to deliver a formal protest over the incident, which represents the U.S.'s boldest challenge yet to China's controversial territorial "This action by the United

States threatens China's sovereignty and security interests and endangers the safety of personnel and facilities on the reef, which is a serious provocation" Vice Foreign Minister Zhang Yesui said.

By mid November 2015 Indonesia's security chief said the Southeast Asian country could become the second in the region to challenge China's claim to all of the South China Sea. That is, if Beijing and Jakarta cannot resolve their territorial dispute through dialogue. China's nine-dash line claim includes Indonesia's Natuna islands.

China sent a warning that appeared directed at the United States to not engage in what it has called "provocative behavior" in the South China Sea. The warning followed news reports 08 October 2015 that the US military was planning to sail warships close to artificial islands Beijing has been aggressively building in hopes of bolstering its claims in the disputed waters. According to the reports, US officials have said they are considering sailing warships inside the 12-nautical-mile zones of the artificial islands that Beijing claims are a legitimate extension of its territory within the next two weeks [ie, before the end of October].

"The Chinese navy has closely monitored the provocative actions of the United States and issued several warnings, while exercising enormous restraint in the interests of safeguarding the overall situation in bilateral relations," said Wu Shengli, commander of the People's Liberation Army Navy, according to a report on the defense ministry's website late on 19 NOvembe 2015. "If the United States carries out repeated provocations despite China's opposition, we have the ability to defend our national sovereignty and security."

Despite many Chinese diplomatic assurances to the contrary, Chinese assertiveness in the South China Sea is an attempt to re-establish traditional Chinese hegemony in the region. China's strategy is taking concrete actions to solidify its claims in the South China Sea, and Chinese officials have underscored such perception.

China has asserted its claims for the South China Sea's rich mineral, oil and fishing grounds by increasing patrols and escorts for its fishing fleets. The ships' excursions regularly raise regional tensions. ASEAN foreign ministers meeting in Brunei in April 2013 agreed to pursue dialogue with China on a Code of Conduct in the South China Sea. ASEAN wants a legally binding agreement to discourage such aggressive moves. It would replace a ten-year pledge by the claimants not to cause conflict, known as the Declaration of Conduct.

China is forging ahead with reclamation projects on at least seven tiny but hotly contested features in the South China Sea, posing a major challenge in the Philippines' international arbitration case against China. Since the beginning of 2015, satellite images of Chinese reclamation work in the Spratly Islands have shown shoals and reefs turning into artificial islands. By April 2015 major harbors that can dock military ships were nearly completed. So were several airstrips and at least three multistory buildings where bare outposts once stood. China's Foreign Ministry expressed serious concern on 27 March 2015 after the Philippines said it would resume repair and reconstruction works on disputed islands in the South China Sea. The ministry accused Manila of infringing on Chinese sovereignty. The Philippines had halted activities in 2014 over concerns about the effect on an international arbitration complaint filed against China.

In September 2015 an agreement was struck between Presidents Barack Obama and Xi Jinping on rules for military air-to-air encounters. The deal, which followed an earlier agreement on encounters between naval ships, was aimed at preventing encounters from escalating or causing crashes. Citing successful implementation of the Code of Unplanned Encounters on the Sea, signed by the two sides in April 2014, Assistant Secretary of Defense David Shear told Congress that he hoped for more positive results from further engagement with China. In February 2014 the United States for the first time explicitly rejected the U-shaped, nine-dash line that China uses to assert sovereignty over nearly the whole South China Sea, experts say, strengthening the position of rival claimants and setting the stage for what could be an international legal showdown with Beijing. Washington had always said that it takes no position on competing territorial claims in the South China Sea among China, the Philippines, Vietnam, Malaysia, Taiwan, and Brunei and opposes any use of force to resolve such issues.

The international community, he said, would welcome China to clarify or adjust its nine-dash line claim to bring it in accordance with the international law of the sea. "I think it is imperative that we be clear about what we mean when the United States says that we take no position on competing claims to sovereignty over disputed land features" in the region, Russel said.

Unlike other countries, Beijing's claim to up to about 90 percent of the South China Sea is not based on claims to particular islands or other features but on a historical map China officially submitted to the United Nations in 2009. The map contains a nine-dash line forming a U-shape down the east coast of Vietnam to just north of Indonesia and then continuing northwards up the west coast of the Philippines. The nine-dash line has been considered by many experts as incompatible with the 1982 United Nations Convention on the Law of the Sea (UNCLOS), which rejects historically based claims.

Deng Xiaoping said "since we can't solve the South China Sea issue, we can leave it to the next generation which will be smarter." It is impossible to resolve the disputes over the South China Sea to the mutual benefit of all. Hypothetically, the claims of other littoral states could be reconciled by sectoral extensions of the Exclusive Economic Zones [as was done in the Gulf of Guinea]. China's claims cannot be so reconciled, since China claims vritually the entire South China Sea, which it views as internal waters.

China claims most of the South China Sea as either territorial water or Exclusive Economic Zone. China's claims cannot be reconciled with the claims of other states in the South China Sea area. The other states have conflicting claims that can be harmonized, the way there were compromises among the conflicting claims for the Gulf of Guinea in Africa. In the South China Sea, each of the littoral states claims areas that are immediately contiguous to their territorial seas, and it would be possible to "split the difference" on competing claims. But China claims the entirety of the South China Sea, so there is no possibility of compromise with China's position, since it is all or nothing.

In July 1977, when Deng Xiaoping emerged as China's leader following the death of Mao Tse-tung, the Chinese foreign minister, Huang Hua, confirmed that China's claim to the South China Sea was "non-negotiable" in the strongest terms. At the same time he commented: "The territory of China reaches as far south as the James Shoals, near Malaysia's Borneo territory... I remember that while I was still a schoolboy, I read about those islands in the geography books. At that time, I never heard anyone say those islands were not China's... The Vietnamese claim that the islands belong to them. Let them talk that way. They have repeatedly asked us to negotiate with them on the issue; we have always declined to do so... As to the ownership of the islands, there are historical documents that can be verified. There is no need for negotiations since they originally belonged to China.... In this respect Taiwan's attitude is all right. At least they have some patriotism and would not sell out the islands..."

Under the United Nations Convention on the Law of the Sea (UNCLOS) coastal states have the right to establish sovereignty over adjacent waters out to a maximum of 12 nautical miles from the nation's coastline, including the coastline of offshore islands. These enclosed waters are known as the coastal state's territorial sea.

During the negotiations of the text of the 1982 UNCLOS military activities in the EEZ were a controversial issue. Some coastal States such as Bangladesh, Brazil, Cape Verde, Malaysia, Pakistan and Uruguay contended that other States cannot carry out military exercises or maneuvers in or over their EEZ without their consent.

In June 1998, the PRC passed the "Exclusive Economic Zone and Continental Shelf Act." This Act created an exclusive economic zone (EEZ) with 200 nautical mile limits from its coastal baseline, and claimed the right, inter alia, to broadly undefined powers to enforce laws in the EEZ, "including security laws and regulations." Based on the Act, the PRC does not recognize the airspace above its EEZ as "international airspace" and has interfered with and protested US reconnaissance flights over its EEZ.

China takes the position that all maritime data collection activities, including military intelligence and hydrographic collection activities, fall within the United Nations Convention on the Law of the Sea [UNCLOS] provisions for marine scientific research and therefore require coastal-state consent before they could be carried out in the two-hundred-nautical-mile EEZ.

The US has protested this sovereignty claim as a violation of international law numerous times since this law was passed. The US Government has long conducted a vigorous freedom of navigation program through which it has asserted its navigational rights in the face of what it has regarded as excessive claims by coastal states of jurisdiction over ocean space or international passages.

When remonstrations and protestations are unavailing, elements of US military forces may sail into or fly over disputed regions for the purpose of demonstrating their right and determination to continue to do so.

ASEAN countries are outward-looking, especially in term of protecting their Exclusive Economic Zones (EEZ). The convergence of interests in conflict areas such as the Spratly Islands affects the relationship among Malaysia, Philippines and Brunei with each claiming parts of the Spratlys. While armed conflicts among the countries of ASEAN overthe Spratly issue may be a remote possibility, it hascompounded historic frictions over unresolved territorial conflicts.

This will continue to be one of the driving force behind arms acquisition which is clearly demonstrated by the expansion of the naval and air forces of Malaysia. All the other ASEAN countries - except for Brunei - have expanded their naval and air arms to safeguard their maritime interests.

Most of the marine traffic in the South China Sea goes to the People's Republic of China and Hong Kong. Vietnam, Indonesia, Taiwan, and the Philippines are largely served by coast-hugging routes outside the PRC's dreaded Nine-Dash-Line.

CHINA PUSHES SOUTH CHINA SEA CLOSER TO A CONFLICT

Notwithstanding China's commitment to implement Declaration of the Conduct of Parties in South China Sea (DOC) based on the norms of International Law and to formulate and implement the Code of Conduct (COC) as well as to resolve the South China Sea disputes peacefully through negotiations, its policies are working just in the opposite direction escalating tension in the region. The serious implications of its aggressive acts and postures are palpable to all who have interests in the South China Sea (SCS).

China following a well-crafted strategy is systematically moving to establish its control over the area it claims in SCS. As a first step, it formed a Committee of thirteen agencies/ departments in February 2012 to fabricate evidence and publicise its claims over the most area in SCS shown through the nine dotted lines. After it made recommendations, China in its new biometric passports projected all the areas in the SCS as belonging to China. These passports also show parts of India as belonging to China. This act of China generated a strong reaction in the neighbouring countries as also in other countries using SCS for trade. While both Vietnam and the Philippines refused to stamp the Chinese travel documents, India began to stamp its own version of the Indian Territory. Jakarta called the Chinese act as counter-productive and the US described these Chinese passports as unhelpful to the resolution of disputes. The second step was the establishment of the prefectural level city of Sansha to administer the Paracel and Ṡpratly Islands in June 2012. Soon after this, China created a military command base there. And as the third step of its strategy, China declared that its police in the Southern Chinese Island of Hainan on the SCS has been authorised to board and search any ship they deem illegal in the "Chinese waters". The new regulations are to be enforced from the 1st January 2013.

All these acts of China are in fact potential triggers for conflicts in the region. China is also continuing with its provocative actions. On 30th November, 2012 Vietnam accused a Chinese fishing boat for cutting the cables of its exploration vessel Binh Minh 02. On expected lines, China on the other hand stated that Vietnam expelled its fishing vessels from its waters. The cutting of cables by China has been criticised even by Chinese security experts like Professor Zhu Feng of International Relations at Peking University. China has also stated that its patrol boats would be around Scarborough Shoal. Such provocative acts can result into a conflict. China is now seen as creator of hurdles in the steps being taken by ASEAN to resolve the issue peacefully. The Chinese reluctance to discuss the issue at multilateral forums continues. The ASEAN July meeting in Cambodia clearly established that China keeps on using its influence on Cambodia, the present Chair of ASEAN to ensure that the SCS disputes are not properly discussed. Even the recent ASEAN Summit reflected that the issue remains hostage to the Chinese policy of not allowing proper discussion and projection of the disputes.

The neighbours of China also see that the Chinese modernisation of the armed forces at a break-neck speed is not meant to defend its interests but to threaten them into submission. The recent landing of J 15 on the newly acquired air-craft carrier has alarmed the powers interested in the region. They also note that Chinese official defence budget has crossed $106 bn this year.

The Chinese policies and posture are causing an armed race in the SCS region. While Vietnam and Philippines are looking to acquire arms to counter the Chinese activities, Japan is also re-orienting its defence policy. Outside powers are now becoming more assertive in stating that they intend to protect the freedom of navigation. In addition, they are also guided by their strategic objectives. US not only have Asia pivot policy but are clearly taking steps to protect the US interests by enhancing their presences in this region. The situation can be rightly termed as alarming. The security experts in China's neighbouring nations are getting seriously concerned about the Chinese activities. Their security experts point out that modernisation of the Chinese Navy is a major security concern. They point out that the Chinese rise is not peaceful. They are suggesting that suitable up-gradation of their armed forces is imperative in view of developing security environment.

An assessment of the situation reveal clearly that the Chinese posturing and activities have moved up from being merely "a concern" to "a serious threat" to the region's stability. Such Chinese activities have made the situation highly explosive. Even an unintended incident can act as a trigger for a conflict. Today the South China Sea stands very close to a conflict than ever before. The moot question is whether something can be done at this stage or not to save the world from a conflict. The Chinese leaders, who have great sense for learning from historical experiences, should be able to see that their activities are not in their interests. They are getting marginalised in the International Community. The present policy of International Community of managing and engaging China has limits and the moment China crosses the proverbial Rubicon, the concerned powers would abandon this policy and resort to arms to protect their interests. It may be recalled that before the Second World War, UK had adopted the policy of "Appeasement" which was also followed by France and others to a point but when Hitler's Germany decided to attack Poland, they abandoned it and the war followed. Peace loving people do not like to hear the "sound of cannons" but when it comes to protecting their national interests, they would not mind listening to cancerous sound of guns.

Chinese new leadership which has interest in expanding the trade with ASEAN, should see that these nations provide an excellent market for their products. Another aspect that the Chinese should realise is the fact that the South China Sea disputes are multi-lateral in nature and have to be discussed at multi-lateral forums involving all parties in the disputes. Fortunately there are some experts in China who understand this aspect.

The International Community too has a responsibility in nudging and pressurising all the involved nations to come to an agreement. There had not been sufficient pressure on China to abandon the present posture which is not conducive for peace. The International Community has been in fact whetting the appetite of China by following a policy of inaction. There has been a view amongst the security community that China is testing waters by provocative steps and is gauging the tolerance limit. The time has come that a unified approach is adopted to deal with China. Keeping in view the Chinese economic interests, China would not be able to ignore such an action. The International Community should put pressure on China to stop provocative steps and take steps for the resolution of the issue. There are number of drafts which have been produced by experts for Code of Conduct (COC) for South China Sea. These should be seriously considered rather than waiting for suitable environment. The implementation of an agreed COC would at least ensure that no untoward incident takes place.

The coming India ASEAN meet in the third week of this month would be another opportunity to discuss the South China Sea issue and come up with some reasonable suggestion. It is understood that final resolution may be difficult to arrive at but COC can be evolved for ensuring peace in the region. The India should take a lead in this direction. India has sufficient experience in dealing with China. Despite 15 rounds of talks there has been practically no progress on the border issue. In addition like in the SCS China continues with provocative actions like intruding on the Indian Territory, writing China on the Indian rocks and objecting presence of Indians from the North East India or J&K in military delegations. Two former

Special Representatives and former National Security Advisors of India had noted the Chinese game plan. While Sri M.K.Narayanan had stated that China is playing a waiting game, late Sri Brijesh Mishra had pointed out the need to take help of US to resolve all the issues including our interests in the SCS. The recent round of talks clearly indicated the Chinese strategy of not dealing with the issue of the border dispute but avoiding the main issue by projecting that the talks have broader goals of development, mutual cooperation and inclusive growth. In the past Chinese had come up with double meaning guidelines and frameworks. Indian leadership needs to see this clearly and work out a strategy with ASEAN and other nations for the resolution of its border issue and the SCS which is important to all.

ASEAN REBOOTS ON SOUTH CHINA SEA

Recent Association of Southeast Asian Nation (ASEAN) summit meetings have been subsumed by unresolved territorial disputes in the South China Sea. The controversy has not only strained ASEAN's key operating principles, including consensus among its 10 member states, but has also highlighted the rising rivalry between China and United States, two countries which are jostling for a strategic upper hand in Southeast Asia.

The unresolved and escalating issue has raised questions on the often celebrated success of regionalism in Southeast Asia, particularly with the implementation of a new ASEAN Economic Community scheduled for 2015. Questions are thus rising over whether ASEAN can stick to its founding objective of maintaining a unified, strategic balance against larger regional powers, namely China.

Pragmatic leadership has been the glue that has held ASEAN together and guided the grouping through difficult strategic issues in the past. The debacle of last year's ASEAN summit held in Phnom Penh, where group members failed for the first time in the association's history to issue a joint statement, highlighted the growing inherent contradictions and competing national agendas of member states.

Cambodia's stance against including any mention of the South China Sea disputes in a joint communique was viewed as acquiescence to external Chinese pressure. Perceptions of outside manipulation of the association's inner workings was a deciding factor in the Philippines decision to take its complaint against China to a United Nations tribunal rather than rely on ASEAN to arrive at a mutually agreed code of conduct in the South China Sea.

The Philippines' decision to use alternative forums to safeguard its territorial claims vis-a-vis China has weakened ASEAN's standing as a unified bloc. Tensions broke out into the open when President Benigno Aquino openly accused host Cambodia of sabotaging ASEAN's interest for bilateral concessions from China. Indonesia helped to bridge the differences through face-saving shuttle diplomacy, but to many analysts the damage to group cohesion had been done.

While the small sultanate of Brunei is ASEAN's chairman this year, much depends on Indonesia's role. In recent consultations among ASEAN senior ministers, Indonesian Foreign Minister Marty Natalegawa has apparently taken the lead in working towards developing a mutually acceptable code of conduct for the South China Sea.

While there have been some signs of positive momentum, including at the recently concluded summit meeting in Brunei, claimant countries have not yet acted on an Indonesian proposal to establish hotlines to avoid conflicts from spiraling out of control in the disputed territories.

Brunei Sultan Haji Hassanal Bolkiah said after last week's ASEAN summit meeting that members agreed to a broad "two step" approach to dealing with the maritime disputes. "Firstly, the overlapping claims are for the claimant states to deal with. Secondly, both ASEAN and China wish to promote a calm and peaceful atmosphere and to urgently work on the code of conduct."

Malaysia and Singapore have been the other two major countries that have been influential in steering ASEAN over the years. Singapore's small size has been a limitation but its strategic location has given it the leverage to deal with major world powers. Its robust relations with the US in particular have raised doubts among certain neighbours who see external powers as intrusive in regional affairs. Its role in pushing through ASEAN trade cooperation has been universally welcomed.

Indonesia, Malaysia and Singapore have led the way in strategic cooperation. The three ASEAN members established a trilateral naval cooperation arrangement known as MALSINDO to patrol the pirated-infested and strategically important Malacca Straits. While nobody has yet to propose similar joint patrols in the South China Sea, ASEAN claimant states like the Philippines and Vietnam that have locked horns with China clearly want ASEAN to play a more decisive role in the disputes.

Some believe Brunei, ASEAN's current chair, is uniquely positioned to cobble together a new grouping consensus on the South China Sea. Brunei, a small oil-rich sultanate of less than half a million people with small claims in the South China Sea, became a member of ASEAN in 1984, the first country to be included after the organization was originally formed in 1967. Although Brunei's trade with China is relatively large, estimated at US$1.3 billion last year, some analysts believe it has strong diplomatic incentive to reaffirm ASEAN's standing as a unified, strategic bloc.

To be sure, consensus inside ASEAN is becoming harder to achieve, especially as China plays divide-and-rule politics among certain member states like Cambodia. In view of Myanmar, another China ally, assuming ASEAN's chairmanship in 2014, the Philippines in particular may feel that if Brunei can not make significant progress towards developing a binding Code of Conduct (CoC) in the South China Sea, ASEAN will be impotent in playing a meaningful role until at least 2015 and will look to outside actors like the US to bolster its claims.

Although the Philippines has applied for international mediation under the United Nations Convention on the Law of the Sea (UNCLOS), it has also reaffirmed its commitment to support any ASEAN effort to bring about a consensus on the disputes. Philippine Foreign Minister Albert del Rosario said after summit meetings held last week in Brunei that there was "solidarity in terms of readiness to convince China that we should move on with the CoC".

China has consistently expressed a preference for dealing with the territorial disputes on a bilateral basis. Beijing will host a meeting with senior ASEAN foreign ministers meeting later this year. Del Rosario told reports that ASEAN member Thailand proposed a pre-meeting gathering among ASEAN foreign ministers to reinforce their solidarity on the South China Sea issue before they meet with China.

Leadership will play a strong role in ASEAN's direction and decision making in the months ahead. Brunei's claims in the South China Sea are small compared to the Philippines and Vietnam and it has been the least vocal claimant in pressing its maritime claims. That can be viewed as both a strength and weakness, analysts say.

The grouping's members realize that they cannot isolate any major power from their calculus in the evolving system in world affairs and rising economic integration, including with China. But if not properly handled, escalating disputes in the South China Sea threaten to upset the regional peace and stability that has fostered recent unprecedented economic growth in the region, much of it driven by growing trade with China.

China no doubt realizes that other regional powers, including the US, are quietly observing developments in the maritime disputes and making their own strategic calculations. After years of peaceful commercial diplomacy, Beijing would seemingly prefer to avoid pushing ASEAN towards these regional competitors while weakening its strategic position in its own perceived sphere of influence.

In this complex geopolitical game, regional powers like Indonesia will be compelled to hold ASEAN together and support smaller claimant states such as Brunei to benefit from its distinctive position vis-a-vis China. An ASEAN consensus on the South China Sea would represent a powerful strategic counterweight to China and mitigate the risks of over-reliance on outside powers like the US to provide strategic balance. To maintain the regional peace, ASEAN needs to recommit to its founding principles of unity and consensus. While Brunei may have the intention and incentive to push that agenda, it is still not clear it has the weight or authority to bring ASEAN back together and achieve a meaningful peace vis-a-vis China in the South China Sea.

SOUTH CHINA SEA: THE FRENCH ARE COMING

China's aggressive territorial push in the South China Sea has resulted in turning this busy international trade route into one of the most volatile spots in the world. The U.S.-led international efforts to defend the freedom of navigation guaranteed by the UN Convention on the Law of the Sea (UNCLOS), aiming at preventing the entire South China Sea from becoming an exclusive Chinese lake, has just received a powerful boost in the form of the July 12 ruling of The Hague-based UN Permanent Court of Arbitration. Much to China's anger, most of its sovereignty claims over the South China Sea are rejected in this ruling.

To the surprise of many, a seemingly unrelated European power, France, has announced its intention of coordinating the navies of fellow European Union nations to conduct Freedom of Navigation Operations or FONOPs in South China Sea. On June 5, at the Shangri-la Dialogue in Singapore, French Defense Minister Jean-Yves Le Drian mentioned this initiative for joint EU patrols of "the maritime areas of Asia" and for a "regular and visible presence there."

Enjoying this article? Click here to subscribe for full access. Just $5 a month. Although China was not named in Le Drian's speech (China is not the only country with sovereignty claims in the South China Sea), the French initiative was generally interpreted as a bad news for Beijing, who was already irritated by what it sees as "outside interference" by the United States and its allies in China's territorial feuds with countries bordering South China Sea.

From a strictly strategic viewpoint, France's announced plan will not have a determining impact on the situation in the South China Sea. After all, despite being a major military power with global reach, France's military presence in the region is limited. Besides, outside of France, what other EU nation has a permanent naval and air presence in the Pacific? But however small the strategic impact may be, the French initiative promises to weigh in heavily on the diplomatic front, adding significantly to China's already stark isolation in this case.

The scope of this diplomatic impact should be measured in the wake of the July 12 ruling of the UN Permanent Court of Arbitration, in a context where China is attempting, without much success, to put together a "coalition of the willing" of countries presumably supportive of its position in the South China Sea.

The French initiative thus has the potential of further weakening China's position by conspicuously bringing Europe in as an additional heavyweight to the international pressure for respecting the rule of law, represented by The Hague-based arbitration court's ruling.

France in the Asia-Pacific

Contrary to general perception, France is no stranger in this volatile theater in the Far East. The announced French initiative may not be so surprising when one recalls that France is also an Asia-Pacific nation with vital interests in the region. It has territories in the Southern Pacific: French Polynesia, New Caledonia, and Wallis & Futuna islands. Combine this to territories in the Indian Ocean (La Reunion, Mayotte, Kerguelen, etc.), and France is also an Indo-Pacific nation.

These overseas territories add to those in the Caribbean's to give France the world's second largest Exclusive Economic

Zone (EEZ) (11 million square kilometers) after the United States, 62 percent of which is located in the Pacific and 24 percent in the Indian Ocean. 1,500,000 French citizens live in the French Indo-Pacific territories (500,000 in the Pacific) besides the 130,000 French nationals in various Asia-Pacific countries.

These territories, EEZ, and population necessitate adequate protection and policing. This explains the permanent presence of 8,000 French military personnel in the Indo-Pacific area (2,800 in the Pacific). In the Pacific area alone, France operates two surveillance frigates, four patrol vessels, two multi-mission ships, five maritime surveillance aircraft, four tactical transport aircraft, and seven helicopters.

Although the European Union as such does not particularly shine as a visible strategic presence in the Asia-Pacific region, France, through various treaties and agreements, maintains a network of "strategic partnerships" with Asian countries such as Japan, China, India, Indonesia, Australia, Singapore, and Vietnam.

France also has developing strategic relationships with Malaysia and New Zealand. And it takes part in almost every major regional strategic forum such as the Shangri-La Dialogue in Singapore, the ASEAN Regional Forum, and the Pacific Coast Guard Forum, to mention only a few. France is the first of EU nations to have signed up to the Treaty of Amity and Cooperation in Southeast Asia, the TAC.

Moreover, France is a major provider of defense equipment in Asia. It has recently inked a deal to provide 12 new submarines to Australia. It is in the process of selling Rafale jet fighters to India and it has assisted Malaysia in setting up its submarine force. France also maintains research cooperation on defense matters with Singapore. Few people know that fighter pilots of the Singapore Air Force train on a permanent basis in southern France.

On a historical note too, France is not new in the region. According to Professor Shawn McHale writing in May 2016 for the "Rising Power Initiative," France, as colonial ruler of

Vietnam at the time, in 1931 asserted its sovereignty over part of the South China Sea. French sovereignty was challenged by Japan throughout World War II and both stopped their claims only in the 1950s.

Why France and the EU?

Given this background, questions may still linger on why France, which, along with other European countries, has important trade interests with China, would choose to ruffle Chinese feathers at this point by entering the fray in the South China Sea. In fact, the French initiative stems from a mounting concern in Europe that the aggressive Chinese expansion in the South China Sea and China's rejection of the Permanent Court of Arbitration's authority would constitute a serious issue for global governance and the rule of law, which will have far reaching consequences beyond Southeast Asia.

This concern, expressed in the March 11 declaration by the EU High Representative for Foreign Affairs, was repeated in the communiqué of the June G7 summit in Japan and was echoed in various statements by European officials and scholars. Coincidentally, the Arbitration Court's award came on the very opening day of the 2016 EU-China Summit in Beijing. This has allowed EU President Donald Tusk to insist diplomatically to his Chinese hosts that, regarding the South China Sea, "the rule-based international order is in our common interest and both China and the EU have to protect it." EU foreign policy chief Federica Mogherini also called on "all parties to respect legal decisions and uphold the UNCLOS including freedom of navigation."

Indeed, as Le Drian said in substance in his speech at the Shangri-La Dialogue, if the rule of law and freedom of navigation are not respected now and here in the South China Sea, tomorrow they will be trumped elsewhere in the world, including in and around Europe itself.

So, France sees an urgent need to back up the EU's common concern with concrete action by conducting FONOPs in this part of the world, preferably under European colors.

It is worth noting that, even before the EU's March declaration of concern and the international court's ruling in July, the French Navy has already been operating in the South China Sea for years. In the most recent cases, French naval ships have carried out joint drills with Australian warships (and Vietnamese navy personnel) off Vietnam's coast (November 2015) as well as with the Malaysian Navy off the northern coast of Borneo (February 2016). Besides, French Navy's "*Jeanne d'Arc* Group," a fleet led by a state-of-the-art helicopter carrier, has been visiting the South China Sea in its annual cruises from the Mediterranean to the Pacific.

Cautious Neutrality

Understandably, some might still wonder how this effort for upholding the rule of law and freedom of navigation in the South China Sea may negatively affect France's (and the EU's) huge trade interests with China, an economic giant with a record of punishing its trade partners for sensitive political motives. For example, in 2008, the French economy suffered severe Chinese reprisals following French condemnations of human rights violations in Tibet. In another case, Norway was commercially punished following the 2010 Nobel Peace Prize award to jailed Chinese dissident Liu Xiaobo.

However, despite what appears to be a challenge to China in the South China Sea, France and the EU have carefully maintained strict neutrality in specific territorial disputes. This neutrality, reiterated by Mogherini on July 13 in Beijing, is after all in line with what China has consistently asked the EU. It should ensure that Beijing would not react beyond mere expressions of displeasure to a French/EU FONOP which, in strict official term, is not aimed at China alone.

Mercantile Aims or Principled Motivation?

It cannot be denied that some skeptics see a different motivation in the French initiative. In their eyes, the fifth-largest arms exporter in the world may see an opportunity in the rising need for new defense equipment in a region made increasingly nervous and volatile by the threat of an assertive China, if not by the saber-rattling North Korea. Rising Chinese maritime assertiveness is pushing countries in the Indo-Pacific area to a rush to modernize their arsenals. This means a need for France to increase its presence in the region with a promising market.

However, as far as France is concerned, I am rather inclined to see a principled motivation behind its new initiative in the South China Sea. France does have an honorable record of persistently upholding international justice, even at the cost of its own economic interests. Such was the case in the above-mentioned 2008 friction over Tibet, putting France at odds with China. Such was also the case when, in 2003, France braved the furious wrath of the United States, its oldest ally and major trade partner, by leading the worldwide opposition to America's invasion of Iraq.

This time around, the ruling of the Permanent Court of Arbitration gives France a new impetus to stand up again in the defense of international justice in the South China Sea, because this also means defending the rule of law elsewhere.

This being said, while the French Navy continues to be present in the South China Sea, the prospect of an EU fleet patrolling these waters may still be a long way away, given the multiple crises and divisions within the European bloc, especially after Brexit. But as a EU founding member most active in pushing for a common defense policy, France is best suited for coordinating such an operation among EU partners.

INDIA'S STAKES IN THE SOUTH CHINA SEA

The South China Sea area comprising of islands, rocks and reefs are considered strategic, economic and political assets for the littoral states in the South China Sea because, they can serve as legal base points for states to project their claims of exclusive jurisdiction over waters and resources in the SCS. The sea is believed to be harboring large reserves of oil and natural gas and is in demand for its rich fishing.

With the rise in demand for energy resources, the disputes in the area have been further exacerbated. It is a critical navigational waterway in this region which is used from the west of the Indian Ocean to East Asia. The island group and the security of the sea lanes (marine terrorism, piracy, marine ecosystems) has been perceived as important since it is an important shipping lane and ASEAN, India, Taiwan, China, Japan and South Korea are all heavily dependent upon international and extra regional trade-most of which is shipped through the area.

As economies develop the SCS is fast becoming the focus of tension. The straits that separate these islands are important not only because restrictions upon passage would seriously disrupt international commerce but also because control over the islands would permit dominance over those routes.

SCS is contested in whole or in part by six littoral parties: China, Taiwan, Vietnam, Philippines, Malaysia and Brunei. (The China and Taiwan claims are in fact a single claim) with each one seeking to give real effect to its sovereign and jurisdictional claims.

The claims made by the parties can be separated into historical, claims of discovery and occupation and claims that rest on the extension of sovereign jurisdiction under interpretation of the provisions of the United Nations Convention on the Law of the Sea (UNCLOS).

Although the assertions of sovereignty, rivalry over maritime resources, nationalism and attempts to consolidate jurisdictional and legal claims have been long standing issues where actions by one claimant or another has drawn reaction from others, it is China's assertive actions backed by modern maritime enforcement capabilities that are proving to be a cause for concern.

As such, China receives the greatest attention because it is by far the most powerful claimant and has the record of using force to pursue its territorial claims. China's economic engine is becoming more dependent on imported energy, and recent

Chinese moves suggest safeguarding its energy sources near and far has become an unstated "core issue".

As defined by the Chinese officially, core issues are those that must be protected and secured by any means including military measures. China has been relentlessly increasing its capacity to exercise control over the Sea by strengthening its capacity and capability to establish its increasing maritime domain (MDA) and its emergence as Asia's pre-eminent naval power.

All this goes in making China a potential game changer in the context of the territorial disputes that leaves the other claimants, who cannot match PLAN's increasing might, at an unenviable situation.

These moves taken by Beijing also indicate its growing aggressiveness and unilateralism, which clearly go against the spirit of the 2002 DOC (Declaration of Conduct of parties), a multilateral political document agreed upon by the ASEAN and China that calls for resolution of 'territorial and jurisdictional disputes by peaceful means, without resorting to the threat of force.'

All of these developments have spilled over impacting India's interest that poses a severe challenge. Indian involvement in the SCS could have implications on other territorial disputes.

China's assertiveness is not good news for the region and especially troubling for India more so since India has unsettled borders with China. As such India cannot afford to simply sit and watch such a situation grow.

INDIA AND THE SOUTH CHINA SEA

Although India is a non claimant to the SCS Island it is concerned with the developments in the SCS. Even though the SCS area may seem far from the Indian mainland but in actual terms it is not so when one considers the Andaman and Nicobar Islands.

It is also important to note that India's trade with Japan and South Korea has been growing and hence, it is crucial that freedom of navigation is maintained in the South China Sea through which the trading routes between India and these East Asian countries pass.

India's sea bound trade that passes through Indian Ocean constitutes 92-95 per cent of its total trade and, there are estimates that nearly 25 per cent (and growing) of this sea bound trade passes through South China Sea. India like China is also energy deficit country and is stretching its resources all over the world to access hydrocarbons in what ever form and quantity available.

India's oil and gas exploration and extractions in Myanmar and Vietnam need to be understood in this respect. Therefore, there is no way that India would retreat from South China Sea just because China or any other country has taken an exception to its economic and naval activities in this region.

Meanwhile, India-ASEAN trade has reached US$ 57.89 billion in 2010-11. Any major conflict in the South China Sea region is bound to impact Indian economic interests.

India is concerned that should an armed conflict break out, the SLOC would be disrupted, which India cannot allow it to happen. Besides, India is worried that if China controls this sea space it will dictate maritime traffic, both civilian and military. Therefore, its priority is to maintain freedom of navigation in the sea both merchant and naval ships. India is of the opinion that the SCS region was a key to its energy security, and that the conflict must be resolved peacefully as per international laws. India has in the recent past increased its activities in that area.

Apart from growing defence ties with Vietnam, India and Japan are building up their own defence relationship. A security interest opposite China is also leading India to a strategic engagement with ASEAN states.

However, India will have to be more proactive to take the lead and evolve proactive policies to influence regional developments in its favor instead of adopting a policy which is more often than not reactive to the China's actions.

Second, India would like to have a voice in a major regional security issue that would confer prestige commensurate with its power status. India is poised to play a greater role in the region, thanks to the growing strength of its Navy.

It is expected to take delivery of the refitted aircraft carrier, the Admiral Gorshkov by next year from Russia while work goes on apace on the indigenous Air Defence Ship (scheduled for completion by 2015.)

Meanwhile, India has started the construction of its first indigenous nuclear submarine in 2009 and has plans to induct a third aircraft carrier by 2017. The Indian Navy has inducted into service the nuclear-powered attack submarine INS Chakra, brought on a 10-year lease from Russia.

India's involvement in the exploration of oil and gas in the region through joint ventures with a claimant state Vietnam has been a subject of great discussion owing to Vietnam China spat in the area.

China raised objection to India's oil exploration in the Vietnamese claimed area of the South China Sea at two levels. Without naming India the Chinese Foreign Ministry Spokesperson said that China hoped that foreign countries will not get involved in the dispute and that they will respect and support countries in the region to solve the dispute through bilateral channels.

The Global Times commented strongly describing India's deal with Vietnam as a serious political provocation and calling upon China to use every possible means to stop this. The People's Daily cautioned saying "it was not worthwhile for Vietnam and India to damage the greater interests of peace, stability and economic development between China and Vietnam, China and India, and in the whole region, for the sake of small interests in the SCS.

The External Affairs Spokesperson while speaking of the Indian official position said that cooperation with Vietnam or any other country is always as per international laws, norms and conventions.

India's Foreign Minister S. M Krishna, who was attending the 14th India-Vietnam Joint Commission Meeting reiterated that India's public sector company, the OVL (ONGC Videsh Limited), will go ahead with oil and gas exploration in Vietnam's off shore blocks being disputed by China as part of its Exclusive Economic Zone (EEZ).

Indian news paper reports on Krishna's talks in Vietnam said that the two sides (India and Vietnam) agreed during the discussions that there is no question of violating any International Law in going ahead with the exploratory work. The meetings on 16 September 2011 have paved the way for expansion of the ONGC Videsh's oil and gas exploration work."

The Foreign Minsiters statement and the official recations that were generated subsequently highlights that India's involvement in the oil exploration was well within Vietnam's EEZ and in accordance with the 1982 UN Convention on the Law of the Sea or UNCLOS. External affairs Minister S.M.

Krishna reacting to the Chinese concern over India's cooperation with Vietnam in the disputed SCS said, "India's position is very clear that these are all international waterways to increase trade among nations, and hence we will have to look at it from that angle."

"We have to strengthen that angle. India is ready to do that with other countries so that relations will get a boost through these waterways." India has in the recent past increased its activities in that area. Apart from growing defence ties with Vietnam, India and Japan are building up their own defence relationship.

Security interests opposite China are also leading the two countries to more strategic engagement with ASEAN states.

Opinion however has been divided in India as to whether India should go ahead with oil exploration in the area.

Among those who caution such a move are the former Navy Chief Arun Prakash and Former intelligence officer (RAW, Research and Analysis Wing) B.Raman who caution because India may not have the military capabilities to protect OVL's exploration activity if China were to take any disruptive action. A clear understanding of India's position on the South China Sea will have to be seen in perspective. The relations between India and Vietnam predate any conflict between India and China as also between China and Vietnam.

15 India and Vietnam have consistently moved forward in the stategic cooperation. The visits of Indian naval ships to Vietnam also date back to 2001, following Indian Defence Minister George Fernandes's visit to Vietnam. Since then Indian ships have been regularly vising the Vietnamese shores.

The ONGC Videsh Limited's (OVL) presence in Vietnam is not a recent phenomenon. India's exploration in Vietnam started as early as 1988 in association with the then Soviet union.

With the discovery of attractive potential of hydrocarbon deposits in Vietnam's territorial waters and EEZ, Vietnam had opened its oil and gas sectors widely to the foreign companies in 1990. In 1992 India's ONGC joined a joint venture with Petro- Vietnam, the Burma Petroleum of the UK and DNSO (Stat Oil) of Norway.

In 2001 India's oil fields in Vietnam were its largest overseas possessions in the energy sector. The ONGC held 45% shares in its joint venture with Petro-Vietnam and the United Knigdom's BP (British Petroleum) group. In November 2002, gas started flowing from the ONGC's joint venture at the Nam Con Son basin inVietnam. Due to lack of facility in India to refine the crude oil received from Vietnam, India sold this oil in the international market.

Its first joint-venture for offshore oil and natural gas exploration in Vietnam's Lan Tay field along with Petro Vietnam and BP became functional in 2003. The OVL of India had signed a production sharing contract with Petro-Vietnam in May 2006. This energy cooperation between the two countries have been strengthened over time. China has been periodically taking exception to any international oil and gas exploration in Vietnam's EEZ in South China Sea, including India.

China also appeared to be taking strong action against unilateral oil exploration activities when it prevented international oil companies BP and Exxonmobil from exploring in Vietnam-claimed areas, reportedly warning them that doing so would affect their own projects in China.

China had offered a reluctant Vietnam to enter into a joint development of the resources in the disputed SCS islands. In 1994, the then Vietnamese Vice Foreign Minister, Vu Khoan reacting to the China's offer of joint development said:" The problem is which sea area we are going to develop jointly... China's intention in proposing the joint development of the Spratlys Islands is an attempt to justify its presence in Vietnam's territorial waters under the name of joint development.

Would you accept an invitation to dinner from a person who was trying to steal a US$100 bill from your pocket...

Vietnam's refusal to enter into joint exploration with China has irked China considerably and it has taken recource to force in asserting its claims. Several incidence of armed confrontation with China has taken place at sea with Vietnam.

The standoff in the region had intensified when China's state –owned oil firm China National Offshore Corporation (CNOOC) called for bids from foreign companies offering exploration of oil in nine blocks in the South China Sea, which Vietnam also claims sparking off protest in Hanoi.

The agreement signed during the India-visit of Vietnamese President Truong Tan Sang, in October 2011, included an accord to promote investments, exploration, refining, transportation and supply of oil and gas in Vietnamese waters of the South China Sea.

A deal for oil exploration was signed between India's state owned oil and Natural Gas Corporation (ONGC) Videsh Ltd (OVL) and Vietnam's Oil and Gas Group, Petro Vietnam. The agreement shall be in a framework coming into force for three areas.

The agreement says the two nations will cooperate on "various fronts in the oil and gas sectors-in upstream activities, in refining, in gas processing in Vietnam... in India and in third countries...as part of ongoing cooperation with Vietnam... We have presence in two blocks-128 and 6.1...." India's state runs Oil and Natural Gas Corporation (ONGC) signed a deal with Vietnam's Petro Vietnam to purchase BP's stakes in oil and gas development in waters off the Vietnamese coast. The block has been at the centre of much diplomatic bad blood among China, Vietnam and India that included demarches, summons and affirmations of sovereignty over the same patch of sea.

The joint communiqué issued at the end of the visit of the Chinese defence minister General Liang Guanglie to India, the first such visit since 1976 said the two sides had agreed to cooperate in the Asia- Pacific region and agreed to "work together to maintain peace and stability of the Asia-pacific region."

The consensus reached was the first clear indication that India has a role to play in the strategically important Asia-Pacific region. Until recently New Delhi wasn't considered to be a power to contend with.

If India and China can at least agree to work in the Asia-Pacific region, it could mean an opening for New Delhi in the South China Sea, where Indian oil companies are prospecting for energy off Vietnam.

While China protests the deal as violating its sovereignty, ONGC and Petro Vietnam claim the area in question is within Vietnamese territorial waters. For all the objections being raised on account of sovereignty over the SCS, Vietnamese President Sang asserted, "...all disputes in the Eastern Sea (SCS) should be settled through peaceful negotiations on the basis of respect for international laws, including the 1982 UN Convention on the Law of the Seas."

It needs to be noted that according to the 1982 United Nations Convention on the Law of the Sea, "... Every State has the right to establish the breadth of its territorial sea up to a limit not exceeding 12 nautical miles, measured from baselines determined in accordance with this Convention."

India remained unfazed by Chinese objection and went ahead and inked an agreement with Vietnam to promote oil exploration in the SCS. Vietnam and India have rejected the claims made by China on the SCS.

At the strategic level, it has been markedly evident that India's growing affinity with Vietnam is expected to be interrupted in a multifarious manner in the region. In a sense, India's relations with regional players like Vietnam are being viewed through the prism of tensions floating in the disputed waters of the SCS.

The Indian Vietnamese ties were further strengthened when the Vietnamese President Truong Tan Sang met Indian Prime Minister Manmohan Singh in New Delhi, with both sides pledging to maintain peace and security in the South China Sea while expanding the contents of their partnership. India's growing engagement with Vietnam, and by extension in the South China Sea, can be seen as a logical expansion of its Look East Policy (LEP). This could not have gone unnoticed by China, when it entered into a joint communiqué with India at the end of General Liang Guanglie to India wherein the two sides have agreed to cooperate in the Asia Pacific region.

Yet China chose to remain silent on this. However, for India, how to manage China and mould its behavior would be its biggest challenge.

Many in India argue that given the high stakes that China and India have in each other's economies, and the fact that the two countries cooperate on issues ranging from climate change to sea bed research, are enough reasons to reduce the likelihood of conflict between the two.

But as developments in SCS exemplify, economic interdependence has never been an antidote to conflict. And to a large extent it is true that economic ties that lack support of strategic partnership tend to be less stable and even volatile, as is apparent from India's economic relationships with China.

Alternatively, China and India can make a close strategic collaboration to lead the way towards freedom, prosperity and stability in the Indo-Pacific region.

The Indian ship INS Airavat was cautined by China through a radio message that the Indian Ship was in China's territorial waters when it was paying a friendship visit to Vietnam.

While the Chinese Foreign office claimed the area and said that it was looking for information through competent authorities, India said that there was no confrontation.

At the same time it made it clear that India "supports freedom of navigation in international waters including South China Sea... in accordance with the accepted international law... to be respected by all."

Again China's action in reaction to the 4 Indian Navy ships, including the indigenously built stealth frigate "shivalik" (F-47), left Philippines en route to South Korea, a Chinese Navy frigate said: " Welcome to the SCS, Foxtrot-47" and stayed alongside the Indian ships for few hours.

Escorting the Indian ship through what India views as international waters underscores for officials how Beijing increasingly views one of the world's most important waterways.

This development clearly indicates that tensions are unlikely to dissipate as China strives to recover sovereignty over these islands. Furthermore the Chinese standoff with Philippines at the Scarborough Shoal and the run-ins with Vietnamese vessels, have emerged as new challenges with competing interests over a crucial international waterway.

With Indian naval ships making ports of call in Vietnam and the Philippines-the two countries with which China has had recent strains- the Vice Admiral stressed that India's "relationships are not at the cost of anybody else" and that there were no "specific reasons" for the port calls.

India supported "freedom of navigation in all waters in the seven seas," he said, and believed bilateral issues between nations "should be resolved peacefully as per international law and international maritime law."

What is more discomforting is the Chinese behavior in the area and the speculation of what if ships, persons and properties of India and the other neighboring states, foreign companies engaged in resource exploration, and even commercial ships become targets of intimidation?

These apprehensions become strong in the face of China's disparity between its oft-stated pledge to uphold freedom of sea lanes and deeds. Therefore, ensuring the freedom of navigation through the South China Sea is the top priority for India together with protecting Indian commercial interests in countries like Vietnam. India will take the China factor into account considering its global and regional presence. And as the Indian Maritime Doctrine suggested in 2007, events in the South China Sea have a bearing on the Indian Ocean region.

It is therefore, in India and ASEAN's mutual interests to pool their efforts to ensure the freedom of navigation in this very important stretch of water, while keeping the channels of communication open with China for the peaceful resolution of all outstanding disputes. The almost-universal acknowledgement of the United Nations Convention on the Law of the Sea (UNCLOS) as international law and the upward trajectory of Indo-ASEAN relations can set a precedent for the peaceful and non-military resolution of future disputes by reinforcing the role of non-littoral states in the South China Sea.

Yet, energy disputes such as this one reflect the disjointed state of the South China Sea dispute. While regional peace and stability may be the cited goal of both India and China, the shadow of intolerance that China casts over energy diplomacy will continue to define the potential paths to conflict resolution in the South China Sea. China's interest as well as the interests of India and other states will need to be addressed through dialogue and negotiation. Till then India will have to remain vigilant in order to safeguard its national interest.

SOUTH CHINA SEA DISPUTES: THE GLOBAL STRATEGIC IMPLICATIONS

South China Sea disputes have today ceased to be a regional concern of East Asia, the Western Pacific and the Asia Pacific.

The chain of developments in the South China Sea conflict increasingly point towards a growing involvement of the extra-regional and international stake holders in the dynamics of these disputes.

Regional disunity in south East Asia and lack of in-region military capabilities to impose even minimal deterrence on Chinese aggressive moves in the South China Sea conflicts opens the way for international stakeholders in the South China Sea region to step-in on the side of the China beleaguered nations.

United States is the countervailing power and Japan and India can be assessed as counterweights that add ballast to United States countervailing power in the Asia Pacific to checkmate China's unrestrained brinkmanship

Russia as an Asia Pacific power also needs to be co-opted towards this end. Russia has already declared its strategic pivot to Asia Pacific and the timing and intentions are open for debate.

At play in the South China Sea conflict is not only the United States undisguised moves of containment of China but also the first tentative moves by Japan and India towards politically checkmating China, if not militarily.

China's aggressive brinkmanship and use of force in the South China Sea conflicts have further reinforced Asian concerns about Chinese military power. In Asian capitals, the perception has taken root that China is not a responsible stakeholder in Asian security and stability.

This is a vast subject and hence only the more salient global strategic implications generated by escalation of South China Sea disputes are being selected for mention. These are as follows

- South China Sea Conflicts Induce Asian Polarisation & Stimulates a New Balance of Power Architecture in Asia Pacific
- South China Sea Conflict Major Spin-off: Western Pacific is No Longer 'Pacific'

- Global Responses to China's Escalated Brinkmanship on South China Sea Disputes
- The Most Significant Strategic Implication: China Generates a New Cold War in Asia Pacific

SOUTH CHINA SEA DISPUTES: THE REGIONAL STRATEGIC IMPLICATIONS

Regional disputes/ confrontations/ conflicts do not occur in a vacuum. They emerge from the contextual security environment that existed, currently exists and is likely to exist in the foreseeable future. Hence the South China Sea disputes need to be viewed in the overall security environment of Asia in the 21st Century. Perceptions play an important role both in the shaping of the contextual security environment and the scope and leeway it offers to prospective regional destabilisers and aggressive revisionist powers.

In the South China Sea disputes China's aggressiveness and brinkmanship on the issue needs to be assessed from China's perceptions of United States commitment to ASEAN security and stability and US ambiguities that China can exploit to further its strategic ends of gaining full control over the entire South China Sea region. China could not care less for ASEAN'S strategic sensitivities conscious that the ASEAN countries even collectively cannot impose deterrence on China's push into the South China Sea.

In terms of regional strategic implications stirred by China's aggressive pushes against ASEAN countries, once again some selected points of salience need to be highlighted from an overall perspective and these are as follows:

- ASEAN Countries Prodded into Arms Build-up/Arms Race
- China's Conflictual Confrontation on South China Sea Generates Japan and India's

Fast Track Military Build-up:

- ASEAN Collective Unity: The Myth Shattered by China

SOUTH CHINA SEA CONFLICTS INDUCE ASIAN POLARISATION

Asia's strategic polarisation today stands stimulated by China's conflictual and adversarial stances on the South China Sea dispute. Taking off from this Asian polarisation is the emergence of new 'balance of power' architectures in the Asia Pacific.

"China's strategic ambitions on the rise of a Sino-centric Asia seem foredoomed as a contemporaneous strategic review of the Asian security environment suggests. China's switch from a Grand Strategy relying on Soft power' to exercise of 'hard power' seems to have generated a strategic polarisation of the Asia Pacific. The Chinese switch in its Grand Strategy seems to have generated perception of a China Threat engulfing the Asia Pacific."

China's use of military aggression, military and political coercion on the South China Sea conflicts against its ASEAN neighbours who made concerted efforts for decades to integrate China in ASEAN dialogue mechanisms, not only betrayed their trust but also in the process has dented China's credibility as a responsible and peace-loving neighbour of ASEAN.

Historically, the Asia Pacific has witnessed different 'balance of power' templates in play at various times.

However United States military interventions in the Balkans in the 1990s and in Afghanistan and Iraq during the 2000s upset the existing 'balance of power' in the region. The ensuing strategic vacuum led to China's meteoric military build-up without any checkmating by the United States.

The South China Sea conflicts erupting in the period post-2009 and their strategic impact nudged the United States back to a strategic pivot to Asia Pacific and restoring the balance sought to be upset by China.

In 2013, the Asia Pacific is witnessing the emergence of new 'balance of power' architecture in the Asia Pacific. Broadly, the United States formulation to this end incorporates the reinforcement of its existing military alliance structure in North East Asia based on Japan, South Korea and the Philippines; remedying absence of US security linkages on the South China Sea littoral states by seeking strategic relationships with Vietnam and Indonesia and evolving a vital strategic partnership with India., besides strategic openings to Myanmar.

"Concluding it can be stated that what United States could not achieve in all the preceding years in terms of strategic polarisation of the Asia Pacific against a probable China Threat, the aggressive policies of China in the first flush of impatience to manifest her new-found military power in Asia seems to have generated a noticeable strategic polarisation in the Asia Pacific, to the consequent disadvantage of China."

PHILIPPINES CLAIMS CHINA IS THREAT TO PEACE IN SOUTHEAST ASIA

In August 2011, AFP reported that Philippine Foreign Secretary Albert del Rosario warned that China's bold claims of control over the South China Sea are one of the biggest threats to peace in Southeast Asia, The threat concerns not only the rival claimants to the hotly contested area, but also all other entities using the waters for shipping, he said in a speech at a Manila university.

"If Philippine sovereign rights can be denigrated by this baseless claim, many countries should begin to contemplate the potential threat to freedom of navigation in the South China Sea," he said.

"The imperative to speak frankly was borne out of an enormous sense of exigency and urgency... to one of the greatest threats to the stability of our progressive Southeast Asian neighbourhood."

Del Rosario repeated calls for UN arbitration on the disputes and for all claimants to jointly develop disputed sections, while asserting Manila's sovereign right to explore for oil and gas deposits on its own in the sea's Reed Bank section.

Filipino Lawmakers Visit Disputed Island

Ship deployed from USS TortugaIn July 2011. AP reported, a group of Filipino lawmakers flew to Pag-asa Island, the Philippine-occupied island in the South China Sea to assert their country's claim to the region in defiance of China's protest that the visit threatens regional stability. Even though the daylong visit upset China, a senior Chinese diplomat at a meeting of Asian security officials in Bali, Indonesia, said that his country has agreed to draft guidelines for behaviour in the disputed region with the 10-member Association of Southeast Asian Nations.

The mission to Pagasa Island was organized by a left-wing legislator, Walden Bello, who, after years of criticizing the United States, now worries more about China. "Just look at their maps and you say: 'My God, how do they come up with these claims?' " Bello said. He sponsored a motion in congress for the South China Sea to be called the West Philippine Sea.

Dozens of Filipino troops and sunburned villagers welcomed the four-member congressional delegation on Pag-asa Island. "This is a historic moment for the congressional delegation. This is Philippine territory," Bello told a small crowd of residents, government officials and troops who greeted him in the intense tropical heat.

Bello carried two new Philippine flags for the island. He and the others sang their national anthem during a flag-raising ceremony in front of a small one-story town hall on the 91-acre (37-hectare) island, which also has a military camp and a small civilian community of about 60 people. Pag-asa, internationally called Tithu Island, lies in the South China Sea about 300 miles (480 kilometres) west of the western Philippine province of Palawan. Kalayaan municipality was established in 1978.

Chinese Embassy spokesman Ethan Sun said Tuesday that China would relay its "great concern" to the Philippine government over the lawmakers' trip. He said it goes against the spirit of a 2002 accord between China and ASEAN, which is nonbinding. The trip "serves no purpose but to undermine peace and stability in the region and sabotage China-Philippine relationship," Sun said in a statement.

Bello said that the trip, which his party calls a "sovereignty mission," aims at peacefully asserting the Philippines' claim to Pag-asa and surrounding territory."We come in peace," he said in a speech on the island. "We support a diplomatic solution, but let there be no doubt in anybody's mind, in any foreign power's mind that if they dare to eject us from Pag-asa, if they dare to eject us from our rightful territories, Filipinos will not take that sitting down. Filipinos are born to resist aggression. Filipinos are willing to die for their soil."

3

South China Sea Conflict and Troubled Waters

The Permanent Court of Arbitration in The Hague today undercut China's claim to maritime territory in the South China Sea by ruling that China's claims have no legal basis. The case was first brought to the court by the Philippines in January 2013. The country argued that under the U.N. Convention of the Law of The Sea (UNCLOS) the Chinese did not have the right to its vast maritime territorial claims in the South China Sea, its reclamation schemes did not constitute legitimate islands and its activities were damaging the marine environment and violating the Philippines' sovereign rights. The court decided in favor of the Philippines.

The court's ruling will strengthen the claims of other countries in the South China Sea against Chinese maritime expansionism. The court's decision is celebrated in Vietnam. China will ignore the ruling. All along it has claimed the Permanent Court of Arbitration did not have jurisdiction. However, the court's decisions and the Chinese policy of nonparticipation and nonacceptance shake their standing as a member in good standing of an international community bound by rules of order and international treaties. China will snub the legal international order and seek bilateral negotiations with the Philippines.

The Philippines has gained from the court ruling by drawing international attention to China's claim and activities in the region. Since the court had no powers of enforcement, the Philippines' victory is a legal one but unlikely to lead to a Chinese back down. The ruling does not make diplomacy any easier for the U.S., which now has to deal with an ally who has won a legal decision but also a rival who will not back down under the muscular pose of President Xi Jinping, even after the court ruling. What is the background to these tensions and what are their likely implications and consequences?

Reassertion of global status

In recent years, China has been asserting claims in the region and has built up atolls and islands to be large enough to stage military exercises. This region is of major economic and geopolitical significance, with its vital commercial shipping lanes, rich fisheries and massive natural gas and oil deposits. China's economic success is obvious. In the past 25 years, it has grown to become the second-largest economy in the world, lifting millions out of poverty in rates of economic growth unparalleled in the modern world.

But it is crucial for non-Chinese to remember that China's leaders see international political standing, not only economic clout, as an important issue. Heightened global stature not only makes up for a century when China was on the wrong end of asymmetrical relations with other powers, especially Japan, and subject to dismemberment and annexations, but it also reclaims China's position as one of the world's preeminent centers of power and influence. China claims a wide swath of territory in the South China Sea. It is often shown on Chinese maps as nine dashes and, indeed, referred to in those words.

Laws and zones

Exclusive Economic Zones (EEZs), first introduced in the 1982 U.N. Convention on the Law of The Sea, are areas where states can claim exclusionary rights over marine resources. They have a limit of 200 nautical miles (370 km) from the coastal baseline, the seaward edge of its territorial sea. Where EEZs overlap, as is the case in some parts of the South China

Sea, it is up to the neighboring states in question to delineate the maritime border.

Matters are made more complex when small islands – rather than a coastline or continental edge – are used to define a nation's EEZ and are claimed by more than one country. A country can establish territorial sea up to 12 nautical miles from a naturally formed island and from there can claim a 200-nautical-mile EEZ. Part of China's strategy in the waters of the South China Sea then is to lay claim over islands, natural and artificial, in order to establish sovereignty to claim the surrounding waters.

MANY ISLANDS IN DISPUTE

China's territorial claim overlaps with the EEZs of Vietnam, the Philippines, Malaysia and Brunei. There are a number of ongoing disputes over the islands in the South China Sea. The Paracel Islands, for example, are claimed by both China and Vietnam. When China moved a giant oil rig to the region in 2013, it was seen as a direct threat by the Vietnamese and undermined China-Vietnam relations. The Chinese have built a surface-to-air missile defense system on Woody Island, one of the largest of the Paracel Islands, and recently added a helicopter base to Duncan Island.

The Scarborough Shoal, a 60-square-mile chain of rocks and reefs, is claimed by both China and the Philippines. In 2012 China took effective control by reconstructing seven islands. Control over the islands in the shoal allows China to monitor U.S. military activity.

It was these actions that prompted the Philippines to take the matter to the court in the Hague in 2013, rather than pursuing bilateral discussion. The Philippines, unlike other states in the region, has fewer economic ties with China and close military ties with the U.S. Today's court ruling firmly denies China's claim to an EEZ based on its activities in the Scarborough Shoal. The election of a new president may, however, herald a new change in Filipino-Chinese relations. Benigno S. Aquino III has suggested the U.S. would need to respond militarily if China develops the shoal to maintain credibility in the region. And incoming President Rodrigo Duterte has said he's open to direct negotiations with China.

And then there are the Spratly Islands, more than 740 reefs, islets, atolls and islands, to which six countries lay claim: China, Vietnam, Taiwan, Malaysia, Brunei and the Philippines.

And all but Brunei have built or claimed outposts there. However, China's activity has ramped up since 2013, when it started to build on existing rock outcrops and reefs to create 2,900 acres of new land. Vietnam and the Philippines have undertaken similar ventures, but China has outpaced every other country combined. Sand is pumped up from the sea floor and spread across islands and even the live coral of submerged reefs that are then concreted over to become bases capable of providing docks for ships and runways for planes. Military runways have been built on Mischief Reef and Subi Reef. In other words, the Chinese have militarized the disputed islands. However, today's court ruling states that Mischief Reef, Second Thomas Shoal and Subi Reef were submerged at high tide in their natural condition and don't generate a 12-nautical-mile territorial sea or EEZ.

PIVOT TO ASIA

China's claim to Scarborough Shoal always lacked any connection with current laws of the sea; I would interpret it as a claiming of world power status and importance. After today it no longer has any international legal authority.

The Chinese look around the region and see the projection of U.S. power: U.S. bases in South Korea, Japan, a nuclear submarine fleet, a military presence in Philippines and Australia and a fleet of super carriers able to project power and influence. The Chinese see the significant military and naval presence in the region as a threat to their regional power status.

The U.S. is the only country capable of proving a credible counter force. The U.S. response is sometimes referred to as the "Pivot to Asia"announced in 2011.

It includes an increase in U.S. Navy assets in the Pacific, a planned deployment of 2,500 marines to Darwin, Australia and a reassurance to regional allies to keep the South China Sea free for navigation and trade. The U.S. Navy has undertaken maneuvers in the region to drive home two points: These are open waters and the U.S. is still a credible force in the region. In October 2015 a U.S. warship passed within 12 nautical miles of a China artificial island. A U.S. guided-missile destroyer passed through the disputed Paracel Islands in January 2016.

TRIBUNAL ISSUES LANDMARK RULING IN SOUTH CHINA SEA ARBITRATION

The wait is over: a judgment has been issued in the *Philippines v. China*South China Sea arbitration. A five-judge tribunal constituted under the Permanent Court of Arbitration (PCA) in The Hague has released its much-anticipated Award concerning the Philippines' challenge to a number of China's maritime claims and activities in the region. The Philippines initiated the arbitration in January 2013 under the dispute settlement procedures of Annex VII to the 1982 United Nations Convention on the Law of the Sea (UNCLOS).

Summary of Key Claims and Holdings

The Philippines' claims fell into four general categories. The ruling of the Tribunal on each category of claims is summarized below: The broadest claim was a challenge to China's "nine-dash line" covering most of the South China Sea. China has never clarifiedwhether the line represents a claim to the islands within the line and their adjacent waters; a boundary of national sovereignty over all the enclosed waters (including, but not limited by, the land features inside the line); or a "historic" claim of sovereignty or some other set of historic rights to the maritime space within the line. The Philippines sought a declaration that the countries' respective rights and obligations regarding the waters, seabed, and maritime features of the South China Sea are governed by UNCLOS. As such, China's claims based on any "historic rights" to waters, seabed, and subsoil within the nine-dash line are contrary to UNCLOS and invalid.

Holding: UNCLOS "comprehensively" governs the parties' respective rights to maritime areas in the South China Sea. Therefore, to the extent China's nine-dash line is a claim of "historic rights" to the waters of the South China Sea, it is invalid.

Reasoning: Whatever historic rights China may have had were extinguished when UNCLOS was adopted, to the extent those rights were incompatible with UNCLOS.

The Philippines sought a determination as to whether certain land features in the Spratly Islands claimed by both China and the Philippines are properly characterized as islands, rocks, low tide elevations (LTEs), or submerged banks. Under UNCLOS, an "island" generates both a territorial sea of 12 nautical miles and an exclusive economic zone (EEZ) of up to 200 nautical miles, subject to delimitation of a maritime boundary with any other countries' overlapping territorial seas or EEZs. A "rock" is entitled to a territorial sea no greater than 12 nautical miles, but not an EEZ. LTEs and submerged banks do not generate any such entitlements.

Holding: None of the features in the Spratly Islands generates an EEZ, nor can the Spratly Islands generate an EEZ collectively as a unit. As such, the Tribunal declared certain areas are within the Philippines' EEZ and not overlapped by any possible Chinese entitlement.

Reasoning: The baseline of analysis is what the features can sustain in their "natural condition" (i.e., not after construction of artificial islands, installation of desalination plants, etc.). Based on historical evidence, none of the features in the Spratly Islands can sustain either a stable community of people or economic activity that is not dependent on outside resources or purely extractive in nature. The current presence of personnel on the features is dependent on outside support and does not reflect the capacity of the features in their natural condition.

The Philippines sought a declaration that China violated UNCLOS by interfering with the Philippines' rights and freedoms within its EEZs. This includes preventing Philippine fishing around Scarborough Shoal, violating UNCLOS's environmental protection provisions through construction and fishing activities that have harmed the marine environment (including at Scarborough Shoal, Second Thomas Shoal, and Mischief Reef), and by dangerously operating law enforcement vessels around Scarborough Shoal.

Holding: China violated the Philippines' sovereign rights in its EEZ. It did so by interfering with Philippine fishing and hydrocarbon exploration; constructing artificial islands; and failing to prevent Chinese fishermen from fishing in the Philippines' EEZ. China also interfered with Philippine fishermen's traditional fishing rights near Scarborough Shoal (without prejudice to the question of sovereignty over Scarborough Shoal). China's construction of artificial islands at seven features in the Spratly Islands, as well as illegal fishing and harvesting by Chinese nationals, violate UNCLOS obligations to protect the marine environment. Finally, Chinese law enforcement vessels unlawfully created a serious risk of collision by physically obstructing Philippine vessels at Scarborough Shoal in 2012.

Reasoning: This set of holdings depended on the Tribunal finding that certain areas are within the Philippines' EEZ and not subject to possible overlapping Chinese entitlements. It also depended on finding that activities such as island construction are, *in accordance with China's own public statements*, not "military activities" and therefore not excluded from jurisdiction under UNCLOS. Once this was established, the Tribunal considered Chinese activities in the relevant areas and found that China had (a) interfered with Philippine petroleum exploration at Reed Bank, (b) purported to prohibit fishing by Philippine vessels within the Philippine EEZ, (c) protected and failed to prevent Chinese fishermen from fishing within the Philippine EEZ at Mischief Reef and Second Thomas Shoal, and (d) constructed artificial islands/installations at

Mischief Reef without the Philippines' authorization. As for Scarborough Shoal, regardless of who has sovereignty, both Philippine and Chinese fishermen have "traditional fishing rights" at the Shoal that were not extinguished by UNCLOS, and China violated the Philippines' rights by entirely preventing Filipino fishermen from fishing near Scarborough Shoal after May 2012. In addition, Chinese artificial island construction has caused "severe harm to the coral reef environment" and China has failed to stop its nationals from engaging in "harmful" and "destructive" harvesting and fishing of endangered sea turtles, coral, and giant clams in violation of UNCLOS. Finally, Chinese law enforcement vessels violated maritime safety obligations by creating a serious risk of collision on two occasions in April and May 2012 during the Scarborough Shoal standoff.

The Philippines sought a declaration that China's recent actions, specifically its land reclamation and construction of artificial islands in the Spratly Islands after the arbitration was commenced, violated the obligations UNCLOS places on states to refrain from conduct that "aggravates and extends" a dispute while dispute resolution proceedings are pending.

Holding: China has aggravated and extended the disputes through its dredging, artificial island-building, and construction activities.

Reasoning: While these proceedings were pending, China has built a large island on Mischief Reed, an LTE within the Philippines' EEZ; caused irreparable harm to the marine ecosystem; and permanently destroyed evidence of the natural condition of the features at issue.

Initial Takeaways

1. Not many people predicted that the Philippines would all but run the table in this case. It's hard to imagine a much more favorable outcome for their legal team.
2. One of the ironies of the Award is that China has vociferously argued in public statements that it is not "militarizing" the South China Sea and that its actions there are for civilian purposes. Those claims turned out

to be crucial to the Tribunal's conclusion that it had jurisdiction to consider the legality of certain Chinese actions such as construction of artificial islands in the South China Sea, because Article 298(1)(b) of UNCLOS excludes disputes concerning "military activities" from compulsory dispute settlement. Despite China's non-participation in the proceedings, the Tribunal went out of its way to review the December 2014 position paper issued by China's Ministry of Foreign Affairs as well as numerous public statements of Chinese leaders. This was an example of where those public statements worked against China's legal interests in the arbitration.

3. The Tribunal rejected the possibility that China could claim the entirety of the Spratly Islands as a single archipelagic feature, as suggested in recent statements by the Ministry of Foreign Affairs as well as a white paper issued last month by the Chinese Society of International Law. As Julian noted earlier, this was a bit of a preemptory legal strike against "any Chinese attempt to draw 'straight baselines' around the Spratlys and thus treat the whole area as a single entity for generating maritime rights."
4. Of all the rulings on the status of features in the Spratly Islands, perhaps none will generate more discussion than the conclusion that Itu Aba (Taiping Island) is a rock and not an island. Many observers thought that Itu Aba, the largest naturally occurring land feature in the Spratly Islands, had the strongest claim to being deemed an island entitled to both a territorial sea and an EEZ. The concepts the Tribunal employed to determine what makes something a "rock which cannot sustain human habitation or economic life of [its] own" are likely to guide future legal determinations of this character.

It will take time to digest this portion of the opinion, but the Tribunal's "habitability and economic life" factors seem to include:

- The objective capacity of the feature in its natural condition (i.e., "without external additions or modifications" and without outside support), to sustain, over an extended period of time, either
  - (a) a stable community of people for whom the feature constitutes a home and on which they can remain, or
  - (b) economic activity that is not
    - (i) dependent on outside resources, or
    - (ii) purely extractive in nature without the involvement of a local population.
- Factors contributing to the natural capacity of a feature to do so "include the presence of water, food, and shelter in sufficient quantities to enable a group of persons to live on the feature for an indeterminate period of time."
- In assessing these "capacity" factors, the Tribunal stated, "the most reliable evidence of the capacity of a feature will usually be the historical use to which it has been put." Applying that standard here, the Tribunal saw "no indication that anything fairly resembling a stable human community has ever formed on the Spratly Islands. Rather, the islands have been a temporary refuge and base of operations for fishermen and a transient residence for labourers engaged in mining and fishing."

Given its sweeping conclusions favoring the Philippines, the Award may seem to have nothing positive in it for China. But the Tribunal offered an important qualification to its judgment, and perhaps a bit of an olive branch toward the end of a decision it knew would not be well received in Beijing.

We should not assume, said the Tribunal, that these disputes are the product of *bad faith* on the part of the PRC; rather, they are the result of basic disagreements about respective rights and obligations and the applicability of UNCLOS. From paragraph 1198 of the Award: "The root of the disputes presented by the Philippines in this arbitration lies not in any intention on the part of China or the Philippines to infringe on the legal rights of the other, but rather—as has been apparent throughout these proceedings—in fundamentally different understandings of their respective rights under the Convention in the waters of the South China Sea. In such circumstances, the purpose of dispute resolution proceedings is to clarify the Parties' respective rights and obligations and thereby to facilitate their future relations in accordance with the general obligations of good faith that both governments unequivocally recognise."

Where does this leave us? China's position all along with respect to these proceedings can be summed up as "no acceptance, no participation, no recognition, and no implementation." The PRC Ministry of Foreign Affairs predictably wasted no time releasing astatement declaring that "the award is null and void and has no binding force."

The Philippine Foreign Affairs Secretary welcomed the decision, stating: "The Philippines strongly affirms its respect for this milestone decision as an important contribution to ongoing efforts in addressing disputes in the South China Sea." No surprises here, especially given that the Tribunal resolved virtually all the key issues in favor of the Philippines. For its part, the U.S. State Department issued a measured statement remarking that "[t]he decision today by the Tribunal in the Philippines-China arbitration is an important contribution to the shared goal of a peaceful resolution to disputes in the South China Sea."

As these statements suggest, the issuance of this Award by no means puts to rest the disputes or the tensions in the South China Sea. The arbitration was never going to resolve issues of sovereignty over the islands and rocks in the South China Sea, because disputes over territorial sovereignty are beyond the jurisdiction of an UNCLOS Tribunal.

And since the Tribunal has no power to enforce its nominally binding decision, questions now turn to what any form of "implementation" might look like and the effect this ruling will have on future negotiations over territorial sovereignty.

China, the Philippines, ASEAN countries, and the United States face a range of strategic questions about the best way forward. Will Beijingdemonstrate its disregard for the decision by engaging in land reclamation at Scarborough Shoal or declaring an Air Defense Identification Zone in the South China Sea, as some have predicted? Will it continue to insist on conditioning any future bilateral negotiations with the administration of new Philippine President Rodrigo Duterte on his government's rejection of the Tribunal's Award? Will it worry that some of these behaviors will push the Philippines and other ASEAN nations closer to the United States? Will we see the U.S. Navy conducting "pure" freedom of navigation operations (FONOPs) within 12 nautical miles of the Spratly Island features the Tribunal says are not entitled to a territorial sea?

WATER WARS: KNOWN UNKNOWNS IN THE SOUTH CHINA SEA

The USS William Lawrence conducted a Freedom of Navigation Operation (FONOP) within 12 nautical miles of Fiery Cross Reef on Tuesday, May 10. Chinese-controlled Fiery Cross Reef is home to a 10,000-foot runway and substantial military and civilianinfrastructure. Last month, Chinese military aircraft landed at Fiery Cross Reef and General Fan Chanlong, vice-chairman of the Chinese Central Military Commission, visited the reef's facilities. Chinaresponded to this week's FONOP by scrambling two fighter jets and directing three warships to tail the USS Lawrence. This is the third FONOP conducted by the US Navy in the South China Sea since consistent exercises began in 2015.

Chinese officials were quick to condemn the US and promised strong countermeasures. PLA Spokesperson Col. Yang Yujun called the "unauthorized illegal entry into Chinese waters near China's Nansha (Spratly) island by the U.S. warships and warplanes.... a serious provocation." Foreign Ministry Spokesperson Lu Kang also condemnedthe US for "waving the banner of navigation and overflight freedom and flexing its muscles in the South China Sea." A day later, the Ministry of National Defense responded by announcing increased maritime and air patrols as well as construction of "various defense capabilities" in the South China Sea. Taiwan, on the other hand, struck a more conciliatory note. The Ministry of Foreign Affairs said that it was "paying close attention" to the situation and reiterated Taiwan's "rights to these island groups and their surrounding waters."

Notwithstanding these reactions, a number of analysts both inside and outside China questioned whether the USS Lawrence's sailby had much legal bite. The Department of Defense stated that this FONOP challenged claims by China, Taiwan, and Vietnam "to require prior permission or notification of transits through the territorial sea" by military vessels "exercis[ing] the right of innocent passage."

Innocent passage is understood as the right of all vessels to pass through a territorial sea (constructed around any rock or island) as long as the vessel does not perform military or intelligence-gathering activities. Euan Graham at *The Interpreter* called this the "least assertive form of surface FONOP" and Julian Ku at *Lawfare* argued that the US should seriously consider "non-innocent passage" operations that would "directly challenge[] the legitimacy of China's artificial islands." An editorial from *The Global Times*, a Chinese publication, was similarlybullish about China's strategic position despite this most recent FONOP.

The Philippines

Rodrigo Duterte is the unofficial winner of the Philippines' presidential election, sending shock waves through the region's foreign policy community. In the run-up to the election, Duterteblamed current President Aquino for China's ongoing reclamation in the South China Sea and was open to the possibility of bilateral negotiations and resource sharing with China. That said, Duterte alsocalled for multilateral negotiations that would include all claimant nations, the United States, Japan, and Australia.

Chinese officials have matched Duterte's wide-ranging comments with equally varied statements. Foreign Ministry Spokesperson Lu Kanghoped that "the future for relations between China and the Philippines can be brighter" while nonetheless reiterating China's preference for bilateral negotiations. An editorial from *Xinhua* also urged the new Philippine president to reject "hawkish politicians in Washington and right-wing extremists in Tokyo."

China

China spent most of the week on the defensive. It began with Ambassador to the UK Liu Xiaoming criticizing Senator McCain'seditorial in *The Financial Times*, claiming that the US has led militarization in the South China Sea. Director-General Xu Hong from the Foreign Ministry reiterated the grounds for China's criticism of the ad-hoc Philippines/China tribunal and Director-General Ouyang Yujing warned that criticism of China could well rebound like a "coiled spring."

China also dealt with a series of unexpected collisions in the East China Sea. Two Chinese fishermen were killed and another 17 went missing after a Chinese fishing boat collided with a Maltese freighter. Twenty crewmembers from the Maltese ship were detained for investigation in the eastern Chinese city of Ningbo. It is unclear where in the East China Sea this incident occurred. A Chinese container vessel also collided with a Liberian boat late last week; all 22 crewmembers were rescued.

Japan

Finishing up last week's trip through Southeast Asia, Foreign Minister Kishida met with Laotian Prime Minister Thongloun Sisoulith to discuss disputes in the South China Sea. Prime Minister Thongloun reportedly agreed to make efforts to resolve the issue and is expected to visit Japan for a G-7 outreach session in late May. The *China Daily*was quick to condemn this charm offensive, claiming that Japan "is both fueling and exploiting tensions in the disputed waters to advance its own economic and strategic interests in Southeast Asia."

Three Chinese Coast Guard vessels entered territorial waters around the Senkaku/Diaoyu Islands on Monday, the twelfth time they have done so this year. It is perhaps unsurprising, then, that Japancontinued to upgrade its military capacity in the southern island chain. Despite continued antagonism, however, Japanese sources reportedthat ministerial-level economic meetings may restart this summer for the first time since August 2010.

Taiwan

The Chinese (Taiwan) Society of International Law, a government-linked group, submitted several hundred pages of evidence that was accepted by the ad-hoc tribunal responsible for the Philippines' case against Chinese claims in the South China Sea. The Society's submission states that, "it is clear that Taiping Island (Itu Aba) is an island which can sustain human habitation and economic life of its own under... UNCLOS." A spokesperson for President Ma Ying-jeou clarified that the submission was not made on behalf of the Taiwanese government, but that it was consistent with its official stance.

Taipei's dispute with Tokyo over the seizure of a Taiwanese fishing vessel near a disputed atoll came to a head last Friday as Japanresponded to Taiwan's deployment of two coast guard vessels with five ships of its own. Taiwan's Ministry of Foreign Affairs has called on the Coast Guard to avoid escalating the issue and President-elect Tsai Ing-wen met with Prime Minister Shinzo Abe's brother to talk about the situation.

Malaysia

Prime Minister Najib Razak's ruling coalition captured 72 of 82 seats in Malaysia's largest state in the first election after a scandal involving a government-backed investment fund rocked the country. Bridget Welsh at *New Mandala* explains why this result is not surprising.

Days later, Foreign Minister Datuk Seri Anifah Aman announced that he and Chinese State Councilor Yang Jiechi agreed to settle South Chin Sea-related disputes through

ASEAN's Declaration on the Conduct of Parties in the South China Sea and intensify negotiations around the much-awaited Code of Conduct in the South China Sea. Minister Anifah also said that Councilor Yang promised to "look into" last month's incursion of Malaysian waters by 100 Chinese fishing vessels.

Vietnam

The Obama administration is deliberating over Hanoi's request to completely repeal a lethal weapons embargo that was partially lifted in 2014. Though reports indicate that defense officials are largely in favor of lifting the embargo, begun after the Vietnam War, Assistant Secretary of State Daniel Russel noted that, "one of the important factors that would make a lift of the ban possible would be to continue forward momentum in meeting universal human rights standards."

A decision, which may be forthcoming during President Obama's upcoming Asia trip, will reportedly hinge in part on ongoing talks with Hanoi led by Assistant Secretary of State for Democracy, Human Rights, and Labor Tom Malinowski.

Singapore

Singapore will expand two military bases in Australia and send an additional 14,000 troops per year as part of a $1.7 billion deal with Canberra to expand defense cooperation. This deal will more thandouble Singapore's current deployment to Australia.

The two countries also plan to enhance military personnel exchanges, start civilian personnel exchanges, and deepen intelligence and information sharing.

Indonesia

Jakarta and Beijing committed to improving trade after a meeting on Monday between President Widodo and State Councilor Yang Jiechi. The agreement to improve bilateral relations in all fields is notable given the fallout after China's Coast Guard interrupted Indonesian authorities arresting a Chinese fishing vessel off the coast of Natuna Island.

In unrelated news, Defense Minister Ryamizard Ryacuduannounced plans to purchase an unspecified number of Airbus A400M military transport aircraft.

Analysis, Commentary, and Additional Information

The rise of President-elect Duterte of the Philippines consumed much of the scholarly world's attention this week. *East Asia Forum* dedicated three articles to examining motivations for his election. Julio Teehankee and Mark Thompson highlight pent-up anger in the middle class, Ronnie Holmes underscores the importance of personality politics, and Imelda Deinla focuses on the rule of law deficit. Pivoting to the international scene, Emily Rauhala in *The Washington Post*provides an overview of Duterte's mixed messaging regarding the Philippines' relationship with China. Jesse Johnson at *The Japan Times*and Matthew Pennington at *Stars and Stripes* outline how President Duterte may upend relationships with Tokyo and Washington. Lindsay Murdoch at *The Sydney Morning Herald* reflects much the same concern for Canberra.

Brookings released a much-read paper by Paul Gewirtz that provides an overview of the Philippines/China arbitration and highlights the likely limits of a decision from the ad-hoc tribunal. Mindful of these limitations, there were a number of articles this week recommending how states should strategize going forward. Zack Cooper and Bonnie Glasser at *The National Interest* begin with the US, parsing the Obama administration's decision to undertake yet another innocent passage FONOP. Tom Switzer at *The Strategist* examines how Australia should proceed after the Lawrence's FONOP and Abhijit Singh explains why Beijing is unlikely to change its strategy in the near future. Marvin Ott and Mick Zloof at *The Diplomat* round out the analysis by looking at Indonesia's strategic options after the Natuna incident.

Buavanh Vilavong at *East Asia Forum* looks ahead to Laos' turn as ASEAN chair and Liu Zhen and Teddy Ng at the *South China Morning Post* explore why ASEAN should start negotiations on a coastguard vessel code of conduct. China, as always, is the elephant in the room. Loke Hoe Yeong at *ASEAN Today* provides an overview of the dispute while Philip Bowring at *The Globalist* argues that China has effectively neutralized ASEAN on the South China Sea.

And finally, we move to Taiwan. Jiye Kim at *East Asia Forum*summarizes Taipei's stance on South China Sea disputes while Tsai Chi-ting at *AMTI* questions this traditional interpretation of Taiwan's position regarding the nine-dash-line. *Stratfor* also released a report on the unintended consequences of Taiwan's dispute with Japan regarding Okinotori atoll.

TROUBLED WATERS

The court ruling will likely create more problems than solutions. Interpreted by China as a U.S.-inspired power move, it will increase rather than decrease geopolitical tensions. Yet, conflict between Washington and Beijing can be managed. There are vast areas of mutual economic interest and shared global objectives. A greater fear is that a local event can spin out of control. An overzealous Chinese lieutenant fires upon a U.S. ship; a U.S. destroyer rams a Chinese fishing boat. A U.S. plane is accidentally shot down by a surface-to-air missile from a disputed island. At the local level the potential for conflict grows to dangerous levels. And often it is events at the local that can influence the global.

4

South China Sea : The 21st Century's Leading Flashpoint

With a population of 660 million and one of the world's most strategically-important locations, Southeast Asia is one of the most pivotal regions in shaping the global economy and the international security environment in the 21st century. Interestingly, this is a region that has, for nearly all of its history, never been dominated by a single power for a prolonged-period of time. Of course, India and China have had a great deal of influence over the region at various points in history, as did Japan for a few years during the Second World War.

However, the region is today comprised of ten very distinct countries, many of which have their own deep internal divisions. Now, Southeast Asia is emerging as one of the leading centers of growth for the global economy and this is resulting in an increased focus on this region by traditional outside powers such as China and India, as well as by newer outside powers such as the United States.

In recent years, the United States has played a much greater role in this region after decades of relatively low-level ties between the world's leading power and most of the countries that comprise Southeast Asia. This was due in large part to the fallout from the Vietnam War that saw US aims for the region offset by the spread of communism in Vietnam, Cambodia and Laos. For most Southeast Asian countries, the modern-day US-led trade, investment and maritime security arrangements have provided the environment needed to help the region to develop export-driven industries that drive some of the fastest-growing economies in the world.

Furthermore, the United States provides the region with an alternative, and a form of protection, against potential Chinese economic and political domination. This has led to a strengthening of ties between the United States and many of its traditional allies in the region, while helping to promote closer ties with former rivals such as Indonesia, Vietnam and Myanmar. Finally, the US' recent pivot towards Asia is likely to continue as the Pacific region has emerged as the world's most important economic and political region, replacing the North Atlantic in this role.

For China, Southeast Asia is often viewed as a region that is entirely within China's sphere of influence and many Chinese leaders believe that this entitles their country to play the leading role in this region. However, this assumption has led China to take a hard line towards defending and reinforcing its claims to the vast majority of the South China Sea, a body of water in which five Southeast Asian countries also have maritime claims. This Chinese assertiveness, together with China's rising economic power, has led many Southeast Asian countries to determine that it is not in their best interest to allow China to dominate the region. Thus, many countries in the region are looking to outside powers such as the US, India or Japan to play a greater role in Southeast Asia. This is a key reason why Myanmar has moved quickly to expand its political and security ties with these outside powers at the expense of its once close ties with China.

On the other hand, China is finding new potential allies in the region, especially two countries that once had very close ties with the United States. First, Thailand's military-led government has been criticized by the US and others for not restoring that country's democracy, and this has led Bangkok to cultivate closer ties with China. Meanwhile, the Philippines' controversial new President Rodrigo Duterte has called for a major shift in his country's foreign policy, aiming to improve ties with Beijing even if this further damages his country's long-standing ties with the United States.

Southeast Asia appears set to be a key battleground in the struggle for influence between the 21st century's two leading powers, the United States and China. Furthermore, the country with the greatest potential to one day become a third leading global power, India, could also play a major role in Southeast Asia's political and economic future, further enhancing the region's role as the center of the struggle for power and influence between this century's leading powers. In fact, Southeast Asia may find itself playing a role similar to that of Europe during the Cold War. That is, Southeast Asia could find itself as a key center of the global economy, but one that it squeezed between two great powers.

For Europe, this led to greater economic and political integration as that region's leading powers found themselves powerless on their own when confronted with the might of the United States or the Soviet Union. Likewise, Southeast Asian countries might find themselves forced to take a similar path in order to avoid being dominated by the larger powers around them. Regardless, there is no doubt that many of the most important flashpoints in the 21st century are found in Southeast Asia and this will focus more of the world's attention on this vital region for the foreseeable future.

HISTORICAL FICTION: CHINA'S SOUTH CHINA SEA CLAIMS

The Spratly Islands—not so long ago known primarily as a rich fishing ground—have turned into an international flashpoint as Chinese leaders insist with increasing truculence that the islands, rocks, and reefs have been, in the words of Premier Wen Jiabao, "China's historical territory since ancient times." Normally, the overlapping territorial claims to sovereignty and maritime boundaries ought to be resolved through a combination of customary international law, adjudication before the International Court of Justice or the International Tribunal for the Law of the Sea, or arbitration under Annex VII of the United Nations Convention on the Law of the Sea (UNCLOS). While China has ratified UNCLOS, the treaty by and large rejects "historically based" claims, which are precisely the type Beijing periodically asserts. On September 4, 2012, China's foreign minister, Yang Jiechi, told US Secretary of State Hillary Clinton that there is "plenty of historical and jurisprudence evidence to show that China has sovereignty over the islands in the South China Sea and the adjacent waters."

As far as the "jurisprudence evidence" is concerned, the vast majority of international legal experts have concluded that China's claim to historic title over the South China Sea, implying full sovereign authority and consent for other states to transit, is invalid. The historical evidence, if anything, is even less persuasive. There are several contradictions in China's use of history to justify its claims to islands and reefs in the South China Sea, not least of which is its polemical assertion of parallels with imperialist expansion by the United States and European powers in the eighteenth and nineteenth centuries. Justifying China's attempts to expand its maritime frontiers by claiming islands and reefs far from its shores, Jia Qingguo, professor at Beijing University's School of International Studies, argues that China is merely following the example set by the West. "The United States has Guam in Asia which is very far away from the US and the French have islands in the South Pacific, so it is nothing new," Jia told AFP recently.

China's claim to the Spratlys on the basis of history runs aground on the fact that the region's past empires did not exercise sovereignty. In pre-modern Asia, empires were characterized by undefined, unprotected, and often changing frontiers. The notion of suzerainty prevailed. Unlike a nation-state, the frontiers of Chinese empires were neither carefully drawn nor policed but were more like circles or zones, tapering off from the center of civilization to the undefined periphery of alien barbarians.

More importantly, in its territorial disputes with neighboring India, Burma, and Vietnam, Beijing always took the position that its land boundaries were never defined, demarcated, and delimited. But now, when it comes to islands, shoals, and reefs in the South China Sea, Beijing claims otherwise.

In other words, China's claim that its land boundaries were historically never defined and delimited stands in sharp contrast with the stance that China's maritime boundaries were always clearly defined and delimited.

Herein lies a basic contradiction in the Chinese stand on land and maritime boundaries which is untenable. Actually, it is the mid-twentieth-century attempts to convert the undefined frontiers of ancient civilizations and kingdoms enjoying suzerainty into clearly defined, delimited, and demarcated boundaries of modern nation-states exercising sovereignty that lie at the center of China's territorial and maritime disputes with neighboring countries. Put simply, sovereignty is a post-imperial notion ascribed to nation-states, not ancient empires.

China's present borders largely reflect the frontiers established during the spectacular episode of eighteenth-century Qing (Manchu) expansionism, which over time hardened into fixed national boundaries following the imposition of the Westphalian nation-state system over Asia in the nineteenth and twentieth centuries. Official Chinese history today often distorts this complex history, however, claiming that Mongols, Tibetans, Manchus, and Hans were all Chinese, when in fact the Great Wall was built by the Chinese dynasties to keep out the northern Mongol and Manchu tribes that repeatedly overran Han China; the wall actually represented the Han Chinese empire's outer security perimeter. While most historians see the onslaught of the Mongol hordes led by Genghis Khan in the early 1200s as an apocalyptic event that threatened the very survival of ancient civilizations in India, Persia, and other nations (China chief among them), the Chinese have consciously promoted the myth that he was actually "Chinese," and therefore all areas that the Mongols (the Yuan dynasty) had once occupied or conquered (such as Tibet and much of Central and Inner

Asia) belong to China. China's claims on Taiwan and in the South China Sea are also based on the grounds that both were parts of the Manchu empire. (Actually, in the Manchu or Qing dynasty maps, it is Hainan Island, not the Paracel and Spratly Islands, that is depicted as China's southern-most border.) In this version of history, any territory conquered by "Chinese" in the past remains immutably so, no matter when the conquest may have occurred.

Such writing and rewriting of history from a nationalistic perspective to promote national unity and regime legitimacy has been accorded the highest priority by China's rulers, both Nationalists and Communists. The Chinese Communist Party leadership consciously conducts itself as the heir to China's imperial legacy, often employing the symbolism and rhetoric of empire. From primary-school textbooks to television historical dramas, the state-controlled information system has force-fed generations of Chinese a diet of imperial China's grandeur. As the Australian Sinologist Geremie Barmé points out, "For decades Chinese education and propaganda have emphasized the role of history in the fate of the Chinese nation-state . . . . While Marxism-Leninism and Mao Thought have been abandoned in all but name, the role of history in China's future remains steadfast." So much so that history has been refined as an instrument of statecraft (also known as "cartographic aggression") by state-controlled research institutions, media, and education bodies.

China uses folklore, myths, and legends, as well as history, to bolster greater territorial and maritime claims. Chinese textbooks preach the notion of the Middle Kingdom as being the oldest and most advanced civilization that was at the very center of the universe, surrounded by lesser, partially Sinicized states in East and Southeast Asia that must constantly bow and pay their respects. China's version of history often deliberately blurs the distinction between what was no more than hegemonic influence, tributary relationships, suzerainty, and actual control. Subscribing to the notion that those who have mastered the past control their present and chart their own futures, Beijing has always placed a very high value on "the history card" (often a revisionist interpretation of history) in its diplomatic efforts to achieve foreign policy objectives, especially to extract territorial and diplomatic concessions from other countries. Almost every contiguous state has, at one time or another, felt the force of Chinese arms—Mongolia, Tibet, Burma, Korea, Russia, India, Vietnam, the Philippines, and Taiwan—and been a subject of China's revisionist history. As Martin Jacques notes in *When China Rules the World*, "Imperial Sinocentrism shapes and underpins modern Chinese nationalism."

If the idea of national sovereignty goes back to seventeenth-century Europe and the system that originated with the Treaty of Westphalia, the idea of maritime sovereignty is largely a mid-twentieth-century American concoction China has seized upon to extend its maritime frontiers. As Jacques notes, "The idea of maritime sovereignty is a relatively recent invention, dating from 1945 when the United States declared that it intended to exercise sovereignty over its territorial waters." In fact, the UN's Law of the Sea agreement represented the most prominent international effort to apply the land-based notion of sovereignty to the maritime domain worldwide—although, importantly, it rejects the idea of justification by historical right. Thus although Beijing claims around eighty percent of the South China Sea as its "historic waters" (and is now seeking to elevate this claim to a "core interest" akin with its claims on Taiwan and Tibet), China has, historically speaking, about as much right to claim the South China Sea as Mexico has to claim the Gulf of Mexico for its exclusive use, or Iran the Persian Gulf, or India the Indian Ocean.

Ancient empires either won control over territories through aggression, annexation, or assimilation or lost them to rivals who possessed superior firepower or statecraft. Territorial expansion and contraction was the norm, determined by the strength or weakness of a kingdom or empire. The very idea of "sacred lands" is ahistorical because control of territory was based on who grabbed or stole what last from whom. The frontiers of the Qin, Han, Tang, Song, and Ming dynasties waxed and waned throughout history. A strong and powerful imperial China, much like czarist Russia, was expansionist in Inner Asia and Indochina as opportunity arose and strength allowed. The gradual expansion over the centuries under the non-Chinese Mongol and Manchu dynasties extended imperial China's control over Tibet and parts of Central Asia (now Xinjiang), Taiwan, and Southeast Asia. Modern China is, in fact, an "empire-state" masquerading as a nation-state.

If China's claims are justified on the basis of history, then so are the historical claims of Vietnamese and Filipinos based on their histories. Students of Asian history know, for instance, that Malay peoples related to today's Filipinos have a better claim to Taiwan than Beijing does. Taiwan was originally settled by people of Malay-Polynesian descent—ancestors of the present-day aborigine groups—who populated the low-lying coastal plains. In the words of noted Asia-watcher Philip Bowring, writing last year in the *South China Morning Post*, "The fact that China has a long record of written history does not invalidate other nations' histories as illustrated by artifacts, language, lineage and genetic affinities, the evidence of trade and travel." Unless one subscribes to the notion of Chinese exceptionalism, imperial China's "historical claims" are as valid as those of other kingdoms and empires in Southeast and South Asia. China laying claim to the Mongol and Manchu empires' colonial possessions would be equivalent to India laying claim to Afghanistan, Bangladesh, Burma, Malaysia (Srivijaya), Nepal, Pakistan, and Sri Lanka on the grounds that they were all parts of either the Maurya, Chola, or the Moghul and the British Indian empires.

China's claims in the South China Sea are also a major shift from its longstanding geopolitical orientation to continental power. In claiming a strong maritime tradition, China makes much of the early-fifteenth-century expeditions of Zheng He to the Indian Ocean and Africa. But, as Bowring points out, "Chinese were actually latecomers to navigation beyond coastal waters. For centuries, the masters of the oceans were the Malayo-Polynesian peoples who colonized much of the world, from Taiwan to New Zealand and Hawaii to the south and east, and to Madagascar in the west. Bronze vessels were being traded with Palawan, just south of Scarborough, at the time of Confucius. When Chinese Buddhist pilgrims like Faxian went to Sri Lanka and India in the fifth century, they went in ships owned and operated by Malay peoples. Ships from what is now the Philippines traded with Funan, a state in what is now southern Vietnam, a thousand years before the Yuan dynasty."

And finally, China's so-called "historic claims" to the South China Sea are actually not "centuries old." They only go back to 1947, when Chiang Kai-shek's nationalist government drew the so-called "eleven-dash line" on Chinese maps of the South China Sea, enclosing the Spratly Islands and other chains that the ruling Kuomintang party declared were now under Chinese sovereignty. Chiang himself, saying he saw German fascism as a model for China, was fascinated by the Nazi concept of an expanded*Lebensraum* ("living space") for the Chinese nation. He did not have the opportunity to be expansionist himself because the Japanese put him on the defensive, but cartographers of the nationalist regime drew the U-shape of eleven dashes in an attempt to enlarge China's "living space" in the South China Sea. Following the victory of the Chinese Communist Party in the civil war in 1949, the People's Republic of China adopted this cartographic coup, revising Chiang's notion into a "nine-dash line" after erasing two dashes in the Gulf of Tonkin in 1953.

Since the end of the Second World War, China has been redrawing its maps, redefining borders, manufacturing historical evidence, using force to create new territorial realities, renaming islands, and seeking to impose its version of history on the waters of the region. The passage of domestic legislation in 1992, "Law on the Territorial Waters and Their Contiguous Areas," which claimed four-fifths of the South China Sea, was followed by armed skirmishes with the Philippines and

Vietnamese navies throughout the 1990s. More recently, the dispatch of large numbers of Chinese fishing boats and maritime surveillance vessels to the disputed waters in what is tantamount to a "people's war on the high seas" has further heightened tensions. To quote commentator Sujit Dutta, "China's unmitigated irredentism [is] based on the... theory that the periphery must be occupied in order to secure the core. [This] is an essentially imperial notion that was internalized by the Chinese nationalists—both Kuomintang and Communist. The [current] regime's attempts to reach its imagined geographical frontiers often with little historical basis have had and continue to have highly destabilizing strategic consequences."

One reason Southeast Asians find it difficult to accept Chinese territorial claims is that they carry with them an assertion of Han racial superiority over other Asian races and empires. Says Jay Batongbacal of the University of the Philippines law school: "Intuitively, acceptance of the nine-dash line is a corresponding denial of the very identity and history of the ancestors of the Vietnamese, Filipinos, and Malays; it is practically a modern revival of China's denigration of non-Chinese as 'barbarians' not entitled to equal respect and dignity as peoples."

Empires and kingdoms never exercised sovereignty. If historical claims had any validity then Mongolia could claim all of Asia simply because it once conquered the lands of the continent. There is absolutely no historical basis to support either of the dash-line claims, especially considering that the territories of Chinese empires were never as carefully delimited as nation-states, but rather existed as zones of influence tapering away from a civilized center. This is the position contemporary China took starting in the 1960s, while negotiating its land boundaries with several of its neighboring countries. But this is not the position it takes today in the cartographic, diplomatic, and low-intensity military skirmishes to define its maritime borders. The continued reinterpretation of history to advance contemporary political, territorial, and maritime claims, coupled with the Communist leadership's ability to turn "nationalistic eruptions" on and off like a tap during moments of tension with the United States, Japan, South Korea, India, Vietnam, and the Philippines, makes it difficult for Beijing to reassure neighbors that its "peaceful rise" is wholly peaceful. Since there are six claimants to various atolls, islands, rocks, and oil deposits in the South China Sea, the Spratly Islands disputes are, by definition, multilateral disputes requiring international arbitration. But Beijing has insisted that these disputes are bilateral in order to place its opponents between the anvil of its revisionist history and the hammer of its growing military power.

SOUTH CHINA SEA: NEXT GLOBAL FLASHPOINT

For, at a time when the world is mainly focused on the twin threats posed by Russia's new spirit of military aggression and the rise of Islamic State (Isil), there is growing concern that not enough attention is being paid to a potentially far more worrying danger emerging from the South China Sea. For more than a year China has been engaged in a massive military build up in the area, where it has turned what was formerly partially submerged reef into a network of artificial islands. By way of announcing the completion of what could prove to be an important strategic asset, China earlier this week began operating a newly-constructed lighthouse on one of these islands.

A statement issued by the Chinese foreign ministry tried to play down the significance of the lighthouse, arguing that it will provide a vital navigational tool for one of the world's most important shipping arteries. A breathtaking $5 trillion in global trade is estimated to pass through the waters each year. But turning on the 55-metre (189 foot) lighthouse has also refocused attention on the deepening tensions that have been created by China's aggressive policy of expansionism in the region.

China's island-building scheme is regarded as an unwelcome provocation by many of its neighbours, which see the programme as blatant bullying tactics aimed at consolidating Beijing's claims over the energy-rich waters of the South China Sea.

This has resulted in both the US and several Asian allies making provocative gestures of their own as a means of signalling their own displeasure with Beijing's actions. Last weekend a Japanese submarine made its first port call to the Philippines for 15 years to demonstrate increased military cooperation between the two countries, while Vietnam seized a Chinese ship for illegally entering its territorial waters.

Meanwhile, Washington has made its own displeasure known by sailing heavily-armed warships through the disputed waters and negotiating a deal with the Philippines to station weapons and troops for the first time in more than 20 years. The question now is whether this dangerous escalation in military tensions will lead to open conflict, one that has the potential to be infinitely worse than the military challenges posed by Russia and Isil.

In an attempt to defuse the crisis US President Barack Obama left Chinese President Xi Jinping in doubt what he though about China's tactics when the two leaders met last week. But while Mr Xi insisted China had no interest in provoking "conflicts or confrontation", the risk of serious military escalation will remain so long as Beijing refuses to resolve its maritime disputes by peaceful means.

SOUTH CHINA SEA VERDICT EXPLAINED

The Philippines has had an historic win in the South China Sea Arbitration founded upon the provisions of the 1982 United Nations Convention on the Law of the Sea. The Tribunal accepted 14 of the 15 claims made by the Philippines in a unanimous award that will set the benchmark for the future resolution of all remaining South China Sea maritime disputes and have implications for all of Southeast Asia. The case was commenced by the Philippines in 2013 following a flare up between the two countries over the Scarborough Shoal, and what the Philippines perceived as a lack of progress in diplomatic talks to try to resolve their many maritime differences.

In bringing the claim the Philippines also sought to directly challenge China's assertion of its so-called "Nine Dash Line", which is a line that appears on Chinese maps of the South China Sea that encircles much of the region and overlaps areas of the sea claimed by the Philippines, Vietnam, Malaysia, Indonesia and Brunei. The Tribunal found Chinese activities had caused irreparable harm to the coral reef ecosystem and breached obligations under six provisions of the Convention.

The Philippines also sought to directly challenge Chinese assertion of sovereign rights over the South China Sea based upon claims over very small islands, islets, reefs and shoals, especially those located in the Spratly Islands group. Finally, the Philippines also challenged China's land reclamation and island building activities throughout the region on the grounds that China had no legitimate basis to undertake those activities which the Philippines argued was causing significant environmental impact.

In considering the "Nine Dash Line" the Tribunal had to first assess a 2006 Chinese Declaration indicating that it did not accept any of the procedures for dispute resolution under the Convention with respect to "historic bays or titles". This raised issues as to whether elements of China's disputes with the Philippines would fall within this exception, including what precisely are the historic titles that China asserts in the South China Sea.

A hollow victory for the Philippines

The Philippines claim also raised issues with respect to South China Sea territorial disputes between the Philippines and China, which substantively would have been beyond the jurisdiction of the Tribunal. In China's written statements released by way of a December 7, 2014 Foreign Ministry Paper, China argued that "the essence of the subject-matter of the arbitration is territorial sovereignty over several maritime features in the South China Sea, which is beyond the scope of the Convention".

However both the 2016 Award and a previous 2015 Award of the Tribunal that solely addressed issues of jurisdiction dismissed China's objections on this ground and made clear that the decision does not directly address any of the territorial disputes that exist in the South China Sea. While China's claims that the Tribunal lacked jurisdiction on this basis were therefore dismissed, the territorial disputes remain a live issue. The first appearance of China's Nine Dash Line with apparent official Chinese government endorsement was in a government internal atlas in 1947, which was then published as a Chinese atlas in 1948.

The Line attained modern significance when China lodged a diplomatic note with the UN in 2009 that directly referred to its claim. On this point the Tribunal conclusively resolved that China's claims to the Line based on assertions of historic rights, sovereign rights or jurisdiction, are unlawful. On its own this decision could significantly rewrite the maritime discourse in the South China Sea given that the Nine Dash Line has been such a dominant basis of China's assertions to maritime entitlements in the region in the past decade.

The Tribunal additionally handed down significant rulings that none of the disputed maritime features in the Spratly Islands in their natural condition, including Scarborough Shoal, Gaven Reef and Fiery Cross Reef are to be equated with islands for the purposes of the law of the sea and, as a result, do not generate entitlements to a 200 mile exclusive economic zone or continental shelf. In doing so the Tribunal confirmed that Mischief Reef and Second Thomas Shoal - which has in recent years been the scene of a standoff between the Philippines military and Chinese government vessels - are within the Philippines maritime domain and not that of China.

When turning to China's controversial land reclamation and island building activities in the South China Sea, the Tribunal found these activities had caused irreparable harm to the coral reef ecosystem and breached obligations under six provisions of the Convention. In the case of these activities at Mischief Reef, the Tribunal directly found that China had breached Articles 60 and 80 of the Convention by undertaking land reclamation without the authorisation of the Philippines and in violation of Articles 60 and 80 of the Convention.

The measured response to date from the Philippines is reassuring that calmer heads may prevail as the dispute moves into its next phase. While the decision is final and binding there are no clear mechanisms for its implementation. The Tribunal did not order China to vacate the islands, rocks, and reefs that it has occupied. There is no international police force to enforce the judgment. Ultimately it will come down to how the Philippines and China decide to resolve their South China Sea disagreements through diplomacy and negotiation.

PARADOXES IN THE SOUTH CHINA SEA ISSUE

The South China Sea controversy is wrapped in paradoxes that are symptomatic of the tension between the practical realities of the geopolitical system of unequal nation-states and the universal norms of an emergent global legal order. China is part of the world system of nation-states, yet it acts like a regional hegemon standing above international law.

The first paradox, of course, is that, while it is called the South China Sea, this body of water does not belong to China. China claims all of it, citing "historic rights" to maritime territory demarcated by a so-called "nine-dash line." We have turned to calling our own side of the ocean the West Philippine Sea. Yet, these are international waters.

Unlike the United States, China has ratified the United Nations Convention on the Law of the Sea (Unclos), which lays down the principles, legal norms, and modes of settlement applicable to maritime disputes. In 2013, the Philippines, an early Unclos signatory, filed a case opposing China's "nine-dash line" at the Permanent Court of Arbitration in The Netherlands. China responded with a "Position Paper" challenging the court's jurisdiction over the case. It also served notice that it would not participate in the proceedings nor would it abide by the court's decision. That is the second paradox: China demands to be heard but it refuses to submit to arbitration. The Philippines is no less caught in this web of paradoxes. In its July 12, 2016, ruling, the arbitral tribunal granted almost all of the Philippine government's claims. Yet, in the face of this unprecedented victory, its incumbent officials have acted as though the country has lost the case. That is the third paradox.

It has taken a lot of nerve for the Philippines to sue a prickly big power like China. Against the counsel of many of its neighbors in the region, it chose to follow what was generally regarded as a reckless, impractical, and futile course. Everyone knew that any ruling would be difficult to enforce. Thus, after paying a heavy cost for alienating China, the Philippines stood to gain nothing but a moral victory. Now it wishes to repair damaged relations and soothe a neighbor's wounded feelings. For, indeed, not even the dry measured language of the arbitral award can mask the excoriation to which the court effectively subjects China.

Unfortunately, the text of the ruling leaves little room, if any, for China to save face. I doubt if the other countries that have staked their claims to the South China Sea are in any position either to help soften the ruling's blow to China's claims. Perhaps, this is the right time for the Association of Southeast Asian Nations to make its presence felt by taking its cue from the tribunal's ruling and speaking up for its members as they seek a just and equitable relationship with China. The Asean could begin by reviving the long-stalled project of a Code of Conduct in the South China Sea.

It has been suggested that the Philippines could initiate the healing process by piously avoiding any reference to the decision when it goes into bilateral talks with China. Indeed, the usually blunt President Duterte has admonished his Cabinet members not "to flaunt" the victory or "taunt" the losing party. But, the real problem, it seems to me, is how any conscientious Filipino negotiator can avoid referring to the tribunal's ruling without appearing to sell the nation's interests and self-esteem to the bully next door. If we fail to give proper recognition and importance to the decision we have just won, we would become the world's laughingstock. No international tribunal would take us seriously from here on. More importantly, we would be undermining the worthy idea of an autonomous global legal order that could regulate relations among nations and formulate rational solutions to conflicts in an increasingly complex world.

The tribunal knew the grave importance of the case before it. It was mindful of the limits of its mandate and authority—that it had no power to decide sovereignty, or to demarcate maritime boundaries. Its jurisdiction was confined to determining the scope of legitimate maritime territory for purposes of exploiting resources.

Here, the governing norm is the 200-nautical-mile exclusive economic zone that Unclos gives to coastal countries. Similarly, an island in the middle of the ocean generates its own EEZ if it can be shown to be capable of supporting human habitation. High-tide rock formations are allowed 12 nautical miles of territorial sea, but not reefs or banks that appear only at low tide. The tribunal ruled that the Spratlys are no more than rock formations, not real islands. Mischief and Subi, where China has built its major bases on reclaimed land, are declared as no more than reefs, with no entitlement to 12-mile territorial sea, or to a 200-mile EEZ.

By its masterful framing of the issues, the tribunal succeeded in using its limited mandate to put to rest the most contentious territorial issues in the South China Sea. Indeed, enforcement is another matter. But, the judges could have made life easier for themselves by simply pleading lack of jurisdiction. That was China's demand. Yet they took the case and did their work. The least we can do to show our appreciation for this exemplary demonstration of professional integrity is to not abandon the conviction that led us to file the case in the first place.

ASEAN'S CODE OF CONDUCT OF SOUTH CHINA SEA

The genesis of ASEAN's 2012 draft COC may be traced back to 1995 when China occupied Mischief Reef, a maritime feature claimed by the Philippines. The Mischief Reef incident marked a turning point. ASEAN foreign ministers issued a statement expressing their "serious concern" and urged the concerned parties "to refrain from taking actions that de-stabilize the situation." The Philippines, as the aggrieved party, sought the backing from its fellow ASEAN members for a Code of Conduct in the South China Sea that would constrain China from further encroachments on Philippines sovereignty. In late 1999 ASEAN members finally reached agreement on a COC.

In March 2000, ASEAN and China exchanged their respective drafts and agreed to consolidate them into one document. Four major areas of disagreement were identified: the geographic scope, restrictions on construction on occupied and unoccupied features, military activities in waters adjacent to the Spratly islands, and whether or not fishermen found in disputed waters could be detained and arrested. A formal ASEAN-China COC proved a bridge too far. In November 2002, ASEAN member states and China signed a non-binding political statement known as the Declaration on Conduct of Parties in the South China Sea (DOC). This document set out four trust and confidence building measures and five voluntary cooperative activities. The parties to the DOC reaffirmed "that the adoption of a code of conduct in the South China Sea would further promote peace and stability in the region and agree to work, on the basis of consensus, towards the eventual attainment of this objective."

The DOC was stillborn. It took a further twenty-five months before senior officials reached agreement on the terms of reference for the ASEAN-China Joint Working Group (JWC) to implement the DOC. In August 2005, ASEAN tabled draft Guidelines to Implement the DOC at the first meeting of the JWC. Point two called for ASEAN consultations prior to meeting with China. China objected and repeated its long-held position that the relevant parties should resolve sovereignty and jurisdictional disputes bilaterally. This proved such a sticking point that another six years of intermittent discussions and twenty-one successive drafts were exchanged before final agreement was reached.

In July 2011, the Guidelines to Implement the DOC were adopted after ASEAN dropped its insistence on prior consultation and agreed instead to promote dialogue and consultation among the parties. A new point was added to the Guidelines specifying that activities and projects carried out under the DOC should be reported to the ASEAN-China Ministerial Meeting. All the other points in the 2011 Guidelines remained unchanged from the original ASEAN draft tabled in 2005.

ASEAN and Chinese senior officials commenced discussions on the implementation of the Guidelines. At a meeting held in Beijing from January 13-15, 2012, agreement was reached to set up four expert committees on maritime scientific research, environmental protection, search and rescue, and transnational crime. These committees were derived from the five cooperative activities mentioned in the 2002 DOC. Significantly no expert committee on safety of navigation and communication at sea was established due to its contentious nature.

The agreement on DOC Guidelines led to the revival of the long-standing proposal by the Philippines for a COC that was included in the 2002 DOC. ASEAN senior officials began drafting the COC with the intention of reaching a common ASEAN position before presenting it to China for discussion. China initially took the position that the implementation of the DOC Guidelines should be given priority over the COC. China stated it would discuss the COC with ASEAN at an "appropriate timing" or when "appropriate conditions" were met.

In January 2012, the Philippines circulated an informal working draft simply titled, Philippines Draft Code of Conduct. The document was eight pages in length and comprised ten articles. In line with official Philippine foreign policy promoting the South China Sea as a Zone of Peace, Freedom, Friendship and Cooperation (ZOPFF/C), the draft COC proposed a Joint Cooperation Area in the South China Sea (Article III), a Joint Permanent Working Committee to implement the ZOPFF/C (Article IV), the Application of Part IX of the 1982 United Nations Convention on Law of the Sea in the South China Sea (Article V), and Dispute Settlement Mechanisms (Article VI). The remaining articles contained standard provisions such as principles (Article I), objectives (Article II), reservations (Article

VII), signature and ratification (Article VIII), entry into force (Article IX) and review and amendments to the code (Article X). In discussions held by ASEAN senior officials during the first quarter of 2012 it became apparent that ASEAN members were divided on Articles III-VI in the Philippines draft. Some ASEAN members also shared reservations about being too prescriptive concerning dispute settlement mechanisms.

It was at this point that China changed tack and sought a seat at the ASEAN discussions. The timing of China's involvement with ASEAN in drafting a COC quickly became a contentious issue within ASEAN. These tensions surfaced at the 20th ASEAN Summit held in Phnom Penh from April 3-4. Cambodia, the ASEAN Chair, pushed for China's inclusion in ASEAN discussions. The Philippines and Vietnam objected strongly and a compromise was reached. ASEAN would proceed on its own to draft a COC, while communication with China would take place through the ASEAN Chair at the same time.

The ASEAN Senior Officials Meeting (SOM) Working Group on the COC concluded its discussions on June 13, 2012 at its seventh meeting. According to an official statement, "The meeting agreed to submit the draft ASEAN proposed key elements of the regional Code of Conduct in the South China Sea to the ASEAN SOM for consideration." The ASEAN SOM met in Phnom Penh from July 6-7 and forwarded the agreed draft to the ASEAN foreign ministers for deliberation at their 45th AMM on July 9. At the end of the AMM formal discussions Kao Kim Hourn, Secretary of State in the Cambodian Ministry of Foreign Affairs, told reporters that the ASEAN foreign ministers had adopted the "key elements" of the COC and "agreed to have the ASEAN senior officials meet with the senior official from China to discuss the (code of conduct) from now on."

According to the document ASEAN's Proposed Elements of a Regional Code of Conduct in the South China Sea, the original Philippine Working Draft was heavily pruned. Articles III-VI were dropped entirely. The ASEAN "key elements" were reduced to a preamble and two articles. A comparison of the Philippine draft preamble with the agreed ASEAN preamble reveals that two items contained in the former were dropped. The first was a reference to "the principles and norms of international law applicable to maritime space, in particular the principles on the peaceful uses and cooperative management of the oceans." The second and more sensitive reference that was deleted referred to "the need to preserve the region from any form of increased militarization and intimidation."

Both preambles began by referencing the 1997 Joint Statement of the meeting of heads of government/state of ASEAN members and China. Next, the Philippines inclusion of the 2003 declaration of the ASEAN-China Strategic Partnership for Peace and Prosperity was replaced with a reference to the more recent 2006 Joint Declaration on Strategic Partnership for Peace and Towards an Enhanced ASEAN-China Strategic Partnership. Both preambles included a reference to the 2002 DOC and its commitment to develop a COC. Both preambles also referred to protection of the environment and biodiversity. The ASEAN draft altered the formulation in the Philippine draft from "advance a lasting and durable solution of disputes" to read "comprehensive and durable solution of disputes." The Philippines original proposal for a "zone of peace, freedom, friendship and cooperation" was modified to read "an area of peace, stability, friendship and cooperation."

Article I of the ASEAN draft COC contained its operative provisions and called on the parties to "respect and adhere to the United Nations Charter, 1982 UNCLOS, Treaty of Amity and Cooperation in Southeast Asia, DOC and the Five Principles of Peaceful Co-existence. However, five of the principles contained in the Philippine draft were deleted in their entirety: respect for freedom of navigation and over flight; the need to define, clarify and segregate disputed areas from the non-disputed areas; full resolution of the territorial and jurisdictional disputes; refrain from undertaking activities that may disrupt the peace and endanger the environment; and build trust and confidence on the basis of equality and mutual respect.

The ASEAN draft contained four principles: (1) to "develop modalities and arrangements for the promotion of settlement by peaceful means of disputes and prevent their escalation...;" (2) to respect the provisions of and take actions consistent with the COC; (3) to encourage other countries to respect the purposes and principles contained in the COC; and (4) to establish an effective mechanism to monitor the implementation of the COC.

Article II of the ASEAN draft enumerated eight obligations: a ministerial level mechanism to monitor the implementation of the COC; prohibition on reservations to the COC; provisions of entry into force; mechanism for settling disputes; amendment of the COC; provisions for other countries to respect the COC; indefinite duration of the COC; and registration of the COC with the ASEAN Secretary General and Secretariat of the United Nations

Article III(4) required signatories to "establish a mechanism for settling disputes relating to the interpretation and application of the Code of Conduct." The ASEAN draft, following deletion of any mention of the joint cooperation area, also dropped reference to a dispute settlement mechanism in the joint cooperation area.

Two dispute settlement mechanisms were included that closely reflected the wording in the Philippine Working Draft on disputes arising from a breach or violation of the COC. The first mechanism is the dispute settlement mechanism included in the ASEAN Treaty of Amity and Cooperation in Southeast Asia (TAC).

The TAC provides for a ministerial-level ASEAN High Council and empowers it to recommend to parties in dispute, subject to their prior agreement, such measures as good offices, mediation, inquiry or conciliation. The High Council also is given the authority to "recommend appropriate measures for the prevention of a deterioration of the dispute..." The People's Republic of China acceded to the TAC in 2003 and undertook in writing "faithfully to perform and carry out all the stipulations therein contained."

In the event that parties are unable to resolve their dispute within the ASEAN framework, the ASEAN COC sets out a second mechanism: the disputants "may resort to dispute settlement mechanism provided under international law, including UNCLOS." This could include taking their case to an international court for adjudication. UNCLOS, however, does not contain any provisions for the settlement of sovereignty disputes over islands and rocks. It does provide for an International Tribunal for the Law of the Sea (ITLOS) to adjudicate disputes over maritime jurisdiction. Under international law "the land dominates the sea" and before disputants can take their case to ITLOS they would first have to determine sovereignty over disputed islands and rocks on which their maritime claims are based.

At the 45th AMM Retreat, the Cambodian foreign minister reported that, "ASEAN-China met twice recently to discuss informally the drafting of [the] COC" and that "Cambodia will host another formal ASEAN China SOM on the COC in the near future." An informal senior-level working meeting was held on July 8 and Japanese media sources reported "ASEAN and China had agreed to start talks on a legally-binding maritime code of conduct to manage the disputes."

A day later the Cambodian Foreign Minister told his ASEAN counterparts that Vice Foreign Minister Fu Ying stated that China was willing to commence talks on the COC in September. Also on July 9, Foreign Minister Yang Jiechi met with Secretary of State Hillary Clinton to discus the South China Sea. After these talks, U.S. officials revealed that "foreign minister Yang gave Secretary Clinton 'a careful indication' that Beijing is willing to join a dialogue on the code as soon as September, ahead of November's ASEAN summit." On July 10, ASEAN Secretary General Surin Pitsuwan also confirmed that the first formal meeting between ASEAN and Chinese senior officials on the COC would take place in Phnom Penh in September.

China's commitment to meet in September to discuss the COC may be in doubt. According to Japanese sources, "on July 11, China's attitude suddenly shifted and it refused to begin talks." Ian Storey argues that Vice Foreign Minister Fu Ying's agreement with ASEAN to begin talks on a COC in September "was overruled by Foreign Minister Yang... At present there is no timetable to discuss a CoC though both sides will meet in September or October to talk about implementing cooperative projects in areas outlined in the DoC."

The document, ASEAN's Proposed Elements of a Regional Code of Conduct in the South China Sea (COC) between ASEAN Member States and the People's Republic of China, has not been officially released and remains an internal draft ASEAN document. At the 45th AMM Retreat Marty Natalegawa promised that "Indonesia will circulate a non paper possible and additional elements of [the] COC. It is meant to be more prescriptive and operational." In other words, ASEAN members will have to meet to approve any further additions to their draft COC before meeting with Chinese senior officials.

Why Was There No Joint Communiqué?

Cambodia, as the ASEAN Chair for 2012, hosted the 45th AMM and related meetings in Phnom Penh from July 8-13. In his opening address Prime Minister Hun Sen stated that "realising the ASEAN Community by 2015 is the top priority for ASEAN." With respect to the ASEAN Political-Security Community, Hun Sen declared, "we should give emphasis to the implementation of the DOC [Declaration on Conduct of Parties in the South China Sea], including the eventual conclusion of *'Code of Conduct (COC) in the South China Sea'*

The AMM has a busy agenda that extends well beyond South China Sea issues. In 2011, for example, the joint communiqué issued at the end of the 44th AMM listed 120 items and ran to twenty-nine pages. At the 45th AMM Cambodia's Foreign Minister, Hor Namhong, assigned responsibility for drafting the joint communiqué summarizing the AMM deliberations to a working party of four foreign ministers: Marty Natalegawa (Indonesia), Anifah Aman (Malaysia), Albert del Rosario (Philippines) and Pham Binh Minh (Vietnam). Their 132-paragraph draft summarized the wide range of issues taken up by the AMM including the terms of reference for the ASEAN Institute of Peace and Reconciliation, the ASEAN Human Rights Declaration and the nomination of Mr. Le Luong Minh as the next Secretary General. The draft communiqué also summarized discussions on the South China Sea including the stand off at Scarborough Shoal between China and the Philippines and Vietnam's concerns about the award of oil exploration leases by the China National Offshore Oil Company within Vietnam's Exclusive Economic Zone (EEZ).

The wording of one paragraph in the South China Sea section of the joint communiqué became such a sticking point between Cambodia and the drafters of the joint communiqué that no communiqué was issued. This was unprecedented. Since ASEAN was founded in 1967 all forty-four previous AMMs had issued joint communiqués. Indeed, a media advisory announcing the 45th AMM, released by Cambodia on July 6, 2002, concluded, "[a] Joint Communiqué will be adopted at the end of the Meeting."

Cambodia argues that the failure of the AMM to adopt a joint communiqué rests squarely with the Philippines and Vietnam and their insistence on including a reference to Scarborough Shoal and EEZs in the final text. According to Cambodia, the actions by the Philippines and Vietnam prevented a consensus from being reached and Cambodia had no recourse but to withhold the joint communiqué. The leaked record of the foreign ministers' retreat held after the AMM reveals a different story.

Discussion on the South China Sea took place in the plenary session under the agenda item "preparation for the upcoming ministerial meetings." All ten foreign ministers spoke in turn with Cambodia speaking last. The Philippines opened the discussion. Foreign Secretary del Rosario stated that ASEAN should adopt a rules-based approach in resolving maritime disputes and territorial claims and adhere to international law to ensure maritime safety and maritime cooperation mechanisms.

He noted that under the DOC the signatories were committed to promote a peaceful, friendly and harmonious environment in the South China Sea. He argued that recent events involved repeated intrusions into Scarborough Shoal, violating the principles of the DOC and universally recognized principles of international law, including the United Nations Convention on Law of the Sea (UNCLOS).

Del Rosario then provided examples of Chinese "expansion and aggression" since the 1990s, including its occupation of Mischief Reef, and numerous intrusions in the Philippines' EEZ all before the confrontation at Scarborough Shoal. China's expansion was premised on ownership of the whole of the South China Sea, he argued. China employed overwhelming force thus preventing "the Philippines from enforcing its laws and forcing the Philippines to retreat from its own EEZ."

Del Rosario stated that the Philippines responded to Chinese actions by exercising patience and restraint under the terms of the DOC. The Philippines entered into negotiations to peacefully resolve the situation at Scarborough Shoal. But China acted in bad faith when it failed to honour its commitment to withdraw its vessels. Del Rosario argued that China's actions challenged ASEAN centrality, leadership and solidarity. The Philippines, as the aggrieved party and one of the founding members of ASEAN, failed to understand the lack of concern by some other members and their "seeming silence" on their commitment to the principles of the DOC, he concluded. Del Rosario then asked rhetorically, "what would be the real value of the COC if we could not uphold the DOC; in Scarborough Shoal the DOC is violated?" He stated that it was "important that ASEAN [make a] collective commitment to uphold the DOC [and this] be reflected in the joint communiqué of the AMM."

Del Rosario then quoted the remarks by Prime Minister Hun Sen at the opening of the AMM: "ASEAN should further demonstrate its ability and role as a driving force for the promotion of dialogue and cooperation on the political and security issues for the cause of peace, stability and prosperity in the region." Del Rosario asserted, "[t]o operationalize this principle [it is] necessary for the joint communiqué to acknowledge the problem rather than ignore [it]. We strongly recommend the [inclusion] of Scarborough Shoal, EEZ and continental shelf in the joint communiqué draft. [There must be] concerted action to address the threat to peace and stability in he region."

Del Rosario thanked ASEAN member states that supported the ASEAN Foreign Ministers' Statement on the Situation in Scarborough Shoal, and in particular he expressed great appreciation for the ASEAN founding fathers. With the creation of the ASEAN Community in 2015, ASEAN members would be "more conscious of our role to ensure peace and security." Finally, Del Rosario concluded his remarks by quoting from the German anti-Nazi theologian, Martin Neimöller:

First they came for the communists, and I didn't speak out because I wasn't a communist.

Then they came for the trade unionists, and I didn't speak out because I wasn't a trade unionist.

Then they came for the Jews, ?and I didn't speak out because I wasn't a Jew.

Then they came for me, and there was no one left to speak out for me.

The Thai Foreign Minister Surapong Tovichakchaikul spoke next. He observed that the South China Sea had attracted a lot of attention. Surapong stated that after discussions with Chinese officials he concluded that they did not want this issue to affect the excellent relations between ASEAN and China. "What is important is for all parties concerned to scale down, calm things down," he said.

Surapong asserted that, "the issue of territorial claims will have to be resolved between the claimant states through negotiation. But we have to recognize the broader implications. Apart from that, there is room for greater dialogue between both sides. Rather than being seen as source of conflict, the South China Sea should be seen [as an opportunity] for cooperation. [ASEAN and China] should build trust and [a] win-win situation." Surapong noted that as the ASEAN Dialogue Coordinator for China (2012-15), "Thailand will try its best towards this end. We will push ahead with concrete implementation of the DOC, while ensuring the COC drafting process that is inclusive and comfortable for all sides. We must get it right from the start."

Surapong concluded, "Last and most important: ASEAN unity; the whole world is watching ASEAN with high expectations; major powers want to be part of this fast growing region; we must ensure that this competition is a healthy one." ASEAN should have a "positive influence on regional and international issues; ASEAN need[s] to speak more with one voice. Our collective voice does matter internationally. Bali Concord II: [ASEAN] unity would enhance credibility and [its] centrality in [the] regional architecture."

Pham Binh Minh, Vietnam's Foreign Minister spoke next. He began by noting, "[o]ver recent months the situation has [been] aggravated due to [a] series of Chin[ese] moves to impose their 9 dash claim. Apart from Scarborough Shoal, China announced the establishment of Sansha City [Hainan, to administer an area] which covers almost all the South China Sea... [The China National] Offshore [Oil] Company invited bidding for nine oil and gas blocks [lying] within Vietnam's EEZ and continental shelf with several points only sixteen miles off Vietnam's coast. [These are] serious violations of Vietnam's sovereignty and jurisdiction over its EEZ and continental shelf [under] UNCLOS. [China's actions] go against the spirit of the DOC, create a serious concern for the maintenance of peace and stability, bring[ing] about long term consequences and implications."

Binh noted, "we have discussed the South China Sea many times [and] agree that territorial disputes should be solved by the parties [directly] involved. But this issue has a much broader implication for maritime security, peace, stability and security in the region. [It is] important for ASEAN to show [a] central role in regional peace and security [and] promote dialogue and cooperation. [ASEAN should] speak with one voice, maintain unity... with agreed common points."

Foreign Minister Binh also quoted approvingly from Prime Minister Hun Sen's remarks at the opening of the 45th AMM on ASEAN's role as the "driving force for the promotion of dialogue and cooperation" in the region and Hun Sen's emphasis on the implementation of the DOC, including the eventual conclusion of a Code of Conduct. Binh then argued "that the joint communiqué should reaffirm further the importance of universally recognized principle[s] of international law, including respect of territorial integrity, sovereignty and sovereign rights and jurisdiction of coastal states in [their] EEZ and continental shelf as stipulated in UNCLOS." Binh noted that the incidents that took place earlier in the year occurred within the EEZs of ASEAN member states. Binh added that "all disputes should be settled through peaceful means through dialogue in accordance with international law, [including] UNCLOS and [the] DOC."

Binh concluded by noting that the ASEAN Senior Officials' Meeting had completed the ASEAN paper on key elements of the COC. He reiterated the COC was an "important legal document [that] contributed to peace, maritime security and safety in the South China Sea; ensuring that disputes will be settled by peaceful means. Based on [the] ASEAN paper, ASEAN should decide to initiate consultations with China on the COC through existing mechanisms, namely the ASEAN-China SOM on the DOC as it is quite appropriate." Binh ended his remarks by re-emphasizing "that during consultations ASEAN should maintain close coordination, unity and speak with one voice, based on the agreed paper."

Indonesia's Foreign Minister spoke next and observed that developments in the South China Sea had been discussed in the past, would likely be discussed in the future, and were unlikely to go away. Marty stated that, "we must have [an] ASEAN outlook... on the matter. It is self-evident whenever ASEAN speaks with one voice we are able to maintain our centrality [and] ensure that we deliver results." He gave as an example ASEAN's contribution to developing the Guidelines to Implement the DOC and the work of the ASEAN SOM in identifying the key elements of the COC. Marty further noted that while the diplomatic process of implementing the DOC was underway, "the situation on the ground at sea is showing signs of concern for all of us. We have been following what has been transpiring. All those developments reinforce the need to get the COC concluded as soon as possible." If there is no progress on the COC "the situation [will] become more destabilizing. [This is] not in our common interest."

Marty further noted that ASEAN's proposed key elements on the COC were "well crafted and well thought through." He asked rhetorically to what extent would the COC guide ASEAN when it faced the situation with China over Scarborough Shoal? Marty concluded: "We want to be sure that the COC is operational in nature, and not simply repeat statements and principles that are available in the DOC. [The] COC must be prescriptive, [provide] rule[s] to avoid incidents in the South China Sea, and provide [the] means whereby the conduct of countries can be better regulated..."

Malaysia's Foreign Minister Anifah Aman spoke on two issues, the DOC and the COC. With respect to the former he noted, "ASEAN and China should continue close consultation and coordination through existing mechanisms [to] fully implement [the] DOC." He proposed that ASEAN "should consider fully utilizing the ASEAN-China Maritime Cooperation Fund [and] look[ed] forward to seeing the details of the fund from China."

With respect to the COC, Anifah Aman noted that ASEAN had concluded a draft of the key elements of the COC. He thanked Cambodia for convening informal consultations with China on this draft. This would contribute to "build[ing] mutual trust and confidence towards peace and stability. As we embark on [the] intergovernmental process on [the] COC [ASEAN and China] should first discuss the [key] elements before discussing the text of the COC [because it was] more practical to do so before the actual drafting begins."

Ȧnifah Aman then turned to a proposal by China, presented to the ASEAN Summit earlier in the year by Cambodia as ASEAN Chair, to establish an Eminent Persons and Expert Working Group. "We should not prevent [the ASEAN-China] SOM from seeking inputs from experts as the need arise[s] on certain technical and legal matters." Malaysia's Foreign Minister then argued that ASEAN should reiterate its position that the "COC aim[s] to create [a] rules based framework; it should not serve as an instrument to resolve territorial disputes. Existing disputes should be resolved between [the] parties concerned based on existing mechanism[s], including UNCLOS."

Next Anifah Aman focused on the proposed paragraph on the South China Sea in the draft joint communiqué. He agreed with Indonesia: "We must talk with a single voice; ASEAN must show [its] united voice; [otherwise] our credibility will be undermined.

We must refer to the situation in the South China Sea, particularly any acts that contravene the international law on EEZ and continental shelves. It is totally unacceptable that we can't have it in the joint communiqué." Brunei's Foreign Minister, Prince Mohamed Bolkiah, spoke briefly. He noted with approval ASEAN's engagement with China on the COS. He then indicated that the proposed key elements in the ASEAN draft COC were acceptable. As for the joint communiqué, Brunei would be "guided by your [ASEAN Chair] decision, [Brunei] can support the statement." It was important for ASEAN and China to have "mutual trust and confidence."

Thongloun Sisoulith, the Laotian Foreign Minister followed Brunei. He noted that there was no doubt the South China Sea was an important issue. "All efforts," he argued, "should be made in order to maintain and promote peace and stability in this part of the world." He was pleased that "ASEAN and China have been engaging in dialogue to contribute to further confidence building and mutual trust. The 5th ASEAN-China SOM on [the] DOC agreed on various activities to implement the DOC including the convening of the joint workshop. Laos fully supports these activities."

The Lao Foreign Minister noted that working toward the eventual adoption of the COC was part of the implementation of the DOC. Thongloun said he was pleased to take note of the proposed key elements in ASEAN's draft COC and these should be for internal ASEAN reference. The Lao Foreign Minister fully concurred "with the proposal that it is time to start the consultation with China on the COC and the upcoming Post-Ministerial Conference should task the ASEAN-China SOM to start talks. The convening of [the] informal ASEAN-China SOM on [the] COC demonstrated the readiness of ASEAN and China to work towards the eventual adoption of the COC." He concluded by noting that "[t]he implementation of the DOC has gained good impetus [and] we should maintain and further strengthen it and therefore contribute to making the South China Sea the sea of peace, cooperation and partnership and prosperity."

Myanmar's Foreign Minister Wunna Maung Lwin spoke briefly on the South China Sea. He reiterated his country's desire that territorial disputes be settled peacefully through dialogue and engagement. He noted the importance of the DOC and its aim to build confidence among the parties and to settle disputes by peaceful means. Myanmar fully supported the Guidelines to Implement the DOC and welcomed the proposal by ASEAN and China to undertake cooperative projects in the South China Sea.

Maung Lwin concluded that Myanmar would "[c]ontinue to support the full and effective implementation of the COC, and support all efforts that ensure [the] peaceful resolution of disputes." He also noted ASEAN's formal engagement with China on the COC and wished "to emphasize that we [ASEAN] have gained positive achievements with China and should keep the momentum of the achievements."

Foreign Minister K. Shanmugam opened his remarks by noting that Singapore was not a claimant state and that "specific claims have to be resolved among [the] parties concerned." Singapore, however, had an interest in seeing that the South China Sea "must be shared by all states, claimant and non claimant," and it was in the common interest to the maintain peace and stability in the region.

Shanmugam asserted that "freedom of navigation [is] very important to all of us. Freedom of navigation can not be respected if the rule of law is not observed." He noted that "recent developments were of special concern" because they "invoke novel interpretations of international law that could undermine the entire UNCLOS regime" and create uncertainty over the future of UNCLOS. Shanmugam said that Singapore welcomed "the internal agreement of ASEAN on possible elements of [the] COC" and suggested empowering the SOM to begin discussions with China. These discussions should proceed in parallel with the implementation of the DOC. He also noted that negotiations on the COC would not be easy, but it was important that ASEAN begin a dialogue with China. Shanmugam concluded by asserting, "it is important that ASEAN has a clear expression of our concerns on the South China Sea in the joint communiqué," and he shared the points made by previous speakers. It would be "damaging to us if we don't say anything. If ASEAN is not united, our negotiations with China will be more difficult and protracted."

Cambodia's Foreign Minister Hor Namhong rounded off the discussion on the South China Sea by bluntly declaring, "[t]here is no consensus, [we should] bracket the entire paragraphs 14-17 for our decision. The most difficult is paragraph 16. It is a complex problem."

According to the Summary of the Cambodia Chair's intervention at the AMM Retreat, Hor Namhong made the following points:

On Scarborough Shoal, we all know it is situated in the South China Sea, and we are talking here about the South China Sea. So why should we specify the Scarborough Shoal precisely in the South China Sea. Up to now, we all know the disputes among the concerned parties [are] in Spratlys and Paracels, but we never mention these name[s] in our talks with China. We always mention only the South China Sea.

On the inclusion of the wording on EEZ and continental shelf, we believe that every one is perfectly aware that the 1982 UNCLOS have precisely defined the EEZ and continental shelf, and other issues related to the sea. Why should we repeat again?

In case we [do] not find a way out, Cambodia as Chair has no more recourse to deal with this issue. So the problem we are facing now is either we have compromise text, [that will] not satisf[y] everyone. If we cannot agree on [the] text, there should be no text at all. For the Joint Communiqué, countries should not try to impose [their] national position, but the common view in spirit of compromise.

ASEAN-China met twice recently to discuss informally the drafting of COC. Cambodia [is] to host formal SOM on COC in near future. All the meetings are steps forward to de-escalate tension... in the South China Sea. We should not take position that may lead in creating or escalating tension in the SCS. What I propose now is in line with what my Prime Minister has proposed, that we have to work for peace, security and stability in the region.

The remarks by Cambodia as ASEAN Chair provoked an interchange with the foreign ministers of Indonesia, Malaysia, Vietnam, and the Philippines. Marty Natalegawa took the floor first and suggested it would be better if the foreign ministers could address paragraph 16 now so they could conclude the AMM Retreat. Malaysia immediately endorsed Indonesia's proposal. Hor Namhong responded by stating that Cambodia was not "talking against anybody or for anybody. We want to move forward the COC to de-escalate the tension. If we put strong wording in the joint communiqué it is not preferable for the solution."

Malaysia's Anifah Aman noted that the 2011 AMM joint communiqué did not reflect the decisions reached at that time. Malaysia was concerned over "how to settle our disputes [and] respect freedom of navigation." With respect to freedom of navigation Anifah Aman argued that the joint communiqué "does not specifically mention the settlement of disputes through international law and UNCLOS. I am concerned that we have left out the most important concern: all disputes must be settled in international law. We have to be mindful of the disputes. UNCLOS and international law should be the mechanism."

Hor Namhong interjected, "now or [in] the near future we can't expect to resolve the disputes. Not ASEAN." Anifah Aman responded: "[the] DOC and COC are the main frameworks. [They are] rules-based frameworks, [they] are not meant to settle the disputes, the mechanisms are based on UNCLOS. We are not happy..."

Vietnam's Pham Binh Minh broke in to raise a question of procedure. "We should discuss this issue right now. Every year the joint communiqué has a paragraph on the South China Sea, [some are] stronger and [other are] milder... There is no question that the joint communiqué does not have that one. Around the table here we have the discussion and [the] ministers already indicated that the joint communiqué must have a paragraph on the South China Sea. Every year we have to update the situation, the development over the South China Sea. This year what happened to the South China Sea? Those incidents occurred not only in the South China Sea but deeper in the EEZs, [these were] new developments. That is why in the draft we have to update the new developments in there. We put here [words] calling [for] the respect of EEZs and continental shelves, these [are] new developments in the South China Sea."

Hor Namhong responded. "We can never achieve [consensus] even though we stay here for the next four or five hours..." Indonesia's Foreign Minister broke in to ask "how detailed are we [going to be in our] references to Scarborough Shoal and EEZs and continental shelves?" Apparently referring to paragraph 16 in the draft joint communiqué Marty read out:

In this context, we discussed in-depth recent developments in the South China Sea, including the situation in the affected Shoal/ disputed area, exclusive economic zones and continental shelves of coastal states, particularly those contrary to the provisions of the 1982 UNCLOS. In this connection, we call upon all parties to respect the universally recognized principles of international law including the 1982 UNCLOS. Further [we call] upon all the parties to resolve the disputes in accordance with universally recognized principles of international law.

Hor Namhong replied, "Up to now there have been disputes in the Paracels and Spratlys but we have never mentioned the names of these. But now why do we include these in the joint communiqué? Second if we need again paragraph 16..."

Del Rosario interjected, "There is no clarity that the disputes must be settled peacefully and in accordance with international law, especially UNCLOS. You refer to freedom of navigation and over flight, it [the joint communiqué] does not mention disputes. Right now there are two gross violations of the DOC. They are in [Scarborough] Shoal and in the oil service contract of the EEZ and continental shelf. These are very clear distinct violations of the DOC. If we are going to be protecting peace and stability and freedom of navigation in the South China Sea we should deal with the problem as it present[s] itself at this point in time. We are also ignoring the fact that there are gross violations of the DOC in the EEZs in the Philippines and Vietnam. It is a challenge to ASEAN's leadership, centrality and solidarity. Why are we ignoring these gross violations instead of identifying them so that we can deal with them?"

Hor Namhong responded: "We are not a tribunal, [we should] not escalate tension but diffuse tension. When we refer to shoal where is the shoal? Are the Spratlys or Paracels shoals? When you say violation of Scarborough Shoal, we have to know to whom it belongs. We are not a tribunal. Maybe it belongs to the Philippines, I don't know. I still don't understand, when we said disputed areas that covers all the areas [that are] disputed. Why should we add the shoal and EEZ and continental shelf? Before we go to [the] concluding session, I propose we delete the South China Sea in the joint communiqué, and [proceed] without paragraph 16. I have no other recourse. Or claimant states will deal directly with China." Indonesia's Marty then asked the Chair to "read again the formulation." Hor Namhong responded, "[where] we refer to [the] shoal?" He then asked if the joint communiqué should include actions contrary to UNCLOS. "UNCLOS already defines the EEZs and continental shelves, should we repeat it again?" he asked.

Del Rosario took up the discussion. "With due respect," he stated, "the first sentence [reads:] 'in this context we discussed in depth the developments [in the South China Sea], including the situation in the Scarborough Shoal and expressed serious concern over such developments in the area, particularly those provisions in the UNCLOS related to Exclusive Economic Zones and continental shelves.' Nowhere in that sentence is ASEAN [taking a] position as to who owns the shoal. We are just calling attention that they are violating the DOC. We are not looking at the resolution of territorial claims here. There is no reference [to] who is owning what."

Malaysia's Anifah Aman declared, "It [violations] is happening. Nowhere did we mention that it [Scarborough Shoal] belongs [to one country or another]. Instead of 'affected shoal' we [should] put it as 'disputed area'." Del Rosario retorted, "There are many disputed areas in the South China Sea but not in the Scarborough Shoal. All we are saying [is] discussion in conflict areas." Anifah Aman replied, "We are trying to find... I don't think we can progress forward if we specifically mention an area... It reflects the united stand of ASEAN to encompass all disputed areas." Marty Natalegawa responded, "We [Indonesia] are not one of those claimant states. We suggested earlier to use the word 'affected shoal.' [We are] trying to be sensitive; affected shoal [is] without prejudice to national claims. Be we can agree to [use the term] disputed area. We don't think that this issue is impossible to resolve. We have discussed in depth the situation [in the South China Sea].

Hor Namhong stated, "I can support the disputed areas, disputed areas covers everything." Vietnam's Pham Binh Minh then interjected, "Disputed area, the EEZ is not a disputed area, certainly not. Some countries [try] to turn an undisputed are into a disputed area. That's for sure [an EEZ is not a disputed area] in accordance with international law." Minh then proposed a break for small group discussion. The notes on the discussions at the AMM Retreat end at this point.

Media and other reporting reveal that discussions on the wording of the South China Sea paragraphs continued until the morning of July 13 without breaking the impasse. Ernest Bower, who spoke to diplomats in Phnom Penh, wrote that after the four-member ministerial committee came up with a draft communiqué, "[r]epeatedly, however, after taking the draft under consideration, Hor Namhong consulted with advisers outside of the meeting room and came back rejecting language referring to Scarborough Shoal and the EEZs, even after multiple attempts to find compromise.

He said Cambodia's view was that those were bilateral issues and therefore could not be mentioned in the joint statement." By one account, the original AMM joint communiqué went through a total of eighteen drafts. Over the four days following the AMM Retreat, the Indonesian and Singaporean foreign ministers made a last-ditch effort to broker a compromise.

They persuaded Vietnam and the Philippines to agree to a compromise on the wording. But repeated attempts to persuade Cambodia's Hor Namhong failed. At their last meeting Foreign Minister Hor Namhong "picked up his papers, and stormed out of the room" arguing it was a matter of principle for ASEAN not to take sides in bilateral disputes. Finally, according to an account by a Philippine official who attended the meetings in Phnom Penh: "[t]he text of the proposed Joint Communiqué's item/subhead on the "South China Sea" was drafted by the ASEAN foreign ministers and several revisions were made to make the text acceptable to all. However, the Cambodian Chair consistently rejected any proposed text that mentions Scarborough Shoal.

Blame Game

The failure of ASEAN foreign ministers to issue a joint communiqué at the conclusion of the 45th AMM led to immediate public recriminations. On the morning of the last day, immediately after a special meeting failed to reach an eleventh hour compromise, the Philippines issued a statement taking "strong exception" to the decision by the ASEAN Chair not to issue a joint communiqué. Foreign Minister Hor Namhong hit back accusing the Philippines of attempting to "hijack" the AMM and declaring that the "joint communiqué has become hostage to a bilateral issue." The Philippine Undersecretary for Foreign Affairs, Erlinda Basilio, penned a personal account entitled, "Why There Was No ASEAN Joint Communiqué" that provoked a Cambodian diplomatic response.

Unnamed diplomatic sources leaked information to the press suggesting collusion between China and Cambodia. One senior diplomat was quoted as stating, "China bought the chair, simple as that" and pointed to comments by Foreign Minister Yang thanking Prime Minister Hun Sen for supporting China's "core interests."

A veteran journalist reported that when the first draft of the joint communiqué was submitted to the ASEAN Chair "the Cambodians, in a breach of ASEAN protocol, showed it to the Chinese, who said it was unacceptable unless the South China Sea reference was removed. So the Cambodians sent it back for amendment."

ASEAN's failure to issue a joint communiqué attracted widespread media coverage and critical commentary by academics and other observers. On July 26-27 Cambodia hit back with a barrage of three letters to the editors.

The first was written by Kou Kuong, spokesperson for Cambodia's Ministry of Foreign Affairs and International Cooperation. This letter was addressed to the Editor-in-Chief of *The Cambodia Daily* in response to a story that quoted critical comments on Cambodia's role as ASEAN Chair by the International Crisis Group. Kou Kuong argued that "two countries...tried to sabotage and hijack our meetings" and held the 45 ASEAN Foreign Ministers' Joint Communiqué "hostage to its [sic] national interests."

The second letter was written by the Cambodian Ambassador to Thailand in response to an opinion piece by Thitinan Pongsudhirak, a well-known academic, published in the *Bangkok Post*. Ambassador You Ay first corrected a common media misperception that the Peace Palace, where the 45th AMM was held, was funded by China.

She then targeted her remarks on comments that were critical of Cambodia's relations with China. Ambassador You pointed out that "China provided assistance only for the construction of the adjacent building and not the Peace Palace.

Next, the Ambassador rejected Thitinan's assertion that China was an "open patron state" of Cambodia as a result of providing U.S. $10 billion in aid and investment. Finally, the Ambassador dismissed (but did not directly deny) as "extremely disparaging and slanderous" Thitinan's claim that Cambodia "shared the draft version of the joint statement with the Chinese, who then vetoed it."

The third letter was written by Cambodia's Ambassador to the Philippines to the editor-in-chief of *The Philippines Star*. Ambassador Hos' letter took direct issue with Undersecretary Basilio's.

Ambassador Hos reiterated Cambodia's argument that the failure to achieve consensus at the 45th AMM was due to the "inflexible and non-negotiable position" of "two countries" [the Philippines and Vietnam]. Cambodia's Ambassador further argued that the "two countries wanted to sabotage and hijack the JC [joint communiqué]" in retaliation for Cambodia's refusal to issue an ASEAN Statement on the Situation in the South China Sea." The Ambassador's parting shot - accusing "the two countries" of "dirty politics" - resulted in two summons by the Philippine Department of Foreign Affairs. The Ambassador failed to appear for either reportedly on the ground of ill health. Shortly after it was announced that Ambassador Hos was being recalled.

Analysts are divided on the details of and extent to which China influenced Cambodia's decision to block the AMM joint communiqué, but few analysts argue that Cambodia's acted independently. Kishore Mahbubani, a former senior Singaporean diplomat, wrote "the whole world, including most ASEAN countries, perceived Cambodia's stance as the result of enormous Chinese pressure."

Amitav Acharya wrote, "[t]here is little question that Hun Sen's refusal to accommodate Philippines and Vietnam resulted at least partly from Chinese pressure. According to a highly placed source, the Chinese specifically reminded the Cambodians that [Norodom] Sihanouk... had accepted the Chinese claims to the South China Sea."

A Chinese scholar close to the Ministry of State Security revealed, "[w]e co-ordinated very well with Cambodia in that case [blocking objectionable wording in the 45th AMM joint communiqué] and... prevented an incident which would have been detrimental to China."

Shuttle Diplomacy

Indonesia's Foreign Minister initiated consultations with the nine other members of ASEAN in an effort to restore unity in ASEAN ranks and commit ASEAN to a common position. Foreign Minister Marty conducted an intense round of shuttle diplomacy flying to five capitals (Manila, Hanoi, Bangkok, Phnom Penh and Singapore) over a two-day period (July 18-19). Marty and del Rosario agreed to a six-point proposal that Marty put to his other ASEAN counterparts. When he obtained their agreement Marty left it to Cambodia's Hor Namhong, as ASEAN Chair, to complete the diplomatic formalities.

On July 20, Hor Namhong, acting in his capacity as ASEAN Chair, officially released ASEAN's Six Principles on the South China Sea. Under the terms of this statement all ASEAN Foreign Ministers reaffirmed their commitment to: the full implementation of the DOC; Guidelines for the Implementation of the DOC; the early conclusion of a Regional COC in the South China Sea; full respect of the universally recognized principles of international law including the 1982 UNCLOS;

continued exercise of self-restraint and non-use of force by all parties; and peaceful resolution of disputes in accordance with the universally recognized principles of international law including the 1982 UNCLOS.

The ASEAN statement concluded: "The ASEAN Foreign Ministers resolve to intensify ASEAN consultations in the advancement of the above principles, consistent with the Treaty of Amity and Cooperation in Southeast Asia (1976) and the ASEAN Charter (2008)."

A Chinese Foreign Ministry spokesperson, Qin Gang, responded to these developments by introducing a pre-condition linking compliance with the DOC and discussions on the COC. Qin Gang stated:

> What concerns people now is that some individual countries, showing no respect for or compliance with the DOC, have time and again resorted to provocative means, which undermined the basic principles and spirit of the DOC and created difficulties for discussing a code of conduct (COC) in the South China Sea.
>
> Therefore, while being open to discussing a COC with ASEAN countries, China believes that all parties concerned must act in strict accordance with the DOC to create the necessary conditions and atmosphere of a COC.

China then dispatched its foreign minister for a fence-mending visit to Indonesia and Malaysia for talks with his counterparts. Foreign Minister Yang Jiechi stated at a joint press conference that China was willing to work with ASEAN to implement the DOC and "on the basis of consensus" to work toward the eventual adoption of the COC.

Foreign Minister Yang held discussions with Malaysian Foreign Minister Anifah Aman in Kuala Lumpur. There was no joint press conference. Anifah Aman stated he was "confident we can resolve this matter [disputes in the South China Sea]... through peaceful means." He then observed, [t]here are overlapping claims by member countries. Let us discuss these among ASEAN countries first before we talk to China. We can only achieve this objective in the South China Sea if all parties agree. Then China can appreciate this and realise it is ASEAN's wish." This statement seemed to imply that ASEAN-China discussions on the COC, if and when they take place, would be a protracted process.

ASEAN's objective of creating an ASEAN Political-Security Community by 2015 is predicated on the assumption that ASEAN members share a common identity and a common responsibility for contributing to "peace, stability and security" in Southeast Asia.

The *ASEAN Political-Security Community Blueprint* states that one of its goals is to "[e]nsure full implementation of the DOC for peace and stability in the South China Sea." In order to achieve this objective the *Blueprint* calls for a continuation of "ASEAN's current practice of close consultation among Member States to achieve full implementation of the DOC... and [w]ork towards the adoption of a regional Code of Conduct in the South China Sea."

The *ASEAN Charter* calls for "[e]nhanced consultations on matters seriously affecting the common interest of ASEAN." ASEAN's failure to issue a joint communiqué after its 45thAMM poses procedural questions about the fate of 128 paragraphs in the draft that recorded decisions on a range of issues other than the South China Sea, including ASEAN community-building and the appointment of a new Secretary General. It also raises questions about the status of ASEAN's agreement on key principles in its draft COC.

The analysis presented in part one clearly shows that the Philippines has made major concessions in its discussions with fellow ASEAN members in order to reach consensus on the key principles in the COC.

The Philippines has been diplomatically circumspect about this. There were no public recriminations when the Philippines proposals for a ZOPFF/C and a joint development area were stripped from its draft COC. As a result, ASEAN was able to reach agreement on the key principles of its COC and approach China informally to discuss the way ahead. ASEAN still has to fine-tune its draft by considering inputs from Indonesia in the form of a "non-paper."

Part two provided a detailed insight into internal ASEAN dynamics as its foreign ministers discussed and debated the South China Sea question and how to word its members' concerns in a joint communiqué.

The analysis clearly demonstrates that the Philippines, as a founding member of ASEAN, expected support on an issue that touched not only on its national sovereignty but regional security as well. The analysis also demonstrates that there was a "majority consensus" to include reference to disputes concerning Scarborough Shoal and oil leasing in Vietnam's Exclusive Economic Zone.

The record indicates that the failure to achieve consensus was the result of Cambodia's handling of its role as ASEAN Chair. Foreign Minister Hor Namhong was not conciliatory at the AMM Retreat and his subsequent actions in rejecting repeated attempts at compromise appear obstinate. At the same time, it is revealing that ASEAN foreign ministers acquiesced to Cambodia's high-handedness in vetoing the draft joint communiqué drawn up by four of their colleagues. No minister directly challenged Hor Namhong's handling of the discussion/debate at the AMM Retreat.

Part three dealt with the recriminations that followed the failure of ASEAN to issue a joint communiqué. It is clear that Chinese influence played a major role in influencing Cambodia to play an obstructionist role. Cambodia's actions indicate that the idea of an ASEAN Community played second fiddle to its relations with China. In the short run the Philippines (and Vietnam) will be hyper sensitive to Cambodia's role as ASEAN Chair in any discussions with China on the South China Sea. In the longer term some ASEAN members will be concerned about China's ability to influence Laos and Myanmar who will assume the ASEAN Chair in 2014 and 2015, respectively. In this respect the events at the 45th AMM may serve as a wake up call and result in amended decision-making procedures.

Part four dealt with Indonesia's decision to engage in a round of shuttle diplomacy in order to obtain unanimous agreement on ASEAN's Six-Point Principles on the South China Sea. Foreign Minister Marty Natalegawa's diplomatic initiative provided a much-needed boost to ASEAN morale. His efforts also helped to dispel the perception outside of Southeast Asia that there was disunity among ASEAN members on how to deal with the South China Sea issue. More importantly, Indonesia's intervention served notice to Cambodia that as ASEAN's chair for 2012 it could not unilaterally control ASEAN's agenda. Natalegawa's intervention was unprecedented in assuming a leadership role that normally would fall to the ASEAN chair and signalled that Indonesia is willing to play a more proactive role in regional affairs.

Current indications are that ASEAN will pursue the implementation of the DOC and discussions on the COC with China in tandem. ASEAN will seek to obtain agreement with China on the key principles and then move on to drafting the final text. China will have to take Indonesia's new role into account and this may prove a positive factor in addressing current tensions in the South China Sea.

5

South China Sea: The State of Crisis and Setting the Stage for Flashpoint

War and peace are no longer binary. The US and its peers are now frequently operating in the gray zone between war and peace. This is the case in the South China Sea where China moves aggressively to solidify territorial claims and influence other claimants. The Chinese, by keeping their actions below the threshold of war, limit the US military response. Tensions increase and decrease based on the actions and responses of the participants. Next moves must be measured in the context of their impact on tensions.

China's claims are built on their 2,000 year maritime history. These claims are being pressed as a part of a broader Chinese strategy of geographic expansion. Developing islands through dredging and infrastructure construction advances the claims from conceptual to physical. If the Chinese are able to influence the claimant countries in the region away from international forums for dispute resolution, these Chinese islands will strengthen Chinese claims. Time will be on the side of an expanding Dragon.

There are roughly half a billion people who live within 100 miles of the South China Sea coastline thus the region's importance cannot be understated. It is a critical fishery, contains potentially lucrative natural resources, and is a critical shipping lane for the world. Approximately 12 per cent of the global fish catch comes from the South China Sea. With thousands of fishing vessels in the region, approximately 55% are Chinese. Many of the disputes in the region are grounded in fishing rights and intrusions. The South China Sea's hydrocarbon reserves of at least seven billion barrels of oil and an estimated 900 trillion cubic feet of natural gas offer tremendous economic opportunity for Malaysia, the Philippines, and Vietnam, and energy security for China's growing economy.

PHILIPPINES V. CHINA

Philippines v. China (also known as The South China Sea Arbitration) was an arbitration case brought by the Republic of the Philippines against thePeoples Republic of China concerning certain issues in the South China Seaincluding the legality of China's "nine-dotted line" claim over the South China Sea under the United Nations Convention on the Law of the Sea (UNCLOS). On 19 February 2013, China officially refused to participate in the arbitration because, according to China, its 2006 declaration under article 298 covers the disputes brought by the Philippines and that this case concernssovereignty, thus it deems the arbitral tribunal formed for the case has no jurisdiction over the issue. On 7 December 2014, a position paper was published by China to elaborate its position. On 29 October 2015, thePermanent Court of Arbitration (PCA) ruled that it has jurisdiction over the case, taking up seven of the 15 submissions made by the Philippines.

On 12 July 2016, the PCA ruled in favor of the Philippines against China overterritorial disputes in the South China Sea. The court unanimously ruled that China has "no historical rights" based on the so-called "nine-dash line" map. The PCA also ruled that Chinese reclamation activity in the south China sea has also caused an irreparable damage to the environment and asked the Chinese government to stop further activities in the South China Sea.

Background

The dispute has been affected by the fact that, after Japan renounced all claims to the Spratly Islands and other conquered islands and territories in the Treaty of San Francisco and Treaty of Peace with theRepublic of China (Taiwan) signed on September 8, 1951, it did not indicate successor states since China was not invited to the treaty talks held in San Francisco. In reaction to that, on 15 August, the Chinese government issued the Declaration on the Draft Peace Treaty with Japan by the US and the UK and on the San Francisco Conference by the then Foreign Minister Zhou Enlai, reitirating China's sovereignty over the archipelagos in the South China Sea, including the Spratly Islands, and protesting about the absence of any provisions in the draft on who shall take over the South China Sea islands following Japan's renouncement of all rights, title and claim to them. It reiterated that "the Chinese government of the day had taken over those islands" and that the PRC's rightful sovereignty "shall remain intact".

On 28 April 1952, the United States presided over the signing of theTreaty of Peace between Japan and the Republic of China. Article 2 of the document provided that "It is recognized that under Article 2 of the Treaty of Peace which Japan signed at the city of San Francisco on 8 September 1951 (hereinafter referred to as the San Francisco Treaty), Japan has renounced all right, title, and claim to Taiwan (Formosa) and Penghu (the Pescadores) as well as the Spratly Islands and the Paracel Islands."

The Philippines bases its claim on its geographical proximity to the Spratly Islands, even though its claim bears no weight on sovereignty ownership because sovereignty of islands is established by legal relations rather than geographical proximity.

In May 1956, the dispute escalated after Filipino national Tomas Cloma and his followers settled on the islands and declared the territory as "Freedomland", now known as Kalayaan for himself and later requested to make the territory a protectorate of the Philippines. Tomas Cloma even stole China (ROC)'s national flag from the Taiping Island. In July 1956, he apologized officially for his act and he surrendered the flag he stole to China's embassy in Manila. On Oct 2nd 1956, he wrote a letter and ensured he would not make further training voyages or landings in the territorial waters of China (ROC).

Philippine troops were sent to three of the islands in 1968, when the Philippines were under President Ferdinand Marcos. In the 1970s, some countries began to invade and occupy islands and reefs in the Spratlys.

The Spratlys were placed under the jurisdiction of the province of Palawan in 1978. The People's Republic of China (PRC) claims it is entitled to the Paracel and Spratly Islands because they were seen as integral parts of the Ming dynasty.

China and Taiwan have these same territorial claims. The Republic of China (Taiwan) took control of the largest island - Taiping Island - in the group since 1946.

Vietnam states that the islands have belonged to it since the 17th century, using historical documents of ownership as evidence. Hanoi began to occupy the westernmost islands during this period. In the early 1970s, Malaysia joined the dispute by claiming the islands nearest to it. Brunei also extended its exclusive economic zone, claiming Louisa Reef.

Participants

The court case involves the Philippines and China.

Philippine stance

The Philippines is contending that the "nine-dotted line" claim by China is invalid because it violates the UNCLOS agreements about exclusive economic zones and territorial seas. It says that because most of the features in the South China Sea, such as most of the Spratly Islands, cannot sustain life, they cannot be given their own continental shelf as defined in the convention.

Chinese stance

China refuses to participate in the arbitration, stating that several treaties with the Philippines stipulate that bilateral negotiations be used to resolve border disputes. It also accuses the Philippines of violating the voluntary Declaration on the Conduct of Parties in the South China Sea, made in 2002 between ASEAN and China, which also stipulated bilateral negotiations as the means of resolving border and other disputes. China issued a position paper in December 2014 arguing the dispute was not subject to arbitration because it was ultimately a matter of sovereignty, not exploitation rights.Its refusal will not prevent the Court from proceeding with the case. After the Permanent Court of Arbration (PCA) verdict, the PRC issued a statement rejecting it as 'null' and having decided not to abide by the court's decision, said it will "ignore the ruling".

Claimants of the South China Sea

Taiwanese stance

The arbitration has not invited Taiwan to join the arbitration, and no opinion of Taiwan has been sought. The Philippines claimed in the court that Taiping Island is a rock. In response, President Ma Ying-jeou of Taiwan rejected the Philippines' claim as "patently false". Taiwan has invited the Philippines and five arbitrators from the PCA to visit Taiping Island; the Philippines rejected the invitation, and there was no response from the court of arbitration.

Vietnamese stance

On December 11, 2014, Vietnam filed a statement to the PCA which put forward three points: 1) Vietnam supports the filing of this case by the Philippines, 2) it rejects China's "nine-dashed line", and 3) it asks the Court to take note of Vietnam's claims on certain islands such as the Paracels.

Other stances

Brunei sent its own claim through a preliminary submission. In May 2009, Malaysia and Vietnam, as well as Vietnam alone, filed claims to the International Tribunal for the Law of the Sea with regard to the islands . This was in relation to extending their claimed continental shelves and Exclusive Economic Zones. The People's Republic of China rejected the claims since those violate the "nine-dotted line". The Philippines challenged the Malaysian claim stating that the claims overlap with the North Borneo dispute. Indonesia made a comment on China's claim by saying that the features are rocks and cannot sustain life, effectively calling the Chinese claim invalid. The Philippines echoed Indonesia's claims, further stating that the islands belong to them through geographic proximity.

Arbitration

Hearings

On July 7, 2015, case hearings began with the Philippines asking the Permanent Court of Arbitration (PCA) at The Hague to invalidate China's claims. The hearings were also attended by observers from Indonesia, Japan, Malaysia, Thailand andVietnam.> The case has been compared to *Nicaragua v. United States* due to similarities of the parties involved such as that a developing country is challenging a permanent member of the United Nations Security Council in an arbitral tribunal.

On 29 October 2015, the court ruled that it had the power to hear the case. It agreed to take up seven of the 15 submissions made by Manila, in particular whether Scarborough Shoal and low-tide areas like Mischief Reef can be considered islands. It set aside seven more pointed claims mainly accusing Beijing of acting unlawfully to be considered at the next hearing on the case's merits. It also told Manila to narrow down the scope of its final request that the judges order that "China shall desist from further unlawful claims and activities." The arbitral tribunal scheduled the hearing on merits of the case from 24 to 30 November 2015.

Award on Jurisdiction and Admissibility

On 29 October 2015, the PCA published its Award on Jurisdiction and Admissibility for the case. The PCA found that the Tribunal has jurisdiction to consider the following seven Philippines' Submissions. The number is the Philippines' Submissions number. PCA reserved consideration of its jurisdiction to rule on No. 1, 2, 5, 8, 9, 12, and 14.

- No.3 Philippines' position that Scarborough Shoal is a rock under Article 121(3).
- No.4 Philippines' position that Mischief Reef, Second Thomas Shoal, and Subi Reef are low tide elevations that do not generate entitlement to maritime zones.
- No.6 Whether Gaven Reef and McKennan Reef (including Hughes Reef) are low-tide elevations "that do not generate any maritime entitlements of their own".
- No.7 Whether Johnson Reef, Cuarteron Reef, and Fiery Cross Reef do or do not generate an entitlement to an exclusive economic zone or continental shelf.
- No.10 "premised on [the] fact that China has unlawfully prevented Philippine fishermen from carrying out traditional fishing activities within the territorial sea of Scarborough Shoal."
- No.11 "China's failure to protect and preserve the marine environment at these two shoals [Scarborough Shoal and Second Thomas Shoal]."
- No.13 Philippines' protest against China's "purported law enforcement activities as violating the Convention on the International Regulations for the Prevention of Collisions at Sea and also violating UNCLOS".

The Tribunal stated in the award that there are disputes in all of the 15 submissions from the Philippines, but for submissions such as No.3, No.4, No.6 and No.7, no known claims from the Philippines prior to the initiation of arbitration exist, and China was not aware or opposed such claims prior to the initiation of arbitration. Chinese Society of International Law (CSIL) states that the PCA was trying to hide its incapability to prove that maritime entitlements of the nine features constitute the disputes.

For Submission No.8 to No.14, the Tribunal held the view that lawfulness of China's activities in the South China Sea is not related to sovereignty. CSIL has asserted that disagreements concern territorial sovereignty, and constitute no dispute with respect to the claims advanced by the Philippines.

Award

On July 12, 2016, the Permanent Court of Arbitration issued an arbitration Award. Conclusions expressed in the award included the following: Regarding the "Nine-Dash Line" and China's claim in the maritime areas of the South China Sea

- The [UNCLOS] Convention defines the scope of maritime entitlements in the South China Sea, which may not extend beyond the limits imposed therein.
- China's claims to historic rights, or other sovereign rights or jurisdiction, with respect to the maritime areas of the South China Sea encompassed by the relevant part of the 'nine-dash line' are contrary to the Convention and without lawful effect to the extent that they exceed the geographic and substantive limits of China's maritime entitlements under the Convention. The Convention superseded any historic rights or other sovereign rights or jurisdiction in excess of the limits imposed therein.

Regarding the status of features as above/below water at high tide.

- High-tide features: (a) Scarborough Shoal, (b) Cuarteron Reef, (c) Fiery Cross Reef, (d) Johnson Reef, (e) McKennan Reef, and (f) Gaven Reef (North).
- Low-tide elevations: (a) Hughes Reef, (b) Gaven Reef (South), (c) Subi Reef, (d) Mischief Reef, (e) Second Thomas Shoal.
- Hughes Reef lies within 12 nautical miles of the high-tide features on McKennan Reef and Sin Cowe Island, Gaven Reef (South) lies within 12 nautical miles of the high-tide features at Gaven Reef (North) and Namyit Island, and that Subi Reef lies within 12 nautical miles

of the high-tide feature of Sandy Cay on the reefs to the west of Thitu.

Regarding the status of features as rocks/islands:

- Scarborough Shoal contains, within the meaning of Article 121(1) of the Convention, naturally formed areas of land, surrounded by water, which are above water at high tide. However, under Article 121(3) of the Convention, the high-tide features at Scarborough Shoal are rocks that cannot sustain human habitation or economic life of their own and accordingly shall have no exclusive economic zone or continental shelf.
- Johnson Reef, Cuarteron Reef, and Fiery Cross Reef contain, within the meaning of Article 121(1) of the Convention, naturally formed areas of land, surrounded by water, which are above water at high tide. However, for purposes of Article 121(3) of the Convention, the high-tide features at Johnson Reef, Cuarteron Reef, and Fiery Cross Reef are rocks that cannot sustain human habitation or economic life of their own and accordingly shall have no exclusive economic zone or continental shelf.
- Tthe high-tide features at Gaven Reef (North) and McKennan Reef are rocks that cannot sustain human habitation or economic life of their own and accordingly shall have no exclusive economic zone or continental shelf.
- Mischief Reef and Second Thomas Shoal are both low-tide elevations that generate no maritime zones of their own [and] that none of the high-tide features in the Spratly Islands are capable of sustaining human habitation or an economic life of their own within the meaning of those terms in Article 121(3) of the Convention. All of the high-tide features in the Spratly Islands are therefore legally rocks for purposes of Article 121(3) and do not generate entitlements to an exclusive economic zone or continental shelf. There is, accordingly, no possible entitlement by China to any maritime zone

in the area of either Mischief Reef or Second Thomas Shoal and no jurisdictional obstacle to the Tribunal's consideration of the Philippines' Submission No. 5.

- Both Mischief Reef and Second Thomas Shoal are located within 200 nautical miles of the Philippines' coast on the island of Palawan and are located in an area that is not overlapped by the entitlements generated by any maritime feature claimed by China. It follows, therefore, that, as between the Philippines and China, Mischief Reef and Second Thomas Shoal form part of the exclusive economic zone and continental shelf of the Philippines.

Regarding alleged interference with the Philippines' sovereign rights in its EEZ and continental shelf.

- China has, through the operation of its marine surveillance vessels with respect to M/V Veritas Voyager on 1 to 2 March 2011 breached Article 77 of the Convention with respect to the Philippines' sovereign rights over the non-living resources of its continental shelf in the area of Reed Bank [and] that China has, by promulgating its 2012 moratorium on fishing in the South China Sea, without exception for areas of the South China Sea falling within the exclusive economic zone of the Philippines and without limiting the moratorium to Chinese flagged vessels, breached Article 56 of the Convention with respect to the Philippines' sovereign rights over the living resources of its exclusive economic zone.

Regarding alleged failure to prevent Chinese nationals from exploiting the Philippines' living resources.

- China has, through the operation of its marine surveillance vessels in tolerating and failing to exercise due diligence to prevent fishing by Chinese flagged vessels at Mischief Reef and Second Thomas Shoal in May 2013, failed to exhibit due regard for the Philippines' sovereign rights with respect to fisheries in its exclusive economic zone. Accordingly, China has breached its obligations under Article 58(3) of the Convention.

Regarding China's actions in respect of traditional fishing at Scarborough Shoal

- China has, through the operation of its official vessels at Scarborough Shoal from May 2012 onwards, unlawfully prevented Filipino fishermen from engaging in traditional fishing at Scarborough Shoal.

Regarding alleged failure to protect and preserve)the marine environment

- China has, through its toleration and protection of, and failure to prevent Chinese fishing vessels engaging in harmful harvesting activities of endangered species at Scarborough Shoal, Second Thomas Shoal and other features in the Spratly Islands, breached Articles 192 and 194(5) of the Convention.
- China has, through its island-building activities at Cuarteron Reef, Fiery Cross Reef, Gaven Reef (North), Johnson Reef, Hughes Reef, Subi Reef and Mischief Reef, breached Articles 192, 194(1), 194(5), 197, 123, and 206 of the Convention.

Regarding occupation and construction activities on Mischief Reef :

- China has, through its construction of installations and artificial islands at Mischief Reef without the authorisation of the Philippines, breached Articles 60 and 80 of the Convention with respect to the Philippines' sovereign rights in its exclusive economic zone and continental shelf [and], as a low-tide elevation, Mischief Reef is not capable of appropriation.

Regarding operation of law enforcement vessels in a dangerous manner

- China has, by virtue of the conduct of Chinese law enforcement vessels in the vicinity of Scarborough Shoal, created serious risk of collision and danger to Philippine vessels and personnel. The Tribunal finds China to have violated Rules 2, 6, 7, 8, 15, and 16 of the COLREGS and, as a consequence, to be in breach of Article 94 of the Convention.

Regarding aggravation or extension of the dispute between the parties:

- China has in the course of these proceedings aggravated and extended the disputes between the Parties through its dredging, artificial island-building, and construction activities [in several particulars itemized in the award].

Regarding the future conduct of the parties:

- Both Parties are obliged to comply with the Convention, including its provisions regarding the resolution of disputes, and to respect the rights and freedoms of other States under the Convention. Neither Party contests this.

THE SOUTH CHINA SEA DISPUTE

A small outcropping of sand occasionally breaks the vast expanse of the South China Sea. These islands are modest, even diminutive, but they form the core of a fierce territorial dispute among six primary claimants: Brunei, China, Malaysia, the Philippines, Taiwan, and Vietnam. These claimants also clash over their rights and duties in the nearby waters as well as the seabed underneath.

The disputes in the South China Sea have the potential to ignite a broader regional conflagration. Multiple claimants contend over issues of sovereignty not susceptible to easy legal resolution. Worse, the stakes are high: the Sea is one of the primary routes for international trade, and many claimants believe that the Sea hides bountiful oil reserves in addition to its plentiful fishing stocks. The disputes are further entrenched by rampant nationalism, as each claimant attaches symbolic value to the South China Sea islands that far exceeds their objective material wealth. And, finally, the disputes are also tinged by great power politics as China and the United States begin to jostle each other for control of the international order.

Over the last year, disputes in the South China Sea have dominated headlines, and they seem sure to continue to generate fresh national security issues. Already, too, they have raised a variety of legal questions that will inform the future course of both the conflict and the region.

Accordingly, *Lawfare* decided to prepare a backgrounder on the South China Sea that proceeds in two parts. First, in this part, I will lay out the history of the disputes and highlight key events necessary to understanding the crises of the day. In the second part (which will run later this week), I will introduce the primary legal issues underlying the disputes.

Centuries of Contested History

As readers can see in the map above, the islands of the South China Sea can largely be grouped into two island chains. The Paracel Islands are clustered in the northwest corner of the Sea, and the Spratly Islands in the southeast corner.

Reflecting the Rashomon nature of the dispute, the claimants have argued bitterly over the "true" history of these island chains. Some have tried to ground their modern claims by proving a long and unbroken record of national control over claimed features. These states assert that, for example, their nationals fished around the islands of the Sea or used them for shelter from storms. In particular, Beijing has taken an active role in subsidizing archeological digs to find evidence of exclusive Chinese usage of the Sea's many features since time immemorial.

It is hard—if not impossible—to wade through these partisan claims (many of which constitute pure propaganda). No impartial tribunal has yet taken on that challenge. To the extent that it is possible to draw any conclusions from the morass, though, it seems fair to say that no claimant has conclusively demonstrated a pattern of exclusive historical control over the South China Sea, or even over isolated parts of it.

A Period of Relative Quiet

In any case, the issue was moot for most of the region's history. Through the first half of the twentieth century, the Sea remained quiet as neighboring states focused their attention on conflicts unfolding elsewhere.

In fact, at the end of World War II, no claimant occupied a single island in the entire South China Sea. Then, in 1946, China established itself on a few features in the Spratlys, and in early 1947, it also snapped up Woody Island, part of the Paracel Islands chain, only two weeks before the French and Vietnamese intended to make landfall. Denied their first pick, the French and Vietnamese settled for the nearby Pattle Island.

But even at this stage, the South China Sea was not seen as a priority by any of the claimants. For that reason, after suffering their cataclysmic defeat at the hands of Mao's Communists, Chiang Kai-shek's forces retreated to Taiwan and abandoned their stations in the South China Sea. Even the French and Vietnamese could not be bothered to take advantage of the lapse in Chinese control, as they were preoccupied with the rapidly escalating war in Vietnam.

The Claimants Rush for Control

However, the next half century saw accelerating interest in the South China Sea. In 1955 and 1956, China and Taiwan established permanent presences on several key islands, while a Philippine citizen—Thomas Cloma—claimed much of the Spratly Island chain as his own.

Once again, this phase of frenetic island occupation was cooled off by a longer period of inertia. But by the early 1970s, the claimants were at it once again. This time, though, the scramble was spurred by indications that oil lurked beneath the waters of the South China Sea. The Philippines was the first to move. China followed shortly thereafter with a carefully coordinated seaborne invasion of several islands. In the Battle of the Paracel Islands, it wrested several features out from under South Vietnam's control, killing several dozen Vietnamese and sinking a corvette in the process. In response, both South and North Vietnam reinforced their remaining garrisons and seized several other unoccupied features.

Another decade of relative inaction was punctuated once again with violence in 1988, when Beijing moved into the Spratlys and set off another round of occupations by the claimants. Tensions crested when Beijing forcibly occupied Johnson Reef, killing several dozen Vietnamese sailors in the process.

Once again, though, tensions deescalated for a few years, only to rise again in 1995, when Beijing built bunkers above Mischief Reef in the wake of a Philippine oil concession.

Diplomatic Developments

The dispute seemed to take a turn for the better in 2002, when ASEAN and China came together to sign the Declaration on the Conduct of Parties in the South China Sea. The Declaration sought to establish a framework for the eventual negotiation of a Code of Conduct for the South China Sea. The parties promised "to exercise self-restraint in the conduct of activities that would complicate or escalate disputes and affect peace and stability including, among others, refraining from action of inhabiting on the presently uninhabited islands, reefs, shoals, cays, and other features and to handle their differences in a constructive manner."

For a while, the Declaration seemed to keep conflict at bay. Over the next half decade, Beijing launched a charm offensive across Southeast Asia, and the claimants refrained from provoking each other by occupying additional features.

Rather than fighting battles out on the Sea, though, the claimants began to needle each other through demarches and *notes verbales*. In May 2009, Malaysia and Vietnam sent a joint submission to the Commission on the Limits of the Continental Shelf setting out some of their claims. This initial submission unleashed a flurry of *notes verbales*from the other claimants, who objected to the two nation's claims.

In particular, China responded to the joint submission by submitting a map containing the infamous "nine-dash" line. This line snakes around the edges of the South China Sea and encompasses all of the Sea's territorial features as well as the vast majority of its waters. However, Beijing has never officially clarified what the line is meant to signify. Instead, it has maintained "strategic ambiguity" and said only that "China has indisputable sovereignty over the islands in the South China Sea and the adjacent waters, and enjoys sovereign rights and jurisdiction over the relevant waters as well as the seabed and subsoil thereof." This could mean that China claims only the territorial features in the Sea and any "adjacent waters" allowed under maritime law. Or it could mean that China claims all the territorial features *and* all the waters enclosed by the nine-dash line, even those that exceed what's permitted under maritime law.

Recent Crises

Since the publication of the nine-dash line, the region has grown increasingly concerned by China's perceived designs on the South China Sea. In 2012, Beijing bore out some of these concerns when it snatched Scarborough Shoal away from the Philippines. The two states had quarreled over allegations of illegal poaching by Chinese fishermen. After a two-month standoff, the parties agreed to each withdraw from the Shoal. Manila did. Beijing did not. Since then, China has excluded Philippine boats from the Shoal's waters.

In response to this escalatory move, Manila filed an arbitration case against China on January 22, 2013, under the auspices of the U.N. Convention on the Law of the Sea (UNCLOS). The Philippine claims center around maritime law issues, although China asserts that they cannot be resolved without deciding territorial issues first. For that reason, Beijing has largely refused to participate in the proceedings, although it has drafted and publicly released a position paper opposing the tribunal's jurisdiction. The Philippines has submitted its memorial as well as a response to China's position paper, and both nations are currently awaiting a decision from the tribunal as to its own jurisdiction.

As the case proceeds in the background, China has adopted an increasingly assertive posture in the region. In early May 2014, a Chinese state-owned oil company moved one of its rigs into waters claimed by Vietnam south of the Paracel Islands. This provocation touched off confrontations between Vietnamese and Chinese vessels around the rig, as well as rioting against foreign-owned businesses in parts of Vietnam. Faced with this pushback, China withdrew the rig in mid-July, a month ahead of schedule.

Additionally, over the last year, Beijing has launched an accelerating land reclamation campaign across the South China Sea. In at least seven locations, Chinese vessels have poured tons of sand to expand the size of features occupied by China. Beijing has also begun construction of infrastructure on much of this reclaimed land, including an airstrip capable of receiving military aircraft. Although other claimants have reclaimed land in the past, China has reclaimed 2,000 acres of new land, more than "all other claimants combined over the history of their claims," according to the U.S. Department of Defense.

The other claimants have condemned this latest project as counterproductive, and President Obama has urged China to stop "throwing elbows and pushing people out of the way" in pursuit of its interests. Thus far, Beijing has not complied with these entreaties, and it is unclear what the next twist or turn in the story of the South China Sea will be.

CONTINUING STABILITY IN THE SOUTH CHINA SEA

East Asia's rapid economic and military development has captured global attention, but pundits are quick to point to the South China Sea, North Korea, and Taiwan as potential obstacles to the region's continued growth. Analysis of news coverage demonstrates that regional economies and tensions have been growing in tandem. The South China Sea has historically been of particular interest because of the number of conflicting claims on the islands and sea-lanes it encompasses. China, Malaysia, Brunei, the Philippines, Vietnam, and Taiwan, among others, have often engaged in bilateral disagreements with resulting spikes in diplomatic tension and even military confrontation. Of note, these conflicts have never escalated to a full-scale regional war. Direct extrapolation suggests that previous restraint in military interactions implies the nations involved do not consider the potential benefits sufficient to justify an upset to the balance of power. However, contemporary changes in economic and security conditions complicate the issue. While current tensions appear unlikely to lead to a full-scale military conflict, the diversion of national resources needed to maintain the status quo is substantial. Institutional changes to increase transparency; clarify US treaties with ASEAN nations; and increase states' internal enforcement of international agreements, although initially costly, would allow the neighbouring states to redirect these resources to long-term growth.

Historically, China has been involved in a majority of the military conflicts in the South China Sea. A 1947 Chinese map delineates China's controversial claim to approximately 80% of the sea. China aggressively used its navy to conclude a dispute with Vietnam in the Battle of the Paracel Islands in 1974 and then in 1988 during the Johnson South Reef Skirmish for the Spratly Islands. Conflict was narrowly averted in 1995 when the Philippines chose not to shell fort-like Chinese military structures on Mischief Reef (China maintained they were only intended as shelter for fisherman); however, the Philippines continues to assert that this is an example of "creeping occupation". This form of venting tensions, while far short of total war, is extremely costly over the long run; the combination of of resources, energy, and lives expended to establish a claim to the islands creates a significant and avoidable opportunity cost. These skirmishes are not merely an imprint of the 20th century but continue today as witnessed by the Chinese establishment of the Sansha garrison-city in 2012 and the Sino-Philippines stand-off in the Scarborough Shoal.

What then is the evidence suggesting a continued reluctance to engage in full-scale military confrontation? Although in the past conflict has often arisen between economically interdependent nations (viz. the previous peak of global trade in 1914), the China-ASEAN relationship is one of fundamental interdependence of production, visible in the prevalence of international supply chaining in manufacturing processes, rather than solely trade and labour movement. The burgeoning economic interdependence and growth of neighbouring states contributes a major incentive to prevent a conflagration. $5.3 trillion of trade, of which approximately 20% is US, transits the South China Sea annually and any interruption would not only severely restrict regional trade revenues, but would also very likely guarantee US military intervention. The Association of South East Asian Nations (ASEAN) is becoming increasingly interconnected and 2015 will mark a key turning point with the opening of internal ASEAN borders for free movement of labour. The ASEAN bloc has also concluded a number of reconciliation agreements with China. Regarding security, both the 2002 Code of Conduct and the 2011 Guidelines to the Code of Conduct are intended to help coordinate diplomacy and maintain peace in South China Sea disputes. Economically China has been ASEAN's largest trading partner since 2009, and at its opening in 2010 the ASEAN-China free trade area (ACFTA) became the largest in the world by population. These arrangements come at a time when growing estimates of the value of the natural resources contained in the South China Sea are generating pressures associated with ensuring energy security.

Economic interdependence between China and ASEAN, however, is not the sole factor at play. In areas with considerable interstate tension sub-state actors have often contributed to the deterioration of international relations, most prominently with the assassination of Archduke Franz Ferdinand tipping Europe into World War I. Recent developments in state-level Chinese political and military discourse reflect a strong interest in cooperation. Chinese President Hu Jintao's 2011 discussions with Filipino President Corazon Aquino firmly expressed the hope that "the countries concerned may put aside disputes and actively explore forms of common development in the relevant sea areas". Additionally in 2011 the Chinese State Council Information Office released a white paper with a similar emphasis on joint development. Yet China is also reported to have developed internal fractures in its South China Sea policy, with a number of different ministries controlling paramilitary units that are not under express government oversight. For example, the Bureau of Fisheries Administration (BFA) now directs a relatively well-equipped law enforcement fleet that is tasked with patrolling Chinese-owned fishing areas.

Such interest groups repeatedly instigate minor disputes with their ASEAN counterparts and the US navy that exacerbate state-level discussions and risk eventually drawing unintended consequences (characteristically, in 2004 two BFA vessels obstructed a US Navy surveillance ship in the Yellow Sea).

The region has also seen a rise in high-tech militarization, with rapid development in areas ranging from aircraft carriers and submarines to cyber-espionage; this is likely to further increase due to the 2011 US "pivot to Asia" and military surge.

The pivot is considered to be a sign that the US intends to continue playing a leadership role in East Asia, a strategy at odds with China's vision.

An associated complication is the imprecise definition of US commitments to its ally nations in the event of disputes in contested territories, especially vis-à-vis the Philippines and Vietnam, and the possibility that alliances will be used to escalate a small battle into a regional affair.

The US is making efforts to address these complications; for the first time since RIMPACS's creation in 1971, China has been invited to participate in a US-led naval exercise. Positive near-term repercussions of growing US involvement have also been postulated; analysts suggest that one of the root causes behind Chinese interest in cooperation is the fear that aggression in the South China Sea will drive other parties to strengthen their ties with the US.

The relative wealth of economic and diplomatic compromises on all sides presents a compelling argument that under current conditions, disputes in the South China Sea will continue to be restrained to small-scale skirmishes that do not threaten overall stability. This is not to say that the increase in regional tension is insignificant, but rather that the involved parties all have a strong interest in maintaining mutual growth and have demonstrated their willingness to make strategic sacrifices to maintain the status quo.

Furthermore as China is the common link in the majority of the disputes, it is probable that it will be at the heart of any conflict — and China has frequently shown restraint in this regard (though not so, for example, in Tibet). In terms of China's priorities, policy analysts tend to agree that if China were to begin a large-scale military campaign, Taiwan would most likely be the focus of its aggression.

My analysis focuses on demonstrating the likely maintenance of the status quo without large-scale war given present circumstances, as well as the high opportunity cost of this outcome.

However the institution of the following policy changes can reduce both interstate tensions and the associated recurring costs: a concerted effort to increase transparency in each nation's territorial claims; a US declaration on the status of disputed territory conflicts in its mutual defence treaties; and internal enforcement of international agreements such as the Code of Conduct.

Establishing these proposals would be costly to all parties in the short term, in part because of the benefits nations derive from ambiguities in their claims and treaties. China has often been reluctant to precisely define its claim to territories in the South China Sea, not least because of its inconsistency with the law regarding Exclusive Economic Zones.

The US intentionally used obscurity in its treaty with Japan to discourage Chinese military intervention in the East China and again in clauses of the US-Taiwan treaty concerning China. Yet ambiguity generates escalating tension as nations attempt to ascertain their positions, and increases room for misunderstanding. Ignoring for a moment China's stated refusal to accept international moderation in the South China Sea, a possible model treaty would be the division of disputed territory by the International Court of Justice in the Qatar-Bahrain conflict over the Hawar Islands. That controversy involved similar economic incentives to the South China Sea due to the significant oil and natural gas reserves in the region of the islands, and the resolution benefited both nations as well as facilitating regional cooperation in other matters. The details of this agreement provide an interesting opportunity to disentangle nationalist and economic disputes in the South China Sea, and may become the foundation of a future China-ASEAN agreement.

SOUTH CHINA SEA TENSIONS

Territorial spats over the waters and islands of the South China Sea have roiled relations between China and countries like Philippines, Vietnam, Taiwan, Malaysia, and Brunei in recent years, and tensions continue to escalate in the wake of U.S. President Barack Obama's announced "pivot" of focus to the region.

A handful of islands comprise the epicenter of the territorial dispute, making up an area known as the "cow's tongue" that spans roughly the entire South China Sea. The region is home to a wealth of natural resources, fisheries, trade routes, and military bases, all of which are at stake in the increasingly frequent diplomatic standoffs. China's blanket claims to sovereignty across the region and its strong resistance to handling disputes in an international arena have mired attempts at resolving the crises and intensified nationalist postures in all countries involved, particularly Vietnam and the Philippines. Experts say the potential for an escalated conflict in the South China Sea—while seemingly distant for now—presents an ongoing crisis for the region, as well as for U.S. interests in the area.

What Territories are Involved and Disputed?

The South China Sea comprises a stretch of roughly 1.4 million square miles in the Pacific Ocean that encompasses an area from the Singapore and Malacca Straits to the Strait of Taiwan, spanning west of the Philippines, north of Indonesia, and east of Vietnam. The South China Sea islands number in the hundreds, although the largest and most contentious territories include the Spratly Islands, Paracel Islands, Pratas Islands, Macclesfield Bank, and Scarborough Shoal, all of which the six major Southeast Asian nations lay various claims to. The islands are mostly uninhabited and have never had an indigenous population, making the issue of historical sovereignty a thorny one to resolve.

The disputes aren't limited to land, however; each country has an Exclusive Economic Zone, prescribed by the 1982 United Nations Convention on the Law of the Sea (UNCLOS), over which it has special rights to marine resources and energy exploration and production. An EEZ spans outward 200 nautical miles from the coast of the each state's territorial sea, and may include the continental shelf beyond the 200-mile limit. These zones come into play during disputes over sea territory, as displayed in China's December 2012 spat with Vietnam (WSJ) *over oil and fishing activity in the waters near the Paracel Islands.*

What is the 9-Dash Line?

The 9-Dash line is a controversial demarcation line used by China for itsclaim to territories and waters in the South China Sea, most notably over the Scarborough Shoal and the Paracel and Spratly Islands—the two most important disputed island groups.

The line, which is contested by the Philippines, Brunei, Malaysia, Taiwan, and Vietnam, encompasses virtually the entire South China Sea region and caused immediate controversy when China submitted a map to the UN in 2009 that included the demarcation. Beijing's issuance of a new passport (Reuters) in late 2012 containing a map of the disputed region based on the line drew fresh international criticism and backlash.

ASEAN countries have contested this boundary, but China has insisted on the historical legitimacy of the line based on survey expeditions, fishing activities, and naval patrols dating as far back as the fifteenth century, putting it at odds with the boundaries UNCLOS has enforced for the region since 1994.

What Resources are at Play in the Region?

The immediate source of conflict in the region is competition over resources, says David Rosenberg, professor of political science at Middlebury College. There are roughly half a billion people who live within 100 miles of the South China Sea coastline, and the volume of shipping through its waters has skyrocketed as China and ASEAN nations increase international trade and oil imports. The need for resources, especially hydrocarbons and fisheries, also has intensified economic competition in the region, particularly given the rapid coastal urbanization of China. "Behind it all, it's essentially the industrial revolution of Asia," Rosenberg said. "And the South China Sea has become the hub of that."

*According to the World Bank, the South China Sea holds proven oil reserves of at least seven billion barrels and an estimated 900 trillion cubic feet of natural gas, which offer tremendous economic opportunity for smaller nations like Malaysia, the Philippines, and Vietnam, and energy security for China's large, growing economy. In December 2012, China's National Energy Administration named the disputed waters as the main offshore site (*NYT*) for natural gas production, and a major Chinese energy company has already begun drilling in deep water off the southern coast. Competitive tensions escalated when India's state-run Oil and Natural Gas Corp announced it had partnered with PetroVietnam (Reuters) for developing oil in the disputed waters. While oil exploration presents one of the higher conflict risks in the region, no major encounters have occurred since June 2011, when Vietnam accused a Chinese fishing boat of cutting cables (BBC) from an oil exploration vessel inside its EEZ.*

Smaller-scale fishing incidents have instead become the hub of maritime confrontation as declining fish stocks have driven fishermen farther into disputed areas to search for supply, as well as highly profitable illegal species. In the most recent clash, the Philippines' naval forces intercepted (al-Jazeera) eight Chinese fishing vessels in the Scarborough Shoal in April, finding what they viewed as illegally fished marine life on board. The attempted arrest of the poachers led to a two-month standoff between the two countries.

Annual fishing bans and arrests of fishermen are a convenient proxy for sovereignty claims since they can be presented as legitimate attempts to enforce marine resources protection, according to a report by the International Crisis Group. "This is an issue that doesn't make big headlines, but 1.5 billion people live there and rely heavily on fisheries for food and jobs," Rosenberg said. "That's where most of the conflict goes on, and most of these have been dealt with on a routine conflict management basis."

6

The Real Secret of the South China Sea Conflicts

To understand the Big Picture, we need to go back to 1890 when Alfred Mahan, then president of the US Naval College, wrote the seminal The Influence of Sea Power Upon History, 1660-1783. Mahan's central thesis is that the US should go global in search of new markets, and protect these new trade routes through a network of naval bases.

That is the embryo of the US Empire of Bases – which de facto started after the Spanish-American war, over a century ago, when the US graduated to Pacific power status by annexing the Philippines, Hawaii and Guam.

Western – American and European — colonialism is strictly responsible for the current, incendiary sovereignty battle in the South China Sea. It's the West that came up with most land borders – and maritime borders — of these states.The roll call is quite impressive. Philippines and Indonesia were divided by Spain and Portugal in 1529. The division between Malaysia and Indonesia is owed to the British and the Dutch in 1842. The border between China and Vietnam was imposed to the Chinese by the French in 1887. The Philippines's borders were concocted by the US and Spain in 1898. The border between Philippines and Malaysia was drawn by the US and the Brits in 1930.

We are talking about borders between different colonial possessions – and that implies intractable problems from the start, subsequently inherited by post-colonial nations. And to think that it had all started as a loose configuration. The best anthropological studies (Bill Solheim's, for instance) define the semi-nomadic communities who really traveled and traded across the South China Sea from time immemorial as the Nusantao – an Austronesian compound word for "south island" and "people".

The Nusantao were not a defined ethnic group; rather a maritime internet. Over the centuries, they had many key hubs, from the coastline between central Vietnam and Hong Kong to the Mekong Delta. They were not attached to any "state", and the notion of "borders" didn't even exist.Only by the late 19th century the Westphalian system managed to freeze the South China Sea inside an immovable framework. Which brings us to why China is so sensitive about its borders; because they are directly linked to the "century of humiliation" – when internal Chinese corruption and weakness allowed Western barbarians to take possession of Chinese land.

TENSION IN THE NINE-DASH LINE

The eminent Chinese geographer Bai Meichu was a fierce nationalist who drew his own version of what was called the "Chinese National Humiliation Map". In 1936 he published a map including a "U-shaped line" gobbling up the South China Sea all the way down to James Shoal, which is 1,500 km south of China but only over 100 km off Borneo. Scores of maps copied Meichu's. Most included the Spratly Islands, but not James Shoal.

The crucial fact is that Bai was the man who actually invented the "nine-dash line", promoted by the Chinese government – then not yet Communist – as the letter of the law in terms of "historic" Chinese claims over islands in the South China Sea.

Everything stopped when Japan invaded China in 1937. Japan had occupied Taiwan way back in 1895. Now imagine Americans surrendering to the Japanese in the Philippines in 1942. That meant virtually the entire coastline of the South

China Sea being controlled by a single empire for the fist time in history. The South China Sea had become a Japanese lake.

Not for long; only until 1945. The Japanese did occupy Woody Island in the Paracels and Itu Aba (today Taiping) in the Spratlys. After the end of WWII and the US nuclear-bombing Japan, the Philippines became independent in 1946; the Spratlys immediately were declared Filipino territory.In 1947 the Chinese went on overdrive to recover all the Paracels from colonial power France. In parallel, all the islands in the South China Sea got Chinese names. James Shoal was downgraded from a sandbank into a reef (it's actually underwater; still Beijing sees is as the southernmost point of Chinese territory.)

In December 1947 all the islands were placed under the control of Hainan (itself an island in southern China.) New maps — based on Meichu's — followed, but now with Chinese names for the islands (or reefs, or shoals). The key problem is that no one explained the meaning of the dashes (which were originally eleven.)

So in June 1947 the Republic of China claimed everything within the line – while proclaiming itself open to negotiate definitive maritime borders with other nations later on. But, for the moment, no borders; that was the birth of the much-maligned "strategic ambiguity" of the South China Sea that lasts to this day.

"Red" China adopted all the maps — and all the decisions. Yet the final maritime border between China and Vietnam, for instance, was decided only in 1999. In 2009 China included a map of the "U-shaped" or "nine-dash line" in a presentation to the UN Commission on the Limits of the Continental Shelf; that was the first time the line officially showed up on an international level.

No wonder other Southeast Asian players were furious. That was the apex of the millennia-old transition from the "maritime internet" of semi-nomadic peoples to the Westphalian system. The post-modern "war" for the South China Sea was on.

GUNBOAT FREEDOM

In 2013 the Philippines – prodded by the US and Japan – decided to take its case about Exclusive Economic Zones (EEZs) in the South China Sea to be judged according to the UN Convention on the Law of the Sea (UNCLOS). Both China and Philippines ratified UNCLOS. The US did not. The Philippines aimed for UNCLOS – not "historical rights", as the Chinese wanted — to decide what is an island, what is a rock, and who is entitled to claim territorial rights (and thus EEZs) in these surrounding waters.UNCLOS itself is the result of years of fierce legal battles. Still, key nations – including BRICS members China, India and Brazil, but also, significantly, Vietnam and Malaysia – have been struggling to change an absolutely key provision, making it mandatory for foreign warships to seek permission before sailing through their EEZs.

And here we plunge in truly, deeply troubled waters; the notion of "freedom of navigation".

For the American empire, "freedom of navigation", from the West Coast of the US to Asia – through the Pacific, the South China Sea, the Malacca Strait and the Indian Ocean – is strictly subordinated to military strategy. Imagine if one day EEZs would be closed to the US Navy – or if "authorization" would have to be demanded every time; the Empire of Bases would lose "access" to...its own bases.

Add to it trademark Pentagon paranoia; what if a "hostile power" decided to block the global trade on which the US economy depends? (even though the premise — China contemplating such a move — is ludicrous). The Pentagon actually pursues a Freedom of Navigation (FON) program. For all practical purposes, it's 21st century gunboat diplomacy, as in those aircraft carriers showboating on and off in the South China Sea.The Holy Grail, as far as the 10-member Association of Southeast Asian Nations (ASEAN) is concerned, is to come up with a Code of Conduct to solve all maritime conflicts between Philippines, Vietnam, Malaysia, Brunei and China. This has been dragging on for years now because mostly the

Philippines wanted to frame the Chinese under a set of binding rules but was only ready to talk until all ten ASEAN members had agreed on them first.

Beijing's strategy is the opposite; bilateral discussions to emphasize its formidable leverage. Thus China assuring the support of Cambodia – quite visible early this week when Cambodia prevented a condemnation of China regarding the South China Sea at a key summit in Laos; China and ASEAN settled for "self-restraint."

WATCH HILLARY PIVOTING

In 2011 the US State Department was absolutely terrified with the planned Obama administration withdrawals from both Iraq and Afghanistan; what would happen to superpower projection? That ended in November 2011, when then Secretary of State Hillary Clinton coined the by now famous "pivot to Asia".

"Six lines of action" were embedded in the "pivot". Four of these Clinton nicked from a 2009 report by the Washington think tank CSIS; reinvigorating alliances; cultivating relationships with emerging powers; developing relationships with regional multilateral bodies; and working closely with South East Asian countries on economic issues. Clinton added two more: broad-based military presence in Asia, and the promotion of democracy and human rights.

It was clear from the start – and not only across the global South — that cutting across the rhetorical fog the "pivot" was code for a military offensive to contain China. Even more seriously, this was the geopolitical moment when a South East Asian dispute over maritime territory intersected with the across-the-globe confrontation between the hegemon and a "peer competitor".

What Clinton meant by "engaging emerging powers" was, in her own words, "join us in shaping and participating in a rules-based regional and global order". This is code for rules coined by the hegemon – as in the whole apparatus of the

Washington consensus. No wonder the South China Sea is immensely strategic, as American hegemony intimately depends on ruling the waves (remember Mahan). That's the core of the US National Military Strategy. The South China Sea is the crucial link connecting the Pacific to the Indian Ocean, the Persian Gulf and ultimately Europe.And so we finally discover Rosebud — the ultimate South China Sea "secret". China under Clinton's "rule-based regional and global order" effectively means that China must obey and keep the South China Sea open to the US Navy.

That spells out inevitable escalation further on down the sea lanes. China, slowly but surely, is developing an array of sophisticated weapons which could ultimately "deny" the South China Sea to the US Navy, as the Beltway is very much aware.

What makes it even more serious is that we're talking about irreconcilable imperatives. Beijing characterizes itself as an anti-imperialist power; and that necessarily includes recovering national territories usurped by colonial powers allied with internal Chinese traitors (those islands that The Hague has ruled are no more than "rocks" or even "low-tide elevations").

The US, for its part, is all about Exceptionalism and Manifest Destiny. As it stands, more than Russia's western borderlands, the Baltics or "Syraq", this is where the hegemon "rules" are really being contested. And the stakes couldn't be higher. That'll be the day when the US Navy is "denied" from the South China Sea; and that'll be the end of its imperial hegemony.

REGIONAL ECONOMIC AND FINANCIAL AGREEMENTS

Regional economic agreements were the main achievements of these meetings. However, the ASEAN Plus Three sessions identified other areas for cooperation, including deeper cooperation in investment and finance, expanded security dialogue and cooperation, expanded cultural exchanges, and periodic progress reviews. Perhaps the most dramatic developments have occurred in regional financial cooperation.

Finance ministers of the ASEAN+3 countries have launched an Asian Bond Markets Initiative and the regional central bankers group set up two Asian Bond Funds in early 2005.

These are key steps in addressing one of the major weaknesses in the region's development as indicated by the currency and financial crisis that struck large parts of the region in 1997: the heavy reliance by firms on short-term bank loans for financing. As Jennifer Amyx notes, many countries in East Asia maintain high savings rates but, because of the absence of stable long-term debt markets, the savings deposited into local banks tended to be funneled out to international financial centres and then back into the region as short-term foreign currency loans. This situation creates a problem referred to as a "double mismatch" — that is, a mismatch between debt maturities (short-term borrowing for long-term investments) and the denomination of this debt (in foreign rather than local currencies).

The ASEAN+3 finance ministers had earlier set up a network of bilateral currency swaps to permit a country beset by a speculative attack to draw on reserves of other nations. The program — the Chiang Mai Initiative (CMI) — went into effect at the end of 2003. Japan, with the largest reserves in the region, led negotiations over swap arrangements and will play the role of arbitrator for currency loans. China, another potential lender with substantial reserves in excess of potential needs, also lent its support to the CMI.

Widespread participation by ASEAN Plus Three members in these initiatives encourages smooth financial liberalization processes and thereby bolsters regional stability. It also reinforces the efforts of various working groups to improve transparency and information dissemination and to strengthen settlement systems and regulatory reforms.

China's shift to a more proactive position on regional financial cooperation has greatly facilitated these recent financial developments. As a result, interdependence between the Chinese economy and other economies in the region has deepened significantly in recent years. Today, trade by ASEAN member nations with China far exceeds trade conducted within the ASEAN grouping, while China is predicted to soon overtake the United States as Japan's top trading partner. Levels of investment in China by countries in the region are also extremely high.

The worst case scenario is not Chinese domination but a Chinese meltdown, as many regional monetary authorities are quick to note.

How to Eliminate Terrorism in the South China Sea?

At the other end of the South China Sea, American officials are primarily concerned by the terrorist threat to the vital sea lane of the Strait of Malacca. Admiral Thomas Fargo, commander of U.S. forces in the Pacific, on a visit to Singapore and Malaysia last year warned that seaborne terrorism must be taken as seriously as attacks from the air, especially in the vital Malacca Strait shipping lane. Fargo noted that the Al-Qaeda-linked Jemaah Islamiyah (JI) terror group was a menace in the region. Defence Secretary Donald Rumsfeld said he hoped U.S. forces would be hunting terrorists in the Strait of Malacca "pretty soon," as they were already doing with Filipino counter-terrorist troops in Mindanao in the Philippines.

To deal with these possible threats, the U.S. has started three major unilateral initiatives, the Container Security Initiative (CSI) the Proliferation Security Initiative (PSI), and the Regional Maritime Security Initiative (RMSI) directed specifically at the Strait of Malacca.

The Container Security Initiative (CSI), first proposed by the U.S. Customs service in January 2002, aims to identify "high-risk" containers and use technology to screen them according to U.S. specifications in the originating ports rather than in the destination ports in the U.S. The program — compulsory inspection at the origin rather than the destination — places an enormous financial and security burden on all ports that ship to the U.S. More than half of the top 20 container ports in the world are in or around the South China Sea.

In order to be approved as a CSI-port, a government must agree to allow U.S. Customs personnel to supervise the screening of containers bound for ports in the U.S., install screening equipment designed to detect illicit narcotics, as well as radiological, chemical, biological or conventional weapons, submit a detailed electronic manifest to U.S. Customs 24 hours in advance of its projected arrival in the U.S., and upgrade to new "smart container" technologies and designs for U.S.-bound shipping traffic.

Remarkably, despite numerous difficulties of implementation, in the first year after the announcement of the CSI, 18 of the top 20 ports that export containers to the United States had complied. In a similar move in December 2004, Australia declared a new 1000-nautical-mile maritime security zone in which all ships travelling to Australia will be required to provide details on their journey and cargo.

All vessels coming within a 200-nautical-mile limit of the Australian coast will be required to give extra details on cargo, ports visited, location, course, speed and intended port of arrival. Indonesian authorities objected to the unilateral measure, saying it infringed on Indonesian waters and violated freedom of navigation. As other countries extend their security zones, complications are bound to arise.

The Proliferation Security Initiative (PSI) aims to seize "shipments of weapons of mass destruction (WMD) and missile-related equipment and technologies" — by sea or air — before they fall into the hands of terrorist organizations or their state sponsors.

Participating states agree to share information related to suspected proliferation activities, interdict the transshipment of WMD, and strengthen national and international laws to allow the "aggressive interdiction of vessels suspected of carrying weapons of mass destruction." The PSI Interdiction Principles further state that countries have a commitment to board suspicious vessels sailing within their national waters, to board suspicious vessels flying their own flag in international waters, and to "seriously consider providing consent" to boardings of their own flagged vessels by other PSI states.

So far, many states have gone along with CSI and PSI. However, the high costs of compliance evoke images of colonialism and hegemony. The stationing of U.S. Customs officials in the sovereign ports of foreign states might be seen as intrusive. PSI and CSI may also limit the rights of commercial vessels operating internationally to remain free from arbitrary search and seizure. The initiatives are directed exclusively toward safeguarding U.S.-bound shipping, not Asia-bound trade or intra-Asian trade. Further, they exclude WMD and related shipments by the U.S. to its allies. On the whole, CSI and PSI lack transparency, reciprocity, and accountability; they are unilateral U.S. measures prompted by the 9/11 attacks.

It may be that this is the necessary cost of increased maritime security in the twenty-first century. If many countries are willing to accept this type of non-consultative and unilaterally-driven process, that would indicate a very significant change in the way international regulations are framed and implemented. It would constitute a major shift from negotiated multilateralism of the post-war system to cooperative unilateralism under post-Cold War American hegemony.

In sharp contrast with the CSI and PSI, the Regional Maritime Security Initiative (RMSI) proposed by the United States, has caused much consternation around the South China Sea. Adm. Thomas B. Fargo, Commander of the U.S. Pacific Command, introduced the RMSI in a speech to the U.S. Congress on March 31, 2004. He remarked that "we're looking at things like high speed vessels, putting Special Operations Forces on high-speed vessels so that we can use boats that might be incorporated with these vessels to conduct effective interdiction in, once again, these sea lines of communications where terrorists are known to move about and transmit throughout the region."

Malaysia and Indonesia immediately and vehemently rejected the idea of U.S. troops in the area, emphasizing their own capabilities in tackling the threat. Malaysian Defence Minister Najib Razak emphasized that the presence of foreign forces in the region or "interdiction" operations in the Strait would not be tolerated.

The U.S. began almost immediately to backpedal on the idea. U.S. Secretary of Defence Donald Rumsfeld and U.S. Navy Pacific Fleet Commander Adm. Walter F. Doran stated that Adm. Fargo's earlier comments on the RMSI had been "misreported," the plan was still very much in its early stages, and it would focus primarily on intelligence sharing not a U.S. troop presence.

Another effort to improve shipping safety and security — the International Ship and Port Facility Security Code (ISPS) — came into effect in July 2004. Initiated by the UN's International Maritime Organization, the ISPS is more comprehensive and provides more transparency and multilateral participation than the RMSI.

EXCLUSIVE ECONOMIC ZONES, PIRATES AND POLITICAL CONFLICT

The most important security issues for many countries in the region between the Straits are not the American priorities of containing China or countering terrorism. They are preoccupied with resource claims in their offshore Exclusive Economic Zones (EEZ's) — in particular, fisheries, oil and natural gas — and in pursuing regional economic integration for their export-oriented economies. Two factors have recently increased concerns about these security issues: the projected increase in shipping traffic and the rise in piracy.

Oil tanker traffic — already high — will increase substantially with the projected increase in Chinese oil imports. Almost all of this additional Asian oil demand, as well as Japan's oil needs, will be imported from the Middle East and Africa. Most will pass through the strategic Strait of Malacca into the South China Sea, although supertankers going to Japan will use the wider Lombok Straight east of Bali.

All the coastal countries around the South China Sea as well as Japan and South Korea — who depend heavily on oil imports — have a common interest in the safety and freedom of navigation through these congested and confined waterways. Major shipping nations and shipping companies are working together to pursue these goals through the APEC Transportation Working Group (TPT-WG) for managing port and cargo traffic and through the Marine Electronic Highway (MEH) program. Funded by the World Bank, United National Development Program (UNDP), and the International Maritime Organization (IMO), the MEH project aims to increase navigational safety through electronic navigational charts and information systems. It can also be extended to search-and-rescue operations, anti-piracy programs, and environmental impact assessment.

The large volume of shipping in the South China Sea/Strait of Malacca littoral has created opportunities for attacks on merchant shipping. Piracy can threaten a disaster through a collision, grounding, chemical or toxic spill or closing of a strait. Since the 1990's, around half of the world's reported piracy took place in the South China Sea. The big increase in piracy in Indonesian waters and ports may be attributed to its economic crisis and domestic instability. It may also result from more sophisticated attacks by organized crime groups.

The response of coastal countries was delayed by uncertainties over legal jurisdiction, disputed sovereignty, and uncoordinated efforts at recovery of crew, cargo, or ships. Even when pirates were detected, "hot pursuit" across national boundaries was seldom attempted. Sensitive to sovereignty issues in their territorial and EEZ waters, coastal countries have slowly started multilateral programs to monitor piracy attacks and bilateral exercises to coordinate anti-piracy patrols. The International Piracy Control Centre in Kuala Lumpur, and the International Maritime Organization's Piracy Reporting Centre in London have stepped up monitoring efforts. The ASEAN Regional Forum convened a meeting of maritime specialists to coordinate coast guard action, information exchange, and investigation of piracy reports.

The most sweeping proposal for eradicating maritime piracy was advanced by Japan, which imports 99% of its petroleum and 70% of its food by sea, mostly through the Strait of Malacca. Ships carry 99% of Japanese exports by volume. Not surprisingly, Japan sees maritime safety as an integral part of its comprehensive security strategy. Its initial anti-piracy proposal envisioned ocean-peacekeeping fleets conducting multinational patrols in both territorial and international waters. This was met with skepticism, if not suspicion, by several Southeast Asian states. Indonesia, in particular, was unwilling to allow Japanese forces to patrol Indonesian waters, and was further reluctant to bear the cost of participating in joint exercises. Faced with disaster relief challenges, separatist struggles, and widespread poverty, Jakarta does not rate piracy as a major security issue. Malaysian policymakers also rejected Japanese joint patrols, concerned about violations of their sovereignty and any limitations on controlling their EEZs. Singapore, possessing interests closely aligned with those of Japan, has been most receptive.

Less ambitious bilateral approaches by the Japanese Coast Guard (JCG), however, have enjoyed relative success. As a safety agency, the JCG is a less controversial vehicle for providing regional police service than the more militarized Japanese Maritime Self-Defence Force (JMSDF). The JCG has provided training, equipment, and funding to all the coastal states of the South China Sea, and has conducted joint training exercises with six Southeast Asian states. The JCG has funded the installation and maintenance of navigational aides and buoy-tenders; it has also provided technical assistance to upgrade marine safety data management systems and hydrographic surveys. These efforts have heightened awareness of the problem, and coastal responses have been emerging. In 2003, Malaysia and Thailand started coordinated maritime patrols along their maritime frontier. In 2004, Singapore, Malaysia, and Indonesia began coordinated patrols of the seaways. Putting aside the conflicting territorial claims in the South China Sea, China has called for joint exercises with its South China Sea neighbours to control piracy and drug smuggling. Anti-piracy programs address region-wide problems; they cannot succeed without regional cooperation. Gradually, they are emerging.

All the major trading countries and their shipping companies in the region have a strong common interest in the safety and freedom of navigation through the perilous, crowded, narrow sea lanes of the South China Sea. They have cooperated in regional and international maritime agencies to combat piracy threatening their vital imports. They have put aside seemingly intractable issues — such as sovereignty claims in the Spratly Islands — and adopted a policy of strategic pragmatism to develop regional institutions to resolve intrinsically regional issues.

The existing maritime forces between the Straits are primarily concerned with policing their waters to assert sovereignty and to secure maritime resources, especially in disputed areas in and around their EEZ's, in relation to piracy, poaching, smuggling, trafficking, and terrorist threats. The limited military modernization that has taken place has primarily been directed toward securing a minimum level of control over their adjacent seas and their new resource claims in their EEZ's, and has not attempted to fill the gap by the apparent withdrawal of U.S. forces after the Cold War or the possibility of an expansionist neighbour, China.

Notwithstanding recent incidents of gunboat diplomacy between Indonesia and Malaysia over oil leases offshore northeast Borneo and violent clashes between Vietnam and China over fishing grounds in the Tonkin Gulf, a modus vivendi has been approached on the territorial disputes in the South China Sea. Many claimants have deployed troops to various islands and reefs within the Spratlys, but total occupation of the Spratlys by any one claimant seems highly unlikely. There have been many low-level incidents, but no major wars in the Spratlys or elsewhere, because no country has any major stakes there. They are not astride any major sea lanes and have little intrinsic military significance. While no one will foreclose options because of the lure of resources, none of the claimants seem likely to attempt a military occupation of the entire Spratly group. No claimant has the power projection capability or the ambition to control them or to defend them. Even if they did, it is highly unlikely that any such claims would be recognized regionally or internationally. Hence, all parties appear to be following a strategy of denial rather than a strategy of conquest.

The shipping of energy through the South China Sea is currently more important than any possible oil resources in disputed waters. As a consequence, there is now a window of opportunity to pursue regional efforts to ensure safe and secure navigation and to promote regional economic integration. Several bilateral and multilateral agreements for joint resource management have been achieved in recent years. For example, China has signed similar bilateral fisheries agreements with South Korea, Japan, and Vietnam for cooperative resource management of their common fisheries in the Yellow Sea, the East China Sea, and the South China Sea. As regional negotiations take shape, more thought needs to be given to finding a creative diplomatic formula for incorporating Taiwan's participation. Taiwan forces occupy the two largest islands in the South China Sea: Pratas Island and Itu Aba. Taiwan has reduced its garrison on Itu Aba; defence responsibilities have been transferred from the ROC Navy to the ROC Coast Guard. This implies that Taiwan is no longer prepared to use force to defend this islet. To the contrary, it is developing facilities for tourism there.

Cross-Strait Conflict and Interdependence

There is a curious pattern of accommodation in PRC-Taiwan relations. On the one hand, the PRC views Taiwan as a renegade province while Taiwan views the mainland with cultural empathy but political disdain. On many South China Sea issues, however, they are often in agreement. They have not had any direct confrontations in the South China Sea. They make the same claims, use the same definitions, baselines, and maps in stating their interests in the region. There is even some direct cooperation between China and Taiwan on technical issues.

Beyond these governmental links, there are very substantial corporate and personal links between China and Taiwan. Taiwanese firms have invested over US $100 billion on the mainland, more than any other country. Much of this involves the relocation of Taiwanese industries to the Shanghai-Suzhou and Fujian areas. To a large extent, Taiwan's continued economic prosperity is tied to reintegration with the mainland. These economic links of investment and trade are reinforced by millions of personal visits as well as mail and email correspondence. Bonds of marriage also strengthen these ties. Nearly 10% of Taiwanese men marry mainland brides, further tying migrant generations to ancestral origins. These deeply-rooted, long-term economic and demographic trends provide a counterbalance to the often strident political clashes. The longer and broader the cross-Strait engagement, the better the prospects for peaceful coexistence.

Unfortunately, the cross-Strait issue has become immersed in domestic politics in Taiwan and China. The recent spate of threats and counter-threats over Taiwan's status is linked to maneuvering among domestic political forces seeking popular support. For example, in March 2005, after China passed its anti-secession law, there were widespread protest demonstrations in Taiwan led by Prime Minister Chen Shui-bian's Democratic Progressive Party (DPP).

Soon after, a large delegation of Taiwan's main opposition party, the Kuomintang (KMT, Nationalist Party), visited the mainland to encourage trade and political dialogue with China and to pay respects to the memorial shrine of Sun Yat-sen, KMT's founder. This, in turn, was followed in early April by the visit of right-wing Taiwan Solidarity Union party leaders to the Yasukuni shrine, the Japanese war memorial in Tokyo. Clearly issues of national identity and national sovereignty can generate volatile reactions.

The big danger across the Taiwan Strait is that misunderstanding and miscalculation, fueled by distrust, xenophobia, and opportunism, may lead to escalating conflict.

Senior leaders on both sides of the Strait are beginning to realize the potential consequences if instability erupts into violence. Hu Jintao has recently been signaling that he advocates a long-term policy of stability for eventual reunification. Chen Shui-bian has recently dropped his independence demands. Several Southeast Asian leaders have opposed Taiwan's independence; most explicitly, Singapore's Prime Minister, Lee Hsien Loong. Lee bluntly stated, "If Taiwan goes for independence, Singapore will not recognize it. In fact no Asian country will recognize it. China will fight. Win or lose, Taiwan will be devastated."

The prospect of a military confrontation between the mainland and Taiwan is unlikely, in part because the consequences of such a conflict would be extremely destructive for both sides. Diplomatic efforts are needed to avoid even this remote risk. In the March/April 2005 issue of Foreign Affairs, Kenneth Lieberthal offered a useful proposal to change the focus of negotiations over "independence" and "reunification" to a pragmatic question: what is needed to achieve long-term stability and peaceful coexistence between China and Taiwan? What confidence building measures are needed to reassure security strategists that defensive military developments are not offensive? What legal and administrative means are necessary to resolve routine conflicts that will inevitably occur as commercial and civil relations thicken?

The current U.S. attempts to help Taiwan "contain" China and to mobilize support in its global war on terrorism threaten to complicate if not weaken regional security developments. As Ronald Montaperto notes, "the almost daily manifestations of Chinese economic power, the effort to demonstrate commitment to the 'new' principle that the economic development of individual nations is inseparable from the development of the region as a whole, and the broad perception within the region that the Chinese are willing to engage actively in multilateral, cooperative policies have combined to provide Beijing with an unprecedented measure of influence and even clout."

The Beijing regime is obsessed with economic stability, because it fears that a severe downturn would trigger social and political upheaval.

The last thing it wants is a military confrontation with its biggest trading partner, the United States, or with Japan or Taiwan, each of which are major trade and investment partners. It may go on playing the nationalist card over Taiwan to curry domestic political favour, but there has been no massive military build-up and there is no plausible threat of impending war.

To the contrary, China is investing heavily in creating a regional security framework to pursue its domestic development. The U.S. goal of achieving genuine regional maritime security would best be served through cooperation with China — one of its most important creditors, suppliers, and markets — rather than confrontation.

ASEAN COUNTRIES ARMS BUILD-UP/ARMS RACE COMMENCES

Rather belatedly, the ASEAN Countries woke up to the strategic reality that The China Threat was a reality and since the Chinese threat was basically maritime, ASEAN countries are now concentrating on building up the deterrent capacities of their Navies and maritime surveillance.

ASEAN countries before the escalation by China of the South China Sea conflict can be said to have been complacent in even building up the minimal naval and air capabilities to impose some sort of deterrence on China.

In this connection the ASEAN countries whether claimants in the South China Sea conflicts or non-claimants, both have to band together for the simple reason that South East Asian security and stability is not divisible. Regional security cooperation is a desirable goal for ASEAN as China emerges stronger and aggressive.

The significant implication that needs to be noted here is that not only the ASEAN countries are upgrading their military capabilities but those other major powers having a stake in

South China Sea security and stability may also join-in in capacity building of ASEAN's deterrence capabilities.

China's Conflictual Confrontation on South China Sea

China's conflictual stances are not limited only to the South China Sea conflicts as China is similarly involved in territorial disputes and military stand-offs with Japan and India also. China's intense brinkmanship on the South China Sea conflicts has fortuitously given a wake-up call to Japan and India to review their own deterrence capabilities against a militarily rising China.

Japan and India with sizeable stakes in Asian security should have realised years back that both singly and jointly they needed to provide an Asian counterweight to China's burgeoning military power. Japan and India both have been subjected to Chinese aggression and brinkmanship on their territorial disputes with China.

Japan has taken the first tentative steps towards greater self-reliance in its defence and deterrent postures against China. China' brinkmanship on the Senkaku Islands would have further convinced that a military capability independent of the United States needs to be created. China's full control of the South China Sea could result in the economic and strategic strangulation of Japan, and Japan can be expected to forestall that eventuality.

Japan so far had been constrained by the United States in adopting assertive policies towards China. Japan in its approaches to China had to subsume its own national security interests to US strategic sensitivities on China. Post-South China Sea conflicts and extension of conflicts to East China Sea has forced Japan not only to re-examine its Peace Constitution but also building up deterrent military capabilities against China

India finally is seeing through the Chinese game of non-resolution of the India-Occupied Tibet boundary dispute and the strategic encirclement by China of India. India has also woken up to the unfolding Chinese naval challenge materialising against it in the Indian Ocean. From that perspective, India now emerges as a concerned stakeholder in South China Sea security and stability.

Both India and Japan have lately evinced a more active interest in the South China Sea conflict and have a strategic congruence on the 'Defence of the Global Commons'. Expectedly, the military build-ups in Japan and India would provide existential counterweights against China at the two ends of the South China Sea. This should be a source of comfort to the ASEAN countries and induce them to be no longer fence sitters in relation to China.

7

China and Japan: Sea Islands on the Frontline of a New International Flashpoint

The Chinese flotilla arrived at the start of August, more than 300 fishing boats escorted by 15 vast coastguard ships, some of them armed. They circled the Senkaku Islands for a week, drifting into and out of Japanese territorial waters as Tokyo's own coastguard played cat and mouse with the intruders.

Then they were gone, but the message they left behind was clear. China had upped the stakes again in a simmering territorial dispute that has made the southern tip of Japan's island archipelago one of the most dangerous places in the region.

CHINA ACCUSES JAPAN OF THREATENING PACIFIC PEACE WITH MILITARY LAW

Ishigaki Island does not look like a frontline. Japan's own tropical idyll, it is a sleepy place of pineapple fields and mango orchards, where thousands of tourists potter along white sand beaches and scuba dive in crystal clear seas. Yet this tiny dot on the edge of the Pacific is the closest Japanese town to the uninhabited but fiercely disputed Senkaku Islands, once inhospitable home to a tuna processing factory, now abandoned but key to lucrative fishing grounds, oil and gas fields and a strategic shipping route. Under other circumstances the rocky outcrops – their name means sharp pavilions – would have only a unique species of mole as their sole claim for international attention. But their location, and competing claims of ownership from China, Japan and Taiwan have made them a potential flashpoint for war and focus of extreme anxiety from Tokyo to Washington.

Beijing's maritime ambitions have been thrown into sharp focus by its extraordinary creation of a chain of islands from previously open seas over the past few years. It has shored up ambitious claims to swaths of ocean far from the Chinese coastline with the frantic construction of artificial islandsthat has seen runways, radar and guns appear on what were submerged coral reefs just five years ago.

Its strategic plans for the East China Sea have drawn less attention, perhaps because developments have not been so dramatic. But the prospect of tensions escalating into hostilities is real.

THE LATEST MAJOR TRUMP RESIGNATIONS AND FIRINGS

It faces in Japan a more powerful rival than any farther south, and one that has the US as a protector, bound by treaty to come to Tokyo's aid if its territory is attacked. Relations between the uneasy neighbours are so strained that they have not even got a hotline set up for military communication in a crisis, despite years of talks aimed at establishing one.

The issue is so pressing that when new US defence secretary James Mattis visited Tokyo last week, confirming America's commitment to defend the islands was top of the foreign minister's agenda.

"Secretary Mattis made clear that the Senkaku Islands are in the territories under the administration of Japan," Fumio Kishida said after the meeting. China promptly responded with a warning that the American politician's "wrong remarks" put Asia's stability at risk.

Few tourists visiting Ishigaki notice the trouble that is brewing in paradise, but those who live on the island have seen a slow escalation in tensions transform their town and lives, particularly those of the fishermen chased away from the Senkakus by Chinese boats.

"What is frightening for us is that when we go there, the Chinese government ships aggressively approach us, they are much larger than our fishing boats and we are afraid of collisions," said Manabu Namisato, 53, who has been fishing for three decades.

Four years ago a Chinese coastguard ship around 150 times the size of his 10-tonne tuna fishing vessel nearly rammed him on the high seas. "I don't know if they are coming towards us intentionally or not," he said, but the memory still unnerves him. "If that boat had hit me I wouldn't be here today."

The fishermen have been warned for their own safety to stay away, but don't need to be told. "It's not that we don't want to go there, it's that we can't go there. We have agreed to talk to you, because we are afraid the situation may get worse."

The fleet that arrived last August was exceptionally large, but comes after years of regular incursions – and the government fears another influx this summer.

From Ishigaki to Tokyo, many Japanese fear that the aggressive coastguards and the fleets they shepherd to the Senkakus are part of a plan from Beijing to bolster China's claim to the islands by establishing de facto control of the area's fishing ground.

"There is possibility the Chinese government will use this fact that our fishing boats are not going there," admitted an official from the ministry of foreign affairs, adding that the argument would have little standing under international law.

Still, rising numbers of Chinese boats flooding into the area each year have put Japan in a difficult position. It does not want to look weak but fears using military force would give China a long-awaited excuse for further confrontation.

"If we send ships in the Chinese government will use this to further escalate the situation and we don't want that," the official added.

Both sides claim history is on their side, although Japan is the only country ever known to have citizens living on the islands – for two decades last century. China's claim is also slightly undermined by its timing, with the first objection to Japanese ownership claims lodged only after publication of a UN report locating deposits of oil and gas nearby.

There has already been a sharp rise in tensions since 2012 when Japan nationalised the islands. The move warded off a planned sale to Tokyo's then mayor, a hardline nationalist apparently hoping to develop the islands, which would certainly have inflamed sentiments in China.

But Beijing saw, or chose to see, aggression where Tokyo felt it was defending an uneasy status quo. Soon violent protests broke out around China, with Japanese cars, shops and factories vandalised, several firms shutting down production and tour trips abruptly cancelled.

At sea, everything changed. Chinese coastguard ships now regularly sail towards the islands, often escorting fleets of fishing boats. And where once the Chinese boats would stray into Japanese waters perhaps once every couple of years, there has been such a regular pattern of two or three monthly violations in recent years that it is hard not to see a schedule.

Japan says China now has a fleet that includes repurposed naval ships, the largest coastguard patrol in the world, and arms on many vessels. In response Japan has expanded its own coastguard, taking the Ishigaki fleet alone to 16 boats stationed at a newly extended pier.

There are daily patrols to the Senkakus, a trip of five or six hours each way, with teams on standby to show up in greater force. "Right now our current policy is to exceed the Chinese vessels around Senkaku, so if they are showing up with three or four, we want more, if they show up with six or seven we want more," said Hiraki Odagi, spokesman for the

Japanese coastguard. The boats have cannons, and some of the sailors bear arms, but their missions are shrouded in military secrecy. "I'm only at liberty to say we had more than the number of Chinese vessels," Odagi said.

China's air force is also testing Japan's defences, with Japanese fighter jets now scrambled twice a day on average to warn incoming aircraft away from the air space over the islands. There were 22 scrambles in 2008, but 644 last year.

Some in Ishigaki, alarmed by China's encroachment on the islands, feel Japan should have done more to assert its control over the islands decades ago, when China had less money, less military power and less international clout.

"I now think that the Japanese government should have done something," said Yoshitaka Nakayama, mayor of Ishigaki, who is calling on the government to push ahead with plans to deploy a unit of the Japanese military, formally known as the self-defence force, to the island. "Meanwhile China has become a superpower... and if we continue to put this issue on the shelf and not do anything then China will become even more powerful."

Even a small harbour, or pier, on the main Senkaku island where fishermen could take shelter in bad weather might persuade more to risk a trip to the area, while reinforcing Japanese claims, he says. But years of pleas have fallen on deaf official ears, and Nakayama fears Tokyo's caution could pave the way for disaster.

"The situation I am worried about is this – a Chinese ship or fishing boat would come to the island, and fishermen land on the island. Then Japanese police and coastguard officials would go on the island to remove them. Then the Chinese will give a reason to deploy warships to the island, saying 'we need to protect our citizens'."

The dispute goes to the heart of concerns about China's growing ambition, as it looks to project power across a region once dominated by America. And while its expansion in the South China Sea has caused alarm around the world, Japanese officials point out that East China Sea, where the Senkakus lie, is even closer to China's shoreline and on the path out to the Pacific.

In Ishigaki many believe a stronger position is the only way to ward off disaster, with a bullishness that carries a disturbing echo of China's own uncompromising stance.

"I think the Japanese government has prioritised the relationship with China, including economic ties," said Yoshiyuki Toita, secretary general of the Yaeyama Defence Association which brings together more than 100 people on Ishigaki and its surrounding islands to campaign and study.

"If we just worry about temporary economic loss and give in, China may create a military facility in this area, so there will be more national security loss than economic loss. Japanese people should understand that and we should raise awareness about issues of territorial claims."

DISPUTED TERRITORIES

1 DMZ (demilitarised zone between North and South Korea): Pyongyang's nuclear ambitions keep tensions high in a heavily militarised peninsula

2 Kuril islands held by Russia, claimed by Japan as part of its 'northern territories': The Kuril Islands were seized by Soviet forces during the second world war. Failure to resolve the resulting territorial dispute has soured relations between Moscow and Tokyo.

3 Sea of Japan (between North Korea and Japan): Pyongyang fired a series of ballistic missiles into the sea off its coast last summer, after the US and South Korea agreed to deploy a new anti-missile system. The area has seen a history of disputes between Jaopan, Russia and South Korea.

4 Taiwan Strait (between Taiwan and China): China was angered by a controversial Trump phone call, warning Washington its right to the island was 'non-negotiable'.

5 Senkaku islands (East China Sea): Anti-Japan demonstrators in China have denounced Tokyo's 'aggression'

over fishing rights in a contested area rich in oil and gas reserves. It may prove a global flashpoint as armed Chinese coastguard vessels intrude.

6 Paracel islands (South China Sea): Woody Island is the largest of the Paracels, which have been under China's control since 1956. Beijing has installed missile launchers while the US wants to enforce freedom of navigation.

7 Scarborough shoal (South China Sea): There has been a five-year dispute between the Philippines and China over ownership of the territory near Luzon island.

8 Spratly Islands (South China Sea): China has built a runway with capacity for military planes and is using dredgers to build artificial islands. The island above is garrisoned by Vietnam and Hanoi disputes China's ambitions.

CHINA FINDS A SPHERE OF INFLUENCE

In many respects, it is the structure, principles, and process of the Association of Southeast Asian Nations—the now ten-member economic organization formed by Indonesia, Malaysia, the Philippines, Singapore, and Thailand in 1967—that make it vulnerable to Chinese influence as Beijing flexes its regional muscle. With its amorphous objectives of economic growth, social progress, and regional stability,ASEAN has proven so weak that it poses an opportunity rather than a threat to China. The organization lacks a collective security provision, joint military forces, and even a foreign policy solidarity clause—the kind of commitments that prevented the Soviet Union from achieving hegemony over Europe during the Cold War. The "ASEAN Way" stresses state sovereignty and non-interference in the internal affairs of other members, mitigating discomfort with the PRC's authoritarian political system. In this regard, in fact, there is more potential tension with the Western democracies, which focus on human rights, fair elections, and other liberal democratic principles.

Beijing has cleverly used economic enticements to deepen its ties with its Southeast Asian neighbours, making China

ASEAN's largest trading partner. Under the terms of ASEAN's Free Trade Agreement with China, the six original member states, along with China, would eliminate tariffs on ninety percent of their products by 2010, with Cambodia, Laos, Myanmar, and Vietnam having until 2015 to do the same. Beijing has continually promoted economic, military, and political cooperation relationships that are "Asia only"—such as the ASEAN Plus Three (ASEAN, China, Japan, and South Korea). But, unable in recent years to keep the implications of considerable military weight (a double-digit annual growth in defence spending for the last fifteen years) from showing in the region, China has also undermined its "win-win" idea of diplomacy. While upholding mutually beneficial economic ties with their giant neighbour, ASEAN leaders have also, with varying degrees of enthusiasm, encouraged the United States to maintain an active presence in their region as an external balancer to the PRC. One major source of tension between Beijing and some of its Pacific neighbours is their overlapping claims to the South China Sea. This 3.5 million-square-kilometer body of water contains islands, minerals, oil and natural gas reserves, and maritime passages contested by the various littoral states. China and Vietnam assert claims to all the small islands in the South China Sea, whereas Brunei, Malaysia, the Philippines, and Taiwan claim only some of them. The Spratly and Paracel chains are the most prominent of the islands, whose small size and population belie the potential value of the important natural resources, especially oil and natural gas, thought to lie under their surrounding waters. The islands are also surrounded by valuable fishing grounds and straddle shipping lanes through which vital energy resources flow into East Asia from beyond.

During the 1990s, the PRC declared the entire South China Sea to be its territorial waters and indicated a willingness, when it gained the capacity, to enforce these claims. In the early 2000s, however, Beijing changed course and pursued a "smile diplomacy" to reassure ASEANnations worried by its rising military power. In November 2002, China and the ASEAN countries signed the Declaration on the Conduct of Parties in the South China Sea, pledging to resolve sovereignty disputes peacefully through direct negotiations.

For reasons that remain unclear, the PRC modified its low-key approach in March 2010, when Chinese officials declared the South China Sea a "core national interest." In diplomatic language, this term normally means an issue a state is willing to use military force to defend. Until this point, Chinese leaders had applied that term only to Tibet and Taiwan. In July, Ministry of Defence spokesman Senior Colonel Geng Yansheng became more specific when he insisted that "China has indisputable sovereignty of the South Sea, and China has sufficient historical and legal backing."

The Chinese Navy has been developing the strength to enforce this claim. It has built an enormous base on Hainan Island as a home port that places the fleet closer to the disputed waters of the South China Sea. The Chinese military has also been developing a new missile, the Dong Feng 21D, intended to hit an aircraft carrier or other moving target at a distance of 1,500 kilometres, and will soon deploy its own first aircraft carrier, recently purchased from Russia. The Chinese military apparently believes that having such a capacity will lead the US Navy to steer clear of the South China Sea and other disputed regions around China's maritime periphery. In July 2010, partly to affirm the PRC's maritime claims, the People's Liberation Army Navy conducted a massive show of force in the South China Sea, with at least a dozen warships from all three of its navy fleets.

Of all the ASEAN countries, Vietnam has the touchiest relationship with China, sharing a border that has led to centuries of invasions and armed conflicts between the two nations.

Still, most recent Sino-Vietnamese tensions have involved water, specifically the South China Sea. The Vietnamese Navy, under different regimes, fought battles with the Chinese during the mid-1970s and late 1980s over the Paracel and Spratly island chains.

The PRC seized the Paracels in 1974 while Vietnam was preoccupied with the final stages of its war, and has since established and reinforced military garrisons there along with a military airbase. Since these facilities are located southeast of Hainan, they allow the People's Liberation Army to project power from points beyond the China coast. More recently, Chinese authorities have declared unilateral fishing bans in the South China Sea and have seized Vietnamese fishing boats in the area, keeping any catches and equipment and releasing the crews only after they pay fines. They have also been warning Western energy firms not to negotiate offshore drilling agreements with the Vietnamese government if they don't want their business interests in China to suffer.

In response, Vietnamese leaders have cultivated a strong and militant form of national independence that aims to make their country a "poison shrimp" that China cannot digest. They have also returned to an age-old tradition of relying on larger, external powers to help balance China's superior population and other resources. During the Cold War, Vietnam cultivated ties with Moscow as well as Beijing, eventually siding with the Soviet Union following the end of the war with the US. Since most of Vietnam's existing arsenal is of Soviet design, its military has found it most practical for reasons of logistical simplicity and cost effectiveness to continue purchasing Soviet-origin weapons from Russia, such as the Su-30 Flanker fighters and Kilo diesel submarines. But despite this tie, Hanoi has been seeking to develop security ties with the United States as well.

The leaders of Vietnam, however, are not the only ones in Southeast Asia concerned about China's increasing diplomatic and military boldness. In a letter to the United Nations on July 8, the Indonesian government formally challenged the PRC's claims to the South China Sea for the first time after a Chinese warship forced an Indonesian patrol boat to release Chinese fishermen. The Chinese boat had been captured in an area that Indonesia claims lies in its Exclusive Economic Zone, but the PRCdenied the claim. Philippine and Malaysian officials have also communicated to Washington, if less openly, their concerns about the PRC's growing assertiveness in the South China Sea. The concerns of China's neighbours are also evident in the sustained military buildups some of them have begun. According to arms transfer data released by the Stockholm International Peace Research Institute (SIPRI), the value of the major conventional weapons systems delivered to Southeast Asian countries almost doubled between 2005 and 2009. Malaysia, which contests Beijing's claims to the South China Sea, imported an astounding 722 percent more arms during this period than it did during the previous five years. For Singapore, the increase was 146 percent, while for Indonesia it was 84 percent. The large volume of weapons purchased by Singapore has, in fact, resulted in that country becoming the first state in Southeast Asia to rank among the world's top ten arms importers since the Vietnam War ended in 1975.

The ASEAN countries cannot hope to balance China militarily, of course. Even with the buildup, the PRC significantly outmatches the combined weight of ASEAN members in manpower, equipment, and spending. A Centre for Strategic and International Studies report on the military balance in Asia estimated Chinese military personnel in 2010 at 2,170,000. In contrast, Cambodia, Indonesia, Laos, Malaysia, Vietnam, Thailand, Singapore, and the Philippines combined only have 1,472,000 in uniform. Moreover, the ASEAN militaries have shown little interest in pooling their defence resources and developing a collective military force.

The ASEAN states also have extensive and mutually beneficial economic ties with Beijing that they do not want to jeopardize by directly confronting China over its maritime claims. They would prefer that some other external balancer such as the United States assume that role, with ASEAN providing indirect support. Unlike South Korea, Japan, or Australia, the Southeast Asian states lack bilateral defence treaties with the United States. Nonetheless, some ASEAN officials have been privately pressing Washington to intervene on the South China Sea issue to discourage Chinese adventurism. Unsurprisingly, it has been the Vietnamese who have most eagerly sought to work with their former adversary to balance the regional colossus.

It was therefore probably not an accident that, at the July 2010 ASEANRegional Forum meeting in Hanoi, Secretary of State Hillary Clinton broke with precedent and offered to help launch multilateral talks on disputed South China Sea territories within the ASEAN framework. She also reaffirmed standard US opposition to the use of coercion or threats of force to settle conflicting claims. Clinton justified her statement of concern on this occasion by explaining that "The United States, like every nation, has a national interest in freedom of navigation, open access to Asia's maritime commons, and respect for international law in the South China Sea."

At the May 2010 Shangri-La Dialogue, US Defence Secretary Robert Gates called the South China Sea "not only vital to those directly bordering it, but to all nations with economic and security interests in Asia." Alluding to alleged PRC threats against American and other international oil companies considering cooperation with Vietnam, Gates said, "We object to any effort to intimidate US corporations or those of any nation engaged in legitimate economic activity." When he visited the Philippines in August 2010, the commander of US forces in the Pacific, Admiral Robert Willard, affirmed the American commitment to guarantee free navigation in the South China Sea.

Taken together, these statements by US officials constituted a bold move designed to redirect the PRC from its increasingly aggressive stance by underscoring American unwillingness to allow the region to become an uncontested sphere of influence. The United States has traditionally sought to avoid taking a public position on East Asian sovereignty disputes, but the recent aggressive moves by China, combined with the quiet pleadings of some prominent ASEAN leaders, has galvanized the Obama administration into action.

Not surprisingly, the PRC foreign and defence ministries each criticized Secretary Clinton for intervening in the South China Sea dispute. In late August 2010, a small manned submarine had planted a PRC flag on the sea bed of the South China Sea. On September 21, the Chinese Foreign Ministry spokesperson warned against "any kind of statement that might be issued by the US and ASEAN over the South China Sea" during the September 24 summit, when President Obama would meet with ASEANleaders on the sidelines of the annual opening of the UN General Assembly in New York. The unofficial PRC media described the new US assertiveness over the South China Sea, as well as the US decision to join the East Asia Summit, as an effort, in collusion with the Vietnamese, to contain China.

The Chinese see Washington's more assertive declaratory policy regarding the South China Sea through the lens of the increasingly close economic and strategic ties between the US and Hanoi, despite persistent tensions between the two over human rights.

Along with China and Japan, the United States is one of Vietnam's largest trading partners, export markets, and sources of foreign direct investment. During the past decade, top US and Vietnamese officials have regularly visited each other's capitals, senior US and Vietnamese officers have exchanged numerous visits, and American Navy warships have made port calls at Ho Chi Minh City, Hai Phong, and Da Nang. In 2009, the US Defence Security Cooperation Agency announced its willingness to permit the export of "non-lethal" military equipment, such as naval surveillance radars, to Vietnam. In early August 2010, the Vietnamese Foreign Ministry announced the beginning of US-Vietnamese negotiations on a civil nuclear cooperation agreement, which could result in US assistance to a Vietnamese nuclear energy program. That same month, the United States and Vietnam held their first formal defence talks, and their navies conducted their first joint exercises since the Vietnam War ended thirty-five years ago.

The destroyer USS *John McCain* joined with ships of the Vietnamese People's Navy to conduct training drills for search and rescue, damage control, maintenance, emergency repair, and fire control. At the same time, the nuclear-powered USS

George Washington aircraft carrier, nominally there to help mark the fifteenth anniversary of the normalization of US-Vietnamese ties, also hosted a combined Vietnamese civilian-military delegation while sailing in the disputed South China Sea off the Vietnamese port of Da Nang. The United States has also invited Vietnam to send observers to US-led military exercises in the region, including the large Cobra Gold exercise in Thailand. The United States has offered to train Vietnamese soldiers to participate in UN peacekeeping operations. In October 2010, Vietnam invited foreign navies, constructed by the United States and then also used by the Soviet Union, to consider using the naval base at Cam Ranh Bay for "peaceful purposes." The locale's deepwater harbour and port infrastructure would be important for replenishing American warships operating in the disputed South China Sea and the Indian Ocean.

In November 2010, US Army chief of staff General George William Casey visited the Vietnamese Ministry of Defence in Hanoi, where he and Lieutenant General Nguyen Quoc Khanh of the Vietnam People's Army agreed to continue cooperating on personnel exchanges, military medicine, and minesweeping.

Vietnamese officials have publicly denied that they are seeking an alliance with the United States against the PRC. They correctly point out that Vietnam engages in defence cooperation with many countries, including China itself. And they note that the US has interests of its own in the region. Indeed, according to one calculation, one-third of all the world's commercial shipping traverses waters that Chinese policymakers now claim as their own. Soon after taking office, the Obama administration made clear its determination to contest Chinese sovereignty claims in international waters when Chinese ships and aircraft launched a concerted campaign of harassment against US maritime surveillance ships in the South China Sea. The most infamous episode occurred in March 2009, when Chinese sailors tried to seize the sonar buoy of the USNS *Impeccable*, a non-commissioned auxiliary ship that the US Navy was using to surveil China's new naval base on Hainan and Chinese submarines in the area. In addition to these military measures, the Obama administration has been increasing the US diplomatic and economic military presence in Southeast Asia, ending earlier complaints that Washington was neglecting the region due to American preoccupation with the wars in Iraq and Afghanistan. The United States has joined every ASEAN-related institution it is eligible to join. A flood of US Cabinet members now visit Southeast Asia on a regular basis. In 2008, the US designated Scot Marciel—deputy assistant secretary for Southeast Asia in the Bureau of East Asian and Pacific Affairs—as, concurrently, ambassador for ASEAN affairs and permanent representative to the ASEANSecretariat in Jakarta. The United States signed the ASEAN Treaty of Amity and Cooperation the following year. The first ASEAN-US summit occurred in November 2009, followed by a second in September 2010.ASEAN invited the United States and Russia, both potential great power balancers against the PRC, to join the East Asia Summit in 2011.

Independently of ASEAN, the United States launched the Lower Mekong Initiative, designed to help Laos, Thailand, and Vietnam address multiple ecological, social, and infrastructure issues. Governments from these countries had complained that Chinese damming of the upper Mekong River was inflicting drought and causing other devastating damage on their environment.

In terms of bilateral relations, the US has sustained long-standing military alliances with the Philippines, Singapore, and Thailand and improved security ties with Malaysia and Indonesia, as well as Vietnam. In April 2010, Malaysian Prime Minister Najib Tun Razak met with President Obama in Washington. They discussed Malaysia's contribution to the US-led military efforts in Afghanistan, which includes about forty medical specialists and military personnel engaged in humanitarian assistance. At the same time, the US government formally upgraded the status of its relationship with Malaysia to that of a "strategic partnership." In June, Malaysia elevated its status in the annual multilateral Cobra Gold military exercise from that of observer to full participant.

After a lengthy hiatus, the US has also restored comprehensive military ties with Indonesia, including reestablishing relations with Kopassus, Indonesia's special forces group, which plays a leading role in Indonesia's counterterrorism efforts. The new Indonesian-US bilateral defence framework agreement provides for security dialogue, education, training, equipment sales, and maritime security cooperation. The two governments also launched a "comprehensive partnership" that includes a joint commission headed by Indonesian Foreign Minister Marty Natalegawa and Secretary of State Clinton. American diplomats have also been encouraging Australia, Japan, and especially India to deepen relations with Southeastern Asian countries to further offset the PRC's hegemonic potential.

Despite their growing economic cooperation with the PRC, ASEANnations now acknowledge that improved security ties with the United States offer the safest and most effective way—and a far better one than they could achieve alone—for them to hedge against China's growing power and to exercise influence on Chinese policy. Yet the ASEANcountries also want to keep China and the United States in balance, and do whatever they can to avert a major Sino-American confrontation. While they play both powers against each other to gain advantage and maneuverability, they insist that Sino-American competition remain a civilian contest for regional position, profit, and prestige. Whether the region can maintain that delicate balance in the face of growing American concern over China's new hegemonic potential and ambition is the question that will determine ASEAN's future.

JAPAN, CHINA AND THE US SPAR IN THE EAST AND SOUTH CHINA SEAS

In China's international relations, 2010 has been the Year of Zero Sum. On a series of issues, the Western and Asian democracies have demanded that China accept policies that advance their agendas while sacrificing Chinese interests.

On one level this is the inevitable outcome of the Obama administration's repositioning of its foreign policy away from the amoral, Westphalian-style horse-trading of national interests of the Bush administration.

The United States has now established global adherence to norms championed by the U.S. and its allies—non-proliferation, global warming, democracy, freedom of information, freedom of navigation, open currency markets, and human rights—as the cornerstone of its foreign policy. This does not necessarily mean, of course, that the U.S. holds itself or its allies to such high standards in these realms, notably global warming, but even human rights and freedom of navigation. By accident or design, the insistence on these norms as the driver behind global policy leaves nations, particularly an authoritarian government like the PRC, which is outside of the U.S.-defined mainstream on virtually all of these issues, little scope to define and advance its competing national interests as legitimate.

It also has the effect of isolating China from Western and some Asian democracies—a useful geopolitical windfall for nations anxious about China's rising economic, military, and geopolitical clout and the global gains Beijing made in the first decade of the 20th century while the Bush administration was asleep at the Asian switch.

In 2010, China was called upon to sacrifice its own interests on virtually all of the Obama administration's key initiatives. On global warming, China was asked to abandon the highly favourable terms of the Kyoto Protocol for an economically costly cap on its greenhouse gas emissions even as the U.S. failed to commit to any significant controls. On the issue of Google, the Obama administration (which counts a significant number of Google insiders in its tech-policy brain trust) called on China to tear down that Great Firewall, something that China considers an unacceptable political risk.

On Iran, China was pressed to put its energy security and alliance with Iran at risk in order to join the U.S.-led crusade against Iran's nuclear ambitions. On North Korea, China was told to abandon its useful buffer, the DPRK, and join a chorus of condemnation over the sinking of the Cheonan that would shift the focus toward the reunification of the peninsula under the aegis of the United States and the ROK. On currency, the U.S. has demanded that China substantially appreciate its currency with the anticipated result of reducing its exports so the United States can try to find a way out of its economic difficulties.

Not only did the PRC resist American pressures on each of these fronts, but it also summoned up the energy to protest the awarding of the Nobel Peace Prize to Liu Xiaobo, the imprisoned activist, whose organization receives funding from the U.S. government's National Endowment for Democracy, whose candidacy was championed by the PRC's arch-foe, the Dalai Lama, and whose platform calls for replacing the PRC's political monopoly with a multi-party democracy.

And then there is the issue of the island groups. The East and South China Seas are home to dozens of contested islands, atolls, and sandbars, virtually all of them uninhabited. China has asserted sovereignty over virtually the entire area, including two potential flashpoints: the Paracels, which it seized from South Vietnam in 1974, and the Diaoyutai/Senkaku Islands, which have been firmly under Japanese sovereignty (with an interlude of American occupation) since 1895.

The situation in the Paracels—and China's patent unwillingness to negotiate on the question of the islands while asserting effective sovereignty through measures like organizing Paracels tourism—has provoked the strong resentment of the Vietnamese government. For several years, Vietnam has attempted to cultivate a relationship with the United States and involve Washington on its side in the dispute. This was a temptation the U.S. resisted until this year, when Secretary of State Hillary Clinton declared that the United States had "a national interest" in freedom of navigation in the South China Sea.

This statement was understood as an overt attempt to multilateralize the issue. It was also, therefore, a direct challenge to China, which was asked once again to sacrifice its interests, specifically the advantages of its preferred negotiation strategy: fully leveraging its regional clout by negotiating bilaterally with its smaller Asian neighbours without the complication of placating the ASEAN group as a whole or coping with the intrusive presence of the United States.

The most recent event in China's *annus horribilus* is the dust-up over the Diaoyutai/Senkaku Islands. In this case, the United States may have actually been trying to chart a middle way, but saw its policy blown out of the water by strident Japanese and Chinese nationalism.

A standoff between a Chinese fishing trawler and two Japanese Coast Guard vessels on September 7 off the Diaoyutai/Senkaku Islands led to the Japanese detention of Captain Zhan Qixiong and the provocative assertion that his case would be adjudicated under Japanese domestic law, rather than resolved through quiet diplomacy between Tokyo and Beijing.

On any given day, hundreds of Chinese boats fish within Japan's proclaimed Economic Exclusion Zone (EEZ); a few boats, including apparently Captain Zhan's, don't scruple to cross the line demarcating Japan's territorial waters to fish close to the uninhabited islands.

News reports suggest that Zhan was something of a hothead. All it took was a Japanese over-reaction to make him a national hero. Japan's hawkish minister Maehara Seiji can take a lion's share of the credit or blame for blowing up the incident. The Asahi newspaper reported the timeline as follows: Maehara was still Minister of Land, Infrastructure, Transport and Tourism – in charge of the Coast Guard – at the time of the incident.

Immediately after the trawler collided with Japan Coast Guard vessels on Sept 7, Maehara called Coast Guard Commandant Suzuki Hisayasu and told him, "The captain of the Chinese fishing boat must be arrested."

Maehara also called Chief Cabinet Secretary Sengoku Yoshito and told him, "It is better to persist resolutely against China."

At first, China responded calmly.

Reflecting back on that time, a Chinese government source said, "By sticking to a calm response, China was trying to encourage Japan to release the captain on its own accord."

But Maehara refused to back down.

He told close aides: "The prime minister's office was hesitant so I had to make the decision to arrest the captain. There was no mistake in the handling of the matter."

Maehara was appointed foreign minister on September 21, days after his aggressive intervention in the incident.

It is rather ironic that Japan would demand diplomatic engagement of China in the South China Sea while simultaneously foreswearing it over the Daioyutai/Senkaku Islands. More important, the Diaoyutai/Senkaku story is not simply a matter of Japan standing up to the big Chinese bully.

By distance, geography, and history Taiwan has the best claim on the Diaoyutai Islands (which are a mere 170 km from Taiwan and separated from Okinawa by 410 km and a deep undersea trench), which Japan acquired during the course of imperial skullduggery involving the seizure of Okinawa in 1872.

With its display of undersea terrain, Google Earth provides an interesting perspective on these tiny islands just north of Taiwan, at 25°44'30.48" N 123°28'21.39"E, and separated from Japan's Ryukyu Islands by the Okinawa Trough which, Wikipedia tells us, "marks the edge of the continental shelf of the East China Sea".

Taipei responded to the incident by vociferously advancing its interest. President Ma Ying-jeou, who has played the Diaoyutai card throughout his entire political career, dispatched 12 Coast Guard vessels to shield a boat of Taiwanese activists that made a symbolic approach within 19 miles of the island on September 15. The Japanese Coast Guard warned them off. Taiwanese media reported:

On several occasions the Kan En No. 99," which means "Showing Grace" in the Chinese language, was just two meters from being rammed by Japan's patrol ships.

Taking into consideration the aggressiveness of the Japanese Coast Guard, it is easy to understand how frustration, fear, and anger might have combined with poor seamanship and bullheadedness to produce Captain Zhan's collision. After Captain Zhan's detention was extended, with indictment in a Japanese court apparently imminent, China moved aggressively both in the public and official spheres. Cancelling scheduled negotiations with Japan over undersea oil and gas deposits in the vicinity of Diaoyutai, it also canceled bilateral talks on airline flights and told Chinese travel agencies not to accept applications for tour groups to visit Japan – scuppering two initiatives that Maehara had championed as tourism minister.

China also allegedly cut off exports of rare earth oxides to Japan and the government detained four Japanese employees of Fujita in Shijiazhuang, capital of North China's Hebei province, on charges of espionage-related activity, apparently in retaliation. Three of the men were subsequently released, and the fourth was returned after a period of detention that roughly matched Captain Zhan's. Judging from the Asahi article, Prime Minister Kan was not pleased that his term had begun with a major diplomatic dust-up courtesy of Maehara and his patron, Democratic Party of Japan (DPJ) secretary general Okada Katsuya. Okada and Maehara are the two most powerful proponents of a strong US alliance within the DPJ, whose platform has emphasized accommodation with Japan's Asian neighbours. As exchanges with China became more heated, Maehara recklessly upped the ante by pulling in the United States.

At the time of the crisis, it was well-known to Japan that the Obama administration had little interest in supporting Japanese assertions of sovereignty over the Senkaku Islands.

In August 2010, *The Japan Times* reported:

The Obama administration has decided not to state explicitly that the Senkaku Islands, which are under Japan's control but claimed by China, are subject to the Japan-U.S. security treaty, in a shift from the position of George W. Bush, sources said Monday.

Although the U.S. government has not officially changed its stance that the Japan-U.S. pact applies to the uninhabited East China Sea islets, known in China as the Diaoyu isles, the shift from making a direct reference to them could become a source of concern for Tokyo as it addresses moves by Beijing, the sources said. Taiwan also claims the islets.

The administration of Barack Obama has already notified Japan of the change in policy, but Tokyo may have to take countermeasures in light of China's increasing activities in the East China Sea, according to the sources.

Whether Foreign Minister Maehara's hard line one month later in September was provoked by the perceived need for Japan to stand up to China—or whether it was an affront calculated to force an unenthusiastic Obama administration to side with Japan on the Senkakus—remains to be determined.

After Maehara met with Secretary of State Hillary Clinton in New York, AFP reported:

"According to the Japanese minister, Clinton said that the Senkakus ... are subject to Article 5 of the bilateral security treaty, which authorizes the US to protect Japan in the event of an armed attack 'in the territories under the administration of Japan'," the report said.

Whatever was said in private, publicly the State Department did not inject itself in the controversy by explicitly extending the US security umbrella over the Senkakus. According to the AFP report, State Department spokesperson Philip Crowley limited himself to the observation that the Senkaku issue was "complicated".

It appears that Maehara abused the secretary of state's confidence by making public her sensitive and probably strongly caveated assurances of US support for Japan, in order to secure U.S. military backing for Japan's claim to Diaoyutai/Senkakus, and for his aggressive move in ordering the arrest and prosecution of the Chinese captain.

Hopeful overreach continued with the Japanese press reporting that Defence Secretary Robert Gates and Admiral Mike Mullen, chairman of the U.S. joint chiefs of staff, had, in the words of the Japanese public-service broadcaster NHK, "indicated that the US security agreement with Japan covers the Senkaku Islands."

"Indicated" is much too strong a word.

The actual transcript of the Department of Defence briefing was long on waffling and offered no explicit commitment:

Q Chinese Premier Wen in New York on Tuesday threatened action against Japan if it didn't return the captain of the ship. I'm wondering, does the US security umbrella extend to the Senkakus – the Senkaku islands?

ADM MULLEN: I think we're watching those – that tension very, very carefully, and certainly our commitment to the region remains. And, you know, we're hopeful that the political and diplomatic efforts would reduce that tension specifically, and haven't seen anything that would, I guess, raise the alarm levels higher than that. And obviously we're very, very strongly in support of, you know, our ally in that region, Japan.

Q And second -

SEC GATES: And we'll – and we would fulfil our alliance responsibilities.

In follow-on questions at the September 24 press briefing, the US State Department cited remarks by Jeffrey Bader, chairman of the National Security Council that the dispute was a matter between China and Japan.

Further awkward parsing was pre-empted as Prime Minister Kan cut the legs out from under Maehara and Okada in the best circular firing squad tradition of the hapless DPJ by agreeing to Zhan's release. The two hawks are striving to disguise their embarrassment with escalating anti-Chinese bluster.

At a time that China was saying that the case of Captain Zhan was "basically over ", Maehara told the Japanese media that China's demand for an apology demonstrated its "undemocratic nature". He also made the provocative statement that China might be preparing to violate an agreement with Japan not to drill unilaterally for oil and gas in contested portions of the East China Sea.

Despite Japan's humiliating retreat from its initial aggressive posture, the U.S. nevertheless received a propaganda windfall. Any threat, real or imputed, that China will deploy its military, economic, and financial clout to advance its interests in the East and South China Seas, strengthens the desire of China's neighbours for a closer US alliance, or so U.S. Asia strategists believe.

Doyle McManus, the Washington correspondent of the Los Angeles Times, delivered the conventional US wisdom:

Because of China's truculence, US relations with Japan, Korea and Vietnam have almost never been better.

Actually, the root cause of friction in East Asia in 2010 is the Obama administration's determination to "return to Asia", most evident in the planned series of U.S.-ROK and U.S.-Japan joint military exercises in China's backyard, and the encouragement this has given to anxious nations to pursue confrontations with China they might otherwise avoid. Certainly this has emboldened Japan, Korea, and Vietnam to confront the Chinese dragon.

It was Japanese, not Chinese, truculence that dictated the decision made at the cabinet level to arrest and try Zhan after the collision near Diaoyutai/Senkaku. This comes at a time of Vietnamese efforts to engage the United States as a counterweight to China, particularly over the nagging question of the Hoang Sa/Paracel/Xisha Islands in the South China Seas, which China seized from South Vietnam after a bloody encounter in 1974.

The issue gained heightened visibility with the report that China "formally declared to the United States that the South China Sea is a core interest", implying to Western observers that China regarded the fate of the uninhabited islands and their associated oil and gas deposits as an existential issue presumably worthy of the attention of the People's Liberation Army. In keeping with the theme of dubious, thinly sourced news reports with a Japanese link, however, this news item derived, virtually in its entirety, from a brief report filed by Kyodo News Service's Washington Bureau on July 3, that the Chinese had stated this position to James Steinberg and Jeffrey Bader when they were in Beijing in March 2010.

The report is anonymously sourced from somebody who was apparently not directly involved in the meetings — it states that the Chinese position was "presumably" conveyed by State Councilor Dai Bingguo. It is also interesting that this scoop was leaked to a Japanese news office in Washington; none of the plugged-in American news organizations got the story at that time (the only apparent corroboration is a statement in a July 2010 story by John Pomfret that Dai Bingguo had made the South China Sea a core interest in representation to Hillary Clinton during a "tense exchange" in May; and, as far as can be seen, Steinberg and Bader have not been asked to confirm the report.

It would appear noteworthy that the Chinese saw fit to announce this position to the only party they are attempting to exclude from the South China Sea dispute, the United States, while not conveying it to Vietnam, the Philippines, Malaysia, Brunei, or Indonesia, the interlocutors with whom it is trying to impose a series of bilateral negotiations. The United States is now apparently happy to spread the "core interests" meme, at least in private conversations between U.S. government officials and American reporters, although its accuracy and context have yet to be made part of the public record.

China has never officially confirmed or denied the story. Within China, there is skepticism that the Chinese government made any statement claiming South China Sea core interest.

As far as the public record goes, China remains committed to freedom of navigation in the South China Sea, the Declaration on the Conduct of Parties in the South China Sea (a standstill agreement negotiated with ASEAN in 2002), and negotiated settlements over disputed islands. Yet the fact remains that such statements remain exclusively in the realm of US journalism.

It is possible, of course, that the phrase "core interest" came up in the context of the continual criss-crossing of the South China Sea by the two US Navy surveillance vessels *Impeccable* and *Victory*.

The US Navy exploits a loophole in the Law of the Sea Convention allowing free transit through a nation's exclusive economic zone in order to monitor and map the area near China's strategic submarine base on Hainan Island. As such, U.S. efforts to undercut China's nuclear deterrent—and improve U.S. prospects of intercepting and destroying China's southern submarine fleet in case of a confrontation over Taiwan—could be construed as a matter of China's "core interest" that the Chinese government might want to raise with American diplomats.

In any case, as publicly defined by the United States, China's "core interest" in the South China Sea is a matter of sandbars, not submarines, and this has prompted the U.S. to inject itself in the South China Sea disputes as the champion of the Association of Southeast Asian Nations members, especially Vietnam, against Chinese territorial overreach. The "core interest" story has been a public relations gold mine for the United States as China has watched in dismay and frustration as several ASEAN nations led by Vietnam and Singapore lined up with the United States to push for internationalizing the dispute. However, the welter of islets and rocks presents a nearly intractable problem even if all the concerned parties desire a friendly solution. Even in the unlikely event that the ASEAN countries were to maintain a united front against China with US encouragement, it is unlikely that China will surrender its claims in an adversarial venue.

Benign neglect—in PRC terms, a policy of postponing thorny territorial issues while negotiating joint development of resources in disputed areas—has served the South China Sea pretty well over the last three decades and would probably be the best way to handle the problem in the future. A universal commitment to free passage through the vital waterways of the archipelago – a principle already accepted by all parties to the myriad territorial, fishing, and undersea resource disputes – is probably worth the price of tacit acknowledgement of the less than ideal status quo.

U.S. pressure on China in the South China Sea was quickly joined by Japan. In July, Okada was already pressing the South China Sea issue at the ASEAN Regional Forum. In a deliberate echo of Clinton's July 23 statement injecting the US "national interest" into the South China Sea matter, Okada involved Japan:

Foreign Minister Katsuya Okada on Tuesday expressed his concern over territorial disputes in the South China Sea mainly between China and Southeast Asian nations, saying the instability in the area could hamper Japan's trade and pose a threat to regional peace. "The instability deriving from differing views on territorial issues between China and ASEAN nations could undermine peace in Asia," Okada told a press conference. "We should get rid of such a destabilizing factor as soon as possible."

Given the realities of the situation, the eagerness of the U.S. and Japan to work through the Western press to turn the South China Sea issue into a regional crisis is worth noting.

A September 22 Wall Street Journal piece, entitled "US, ASEAN to Push Back Against China," offered what it sold as a privileged preview of the ASEAN-US joint statement blockbuster:

On Friday, Mr. Obama and the Asean leaders will issue a joint statement in which Washington has proposed text reaffirming the importance of freedom of navigation in the South China Sea, according to the Associated Press.

It said the statement would oppose the "use or threat of force by any claimant attempting to enforce disputed claims in the South China Sea."

The wording is significant – and provocative for China – because it mirrors that of a speech by US Secretary of State Hillary Clinton at another Asean meeting in Hanoi in July.

Japan's NHK obtained a copy of the same draft (bear in mind that Japan was not party to the agreement and not the most likely conduit for a leak). Headline writers throughout the world ran leads like "US backs ASEAN stand against use of force in Spratlys. "

However, the actual text of the joint statement said nothing about disputes in the South China Sea. Apparently, the edifice of US-ASEAN solidarity was not strong enough to withstand a strong, disapproving shove administered publicly by China's Foreign Ministry on September 21 and undoubtedly through numerous private channels.

Having missed the boat on the joint announcement, the *Wall Street Journal*compounded its problems in an untimely encomium celebrating collective Japanese and ASEAN backbone vis-à-vis China:

Japan – the main US ally in the region – is leading the way in confronting China, taking an unusually firm line in a dispute over a collision between a Chinese fishing trawler and two Japanese Coast Guard ships near disputed islands in the East China Sea two weeks ago.

Evidence of the backlash – and its effect on China – is apparent in the current dispute between Beijing and Tokyo over the ship collision near the disputed islands called Diaoyu in China and Senkaku in Japan. Japan has released the trawler and the 14 crew, but continues to detain the ship's captain.

China has summoned Japan's ambassador six times and suspended high-level government exchanges. Mr. Wen, China's premier, personally demanded the captain's release on Tuesday. Yet Tokyo has stood firm, apparently gambling that Beijing doesn't want to damage commercial relations or provoke the kind of anti-Japanese violence that almost spiraled out of control during a similar row in 2005.

"Clinton's stand in Hanoi may have contributed to Japan's demonstration of more backbone than most of us give it credit for having in its current territorial confrontation with China," said Mark Borthwick, director of the United States Asia Pacific Council at the East-West Centre in Washington.

Four days later, Japan folded and returned Captain Zhan.

The unambiguous victory for China makes it hard to give credence to assertions that China's foreign policy is out of control and driven by weakness, arrogance, runaway PLA hotheads, or cadet Politburo members recklessly burnishing their nationalistic credentials in the run-up to China's generational leadership change, due in 2012. Nevertheless, John Pomfret did his best to spin a clear-cut diplomatic victory for Beijing as evidence of China's foreign policy dysfunction and Japanese determination:

The increasingly bitter dispute between China and Japan over a small group of islands in the Pacific is heightening concerns in capitals across the globe over who controls China's foreign policy.

A new generation of officials in the military, key government ministries and state-owned companies has begun to define how China deals with the rest of the world. Emboldened by China's economic expansion, these officials are taking advantage of a weakened leadership at the top of the Communist Party to assert their interests in ways that would have been impossible even a decade ago.

It used to be that Chinese officials complained about the Byzantine decision-making process in the United States. Today, from Washington to Tokyo, the talk is about how difficult it is to contend with the explosion of special interests shaping China's worldview.

The fine lines between spin, self-delusion, and lazy disregard for geopolitical realities seem to be blurring, at least in the foreign affairs quadrant of the Western media.

USA Today pitched in, graciously ignoring Maehara's role in intentionally escalating the confrontation, with a story under the headline, "China's Aggressive Posture Stuns Japan, Experts". McClatchy, at least, indulged in honest sour grapes resentment: "Is a rising China getting too big for its britches?"

The simplest explanation of China's response was that China's elites and public were largely united in their anger at Japan's deliberate high-handedness over the issue of Captain Zhan and fishing rights in the vicinity of Diaoyutai; and the Chinese leadership recognized that any sign of weakness on Diaoyutai might encourage Vietnamese moves on the Paracels with U.S. and Japanese backing.

In Japan, the DPJ government, attempting to deal with the political fallout stemming from its retreat, continues to emphasize its absolute sovereignty over the islands and is reportedly mulling the stationing of a permanent garrison "near" Diaoyutai/Senkaku, presumably on Ishigaki Island, about one hundred miles from Diaoyutai, the nearest major inhabited island and the place where Captain Zhan was detained.

At the September 29 press conference of China's Ministry of Foreign Affairs, Japan was called on to "adopt concrete actions to eliminate the negative effect on China-Japan relations brought by the incident and make practical efforts to mend bilateral relations."

It is not clear what practical efforts China expects, or what Japan can be realistically expected to do in order to reassure Beijing that Tokyo is no longer interested in filling the role of one of America's front-line assets on China's borders.

Asia Times reported in early October that China, which sees no sign that Japan genuinely regrets inflaming the Diaoyutai/Senkaku situation, indicated at an ASEAN get-together in Hanoi that it is not quite ready to consider the issue resolved after all:

Chinese Defence Minister Liang Guanglie's decision to lecture Japan's Defence Minister Kitazawa Toshimi about how the incident near the disputed Diaoyu Islands between the Chinese fishing trawler and the Japanese Coast Guard demonstrated that Japan still does a poor job of handling sensitive issues affecting both countries, and is proof of a lasting chill. Liang wanted to remind Japan that Japan needs to resolve these and other matters in a way that ensures that China's approval will be forthcoming.... This lecture was taking place just as China was issuing a terse announcement about its new maritime enforcement policies. Sun Zhihui, director of the State Oceanic Administration revealed that China intends "to strengthen patrols and supervision in order to protect the country's maritime rights and interests".

At the same time, Chinese Premier Wen Jiabao at a meeting in Brussels informed Japanese Prime Minister Kan Naoto that China had no plans to relinquish its claim to the Diaoyu Islands (called Senkaku by Japan) which the Chinese have always depicted as "an inherent part of the Chinese territory".

"The Diaoyu Islands have been Chinese territory since ancient times," Wen told Kan.

At the same meeting, China rather slyly implied to the United States that its beef was with Tokyo, not Washington (and perhaps rewarded the Obama administration for its equivocal support of Maehara on the issue of Senkaku sovereignty).

The PRC extended to Defence Secretary Gates a longed-for invitation to visit Beijing and printed a picture in state media of Gates and Liang solemnly clasping hands in Hanoi under the heading *Gates to visit China, defence ties normalize.*

Recently, Beijing has been ramping up the rhetoric on the Diaoyutai/Senkaku Islands, seemingly in order to highlight Tokyo's discomfiture and sense of abandonment on the issue—"beating a dog in the water", in Chinese parlance.

Japan has responded in kind. Geopolitical considerations aside, both sides see domestic political advantage in escalating the war of words. Chinese nationalist hotheads were given relatively free reign to stage abusive, anti-Japanese demonstrations in several cities on October 16.

Foreign Minister Maehara responded by calling China's reaction "extremely hysterical"; China's Foreign Ministry, not to be outdone, stated that it was "shocked" at Maehara's statement.

Former Prime Minister Abe emerged from obscurity to toss Hitler into the mix, accusing China of yearning for "Lebensraum" (for some reason, he decided not to run with a more apt World War II analogy and accuse China of harboring ambitions to establish a Greater East Asia Co-Prosperity Sphere).

It appears that the Diaoyutai/Senkaku Islands will remain a low-level and—at least to hardliners in China, Japan, and the U.S.– not completely unwelcome irritant in China's foreign affairs rather than the foundation for a meaningful diplomatic breakthrough in China's relationship with its smaller and anxious neighbours.

There is a remarkable but virtually unnoted parallel between the Diaoyutai/Senkaku case and another confrontation during which the U.S. and its ally pushed, China pushed back, and the U.S. team folded: the Cheonan affair. Faced with U.S. and ROK efforts to use the sinking of the Cheonan as a justification for ostracizing the DPRK and making the fate of the peninsula a matter for the UN Security Council (and not the China-mediated Six Party Talks), China issued a high-level public endorsement of the Kim Jong Il regime and successfully pressured the Lee Myung-bak government to accept a return to the Six Party Talks. The true lesson of the Diaoyutai/Senkaku crisis is that on regional matters China will ferociously oppose would-be US proxies like Japan—and South Korea and Vietnam–if they presume to advance US interests at Chinese expense. The other lesson that China would like its neighbours and enemies to extract from the situation is that the United States is happy to have its allies foment politically useful confrontations with China, but unwilling to alienate China by backing its proxies with determined diplomatic and military escalation when things get tough.

It appears that Beijing can and will deploy its preferred weapons— diplomatic pressure, economic coercion, legal jeopardy for foreign nationals and their interests —with far more speed and determination than the US and its allies can bring to bear despite their overwhelming military superiority. The United States and its Asian partners have done a good job of irritating China and provoking a dangerous crisis; they have yet to prove they can do as good a job of dealing with the consequences.

ANALYSIS: SOUTH CHINA SEA SPAT FRESH THREAT TO SINO-US TIES

China was furious after it was ambushed at Asia's top security forum by a discussion of sensitive territorial claims in the South China Sea, an area rich in energy and key for shipping.

Beijing had kept the South China Sea off the agenda of the ASEAN Regional Forum (ARF) for a decade and a half. But last week in a meeting in Hanoi, 12 of the 27 members — including some with no direct stake in the territorial disputes — raised maritime issues.

An angry summary of the meeting was posted on the Foreign Ministry's website on Sunday evening, eschewing usually opaque diplomatic language to accuse U.S. Secretary of State Hillary Clinton of a barely disguised assault on Chinese interests.

"As expected, the U.S. side chose to ignore China's advice and played up the issue at the meeting," the statement said.

"The seemingly impartial remarks (by Clinton) were in effect an attack on China and were designed to give the international community a wrong impression that the situation in the South China Sea is a cause for grave concern."

The statement was repeated the next day in English, ensuring maximum overseas readership for the broadside, and angry editorials in state-run media have also followed. Experts say the fury is not just for show, and threatens already tense ties.

"China is angry. This is the first public U.S. interference over the South China Sea, which the Foreign Ministry sees as an issue between China and Southeast Asian countries," said Shi Yinhong, International Security professor at Renmin University.

"I think this is quite serious because it dramatically expands the space for disputes between China and the U.S."

Relations between Beijing and Washington have been getting back on an even keel after a disastrous start to the year, marred by spats over everything from Tibet, self-ruled Taiwan and trade and the value of China's currency.

But military ties in particular have been slow to recover, and the latest dispute comes hot on the heels of joint U.S.-South Korean military drills in seas near China, directed at North Korea but also criticized repeatedly by Beijing.

"The Obama administration must clearly understand: are they prepared to fully open up an era of friction with China? If they are not then they are certainly giving the impression that they are," the state-owned but populist Global Times tabloid quoted National Defence University professor Han Xudong saying.

8

South China Sea Dispute and China's Window of Opportunity

The South China Sea (SCS) issue has now arrived at a critical point. China should take the advantages of this opportunity to adjust its South China Sea approach – to steer from a "unilateral win" formula to "multilateral win" formula, so as to take lead in the problem-solving process. This new approach should drive the South China Sea problem-solving process to a faster track, in the process clearing out major obstacles to building a Southeast Asian hub for the 21st Century Maritime Silk Road (MSR).

Based on different opinions regarding sovereignty over islands and reefs and maritime interests and rights, the claimant parties in the South China Sea can be divided into two groups: mainland China and Taiwan, and the four ASEAN claimants (Vietnam, the Philippines, Malaysia, and Brunei). The majority of the ASEAN non-claimants, along with some outsiders — led by European countries, the United States, Japan and Australia — tend to support the claims made by the ASEAN claimants, whereas a minority of the ASEAN non-claimants, Russia, South Korea, and some other outsiders stand neutral. Although there also are some disputes between the ASEAN claimants themselves, for the moment these disputes are considered "minor" in the face of their mutual confrontation with China.

At the moment, the South China Sea is in a relatively peaceful period, but over years of development, it has already been shaped into a trifold game between China and the United States; China and the ASEAN claimants; and China and the ASEAN as a whole. The game between China and the United States is the major conflict, but the game that sees the ASEAN claimants using ASEAN against China is increasingly tense. Because the South China Sea issue is already a flashpoint in China-ASEAN relations, it is considered an indicator for China's overall foreign policy, as well a major tool to the United States' Asia-Pacific rebalancing strategy. The South China Sea issue is also a key security question for ASEAN countries and seen as a touchstone for the ASEAN security cooperation. China, meanwhile, has called for downplaying the South China Sea issue whilst strengthening political, economic, and cultural cooperation with ASEAN countries, but the outcomes so far are barely visible.

The ASEAN countries believe that China has become increasingly assertive regarding the South China Sea issue over the past few years. Along with China's rise, this puts them in an even more disadvantageous position. As a response, the ASEAN claimants propelled the internationalization of the South China Sea issue and became more reliant on the United States and other foreign countries to deal with their security concerns. Only when China and the ASEAN agree on a binding working framework for handling the disputes will the ASEAN claimants then begin economic and cultural cooperation with China, and maybe venture attempts to strengthen security cooperation as well.

It is highly unlikely to see the South China Sea issue resolved in the short term. However, the South China Sea issue may not necessarily get in the way of promoting cooperation between China and the ASEAN claimants. Of course, this outcome requires a relatively more relaxed external environment and a smoother internal environment. The external environment mainly concerns the degree of intervention made by outside countries (i.e. major powers). The internal environment on the other hand, mainly refers to the domestic political stance of the ASEAN claimants and the resulting political relationships between these countries. On both fronts, China currently has a unique window of opportunity to improve its relationships with ASEAN claimants.

External Environment

Considering that populism and the anti-globalization trend have made developed countries less concerned about issues abroad, there is currently a relatively relaxed external environment for resolving the South China Sea issue. For the purpose of this analysis, Japan, the European Union, India, and Russia form the major external powers, with the United States taking the lead.

The Asia-Pacific region is in no doubt one of the United States' most concerned areas. As an experienced hegemon, the United States is well aware that it has to give way to China's rise, but in the meantime, it is hoping to slow down this process, as well as to increase the cost of the rise of China's maritime power. In order to achieve this, the Obama administration shifted its military deployments to the Second Island Chain, strengthened the mobility of the First Island Chain, and urged its allies and partners to make further input so as to form an arc (from northern Japan to Darwin, Australia) to counterbalance China. However, the new Trump administration, whilst promising to "make America great again" and emphasizing "America first," is likely to place more stress on domestic development and demand other countries assume more responsibilities.

Nevertheless, the Trump administration will continue to counterbalance China, but in practice, it might adopt a more tiered approach (e.g. prioritizing the North Korean nuclear issue first, and then the East China Sea and Taiwan, then the South China Sea, and so on) rather than carry on the arc strategy employed by the Obama administration.

If "core interest" is considered as vital to a nation as the brain is to the human body, freedom of navigation, though critical for the U.S. Navy, is not one of the United States' core interests. The key to the U.S. Navy's definition of freedom of navigation is the right to conduct military activities (including intelligence gathering) within other countries' exclusive economic zones. To this end, the United States defined freedom of navigation in its own favor after World War II and promoted its stand with its much superior naval power. The reason behind the establishment of the Freedom of Navigation Program in 1979 is to continuously promote the United States' maritime claims using its own domestic laws and regulations, even after the United Nations Convention on the Law of the Sea (UNCLOS) took effect, and to challenge what the United States regards as "excessive maritime claims."

The Freedom of Navigation Program in practice carries out out Freedom of Navigation Operations (FONOPs) to challenge maritime claims by both allies and opponents. The South China Sea is a major area for carrying out FONOPs, but it is not the only one. In this context, FONOPs in the South China Sea are more of a bargaining chip, just like FONOPs in the Black Sea during the Cold War. Furthermore, after the United States lost its "Filipino arm" when President Rodrigo Duterte scaled back military cooperation with the United States, the significance of FONOPs is also greatly reduced. All told, then, the external environment is more conducive than anytime in recent memory for China to pursue peace in the South China Sea.

Internal Environment

The South China Sea issue involves mainland China, Taiwan, Vietnam, the Philippines, Malaysia, and Brunei. The six other ASEAN countries are non-claimants; of these, Indonesia and Singapore are more influential on the South China Sea issue.

ASEAN Non-Claimants

Even though Indonesia is not one of the parties claiming disputed islands and reefs, there are about 50,000 square kilometers of exclusive economic zone north of its Natuna Islands situated within China's nine-dash line. In order to strengthen its claim, not only has Indonesia been sending immigrants to the Natuna Islands for the past 20 years or so, in recent times, it also boosted military deployments to the area. Overall, though, Indonesia seems to be more discrete and realistic about the South China Sea issue.

When Joko "Jokowi" Widodo assumed the presidency in 2014, he put forward a vision for Indonesia to become a "global maritime fulcrum." With a willingness to promote economic development, he pledged his support to China's Belt and Road Initiative. China regards Indonesia as one of the key players in building the Belt and Road. At this stage, China-Indonesia cooperation has been continuously deepening. More to the point, Jokowi announced publicly during his 2014 election campaign that the South China Sea issue is so complicated that he would not to pay much attention to it unless a good potential solution emerges. That indicates Jokowi will probably keep a sound relationship with China — although during his re-election campaign in 2019, Jokowi might try taking a stronger hand toward the issue in view to fend off his conservative rival, General Prabowo Subianto.

Singapore, as the only developed country of the ASEAN members, with a high dependency on sea trade, is committed to promote ASEAN integration and play a "chief of staff" role. When it comes to the South China Sea issue, Singapore is keen on acting strongly against China. This, in the past few years, has inevitably led to turbulence in the China-Singapore relationship. However, given that Singapore's economy is highly compatible with China's, it has neither the ability nor the intention to openly confront China. Vietnam and the Philippines' preferences to not publicly confront China are also holding back Singapore's ambitions. These together indicate that Singapore will not pursue a radical SCS policy in the near future.

ASEAN Claimants

Of the four ASEAN claimants, Vietnam and the Philippines clearly have more disagreements with China, and they advocate using a multilateral framework to solve the issue. The Philippines in the past even attempted to pursue its interests through third-party arbitration by filing a case with the Permanent Court of Arbitration. Malaysia and Brunei, in contrast, are more settled about the South China Sea issue. Politically, they are more prone to using a bilateral framework to solve the issue, while managing differences and promoting cooperation.

There are two groups of political elites within the Vietnamese government – the Southern Clique and the Northern Clique. The new Vietnamese government is mainly formed by the Northern Clique, which is by and large China-friendly. Thus China and Vietnam are likely to maintain a relatively friendly relationship until 2021. As history suggests, the delimitation of land borders and the maritime boundary in the Beibu Gulf (Gulf of Tonkin) were all achieved under friendly circumstances. In this sense, Vietnam and China stand a good chance of coming to some common understanding over the South China Sea issue under the current Vietnamese government.

Likewise, there is a window of opportunity with the Philippines. The South China Sea policy adopted by former Philippine President Benigno Aquino III drove China-Philippines relationship to a nadir, and directly caused the "globalization" of the SCS disputes. After Duterte's inauguration in 2016, the Philippines' revised SCS policy has made great improvements to the China-Philippines relationship. At present, the prospects for China-Philippines ties are no less optimistic than they were during the Arroyo period, and the impact of SCS issue is kept to a minimum. Until the next presidential election, due in 2022, Duterte is very likely to continue this friendly approach, and limit the impact of SCS issue on bilateral relations.

As for Malaysia, since Prime Minister Najib Razak came to power in 2009, China-Malaysia relations has seen their best era in history. Najib insists on dealing with the SCS issue through a bilateral framework, and quietly resolved the recent

Luconia Breakers dispute. Compare that to the previous prime ministers who set foot on Swallow Reef to claim ownership. At the moment, Najib is most likely to continue his premiership for another four years after the next election.

Finally, there has been an obvious increase in economic cooperation between China and Brunei in recent years. When it comes to jointly developing offshore oil and gas resources, Brunei holds a positive attitude and co-signed a joint declaration with China on the subject in 2013. Given that this joint development was hugely delayed due to Malaysia's objection, a commonly understood solution to the South China Sea issue is in no doubt in Brunei's favor.

Taiwan

Taiwan's South China Sea stand mainly comes from the South China Sea Policy Guidelines established in 1993, which clearly stated that the waters within the nine-dash line are its "historic waters." Although Taiwan is very unlikely to have a seat at the negotiation table over the South China Sea issue, there is still the possibility that it could carry out cooperation with the ASEAN countries. However, given her leanings toward "Taiwan independence" it's likely that Tsai Ing-wen will be less concerned about the South China Sea issue than Ma Ying-jeou was.

Mainland China

In China, Xi Jinping might be the most powerful leader since Mao Zedong. While he is fully capable of making and implementing major foreign policies (e.g. the Belt and Road Initiative), including pursuing a resolution to the South China Sea disputes. The key lies in making the case that such foreign policy initiatives are necessary.

The Belt and Road Initiative is a top-level blueprint for foreign relations determined by the new Chinese government under Xi. Centering on economic development, it emphasizes promoting infrastructure and manufacturing throughout the Asia-Pacific, Eurasia, and even parts of Africa. In the promotion of the BRI, China has shown the leadership and responsibility of a great power to some extent, but at the same time, it also should realize that there still are political, security, and cultural differences slowing down the process. One of those is the South China Sea issue.

As the biggest coastal country of the South China Sea, it falls to China to come up with a "win-win" plan to sort out the SCS issue and take the lead in the process. Other claimants do not have the capacity to do so. At present, China is swinging between "protecting rights first" and "keeping SCS stability first." The former focuses on China's own national interests rather than those of the other claimants; the latter focuses on controlling differences, so as to keep the impact of the South China Sea issue to a minimum and carry on cooperation in other aspects. Given that both of these ideas center on China's unilateral interests, they neither facilitate avoiding tensions nor help resolve the fundamental issue.

In addition to promoting economic cooperation with its neighboring countries, China, as a rising great power, should also take into consideration their security concerns and gain their trust in cooperation with China. Otherwise, China will see its neighboring countries turn to other partners. China must remember that the SCS dispute is the most important regional security issue for ASEAN countries.

As it stands, the SCS disputes have already gotten in the way of building the Southeast Asian hub of the Maritime Silk Road (MSR). Not only did the disputes sabotage the enthusiasm of the ASEAN claimants, but also wounded the participation of non-claimants. This is the main reason why Vietnam continuously replies that it "has to further observe" the Belt and Road Initiative before making a decision. The South China Sea issue is now like an infection in the China-ASEAN relationship; the treatment is a binding multilateral working framework.

Based on the above discussion, both the external environment and internal environment for resolving the South China Sea issue are in China's favor at the moment. Should

China miss this time window, there is a good chance that this "infection" will flare up once again at the slightest touch.

The next few years provide a window of opportunity for the claimants to work together to push forward a solution to the South China Sea issue. Rather than settling in to this seemingly peaceful but temporary situation, China should take this opportunity to initiate a new approach to the South China Sea issue so as to take the lead in the problem-solving process and fundamentally end this passive situation. The key to this new approach should be the idea of a win-win, comprehensive plan to resolve the South China Sea issue. Not only is this China's obligation as a rising great power, but it is also the solution to the security concerns of the Southeast Asian countries, as well as the key the building the Southeast Asian hub of the MSR.

TALKS BETWEEN THE PHILIPPINES AND CHINA OVER THE SOUTH CHINA SEA

U.S. Ships Operate in Formation

in the South China SeaIn July 2011, the Philippines and China have agreed not to let disputes in the South China Sea affect friendly relations.

After Philippine Foreign Affairs Secretary Albert del Rosario and Chinese Foreign Minister Yang Jiechi held talks in Beijing the two countries issued a joint statement that read: "The two sides reaffirmed their commitments to respect and abide by the Declaration on the Conduct of Parties in the South China Sea...Both ministers exchanged views on the maritime disputes and agreed not to let the maritime disputes affect the broader picture of friendship and cooperation between the two countries." Chinese Vice President Xi Jinping described the meeting as "productive".

In August 2011, Philippines President Benigno Aquino met his Chinese counterpart, Hu Jintao, during a four-day visit to Beijing.

The two leaders agreed on the need for a binding code of conduct in the sea. Aquino told Hu of his wish that the territorial dispute be settled with a "regional" solution. "President Aquino initiated (the discussion on the West Philippine Sea) and he mentioned that we have differences but these differences should not deter us from moving forward.

The President also mentioned the position of the Philippine government or the Philippine side, because this is a regional problem, it requires a regional solution," a Philippines government spokesman said. "On the side of the Chinese, they also mentioned that they continue to hold their consistent position that it should be resolved peacefully and they would encourage that the region be developed or the South China Sea be developed as a sea of friendship, peace and cooperation. So both sides were very positive in addressing the issue in the South China Sea," he added.

Philippines Energy Projects in the South China Sea

China has not objected to a big existing natural gas field off Palawan developed by a state-owned Philippine company, Shell and Chevron but has demanded that Manila stay away from potential energy wealth in the nearby Spratlys. The Department of Energy in Manila is nonetheless now taking bids for 15 new offshore exploration blocks, three of them in or near contested waters.

The Malampaya gas field is to the east of Palawan island in an area of the South China Sea not claimed by China. The $4.5 billion Malampaya project, estimated to hold 2.7 trillion cubic feet of natural gas and 65 million barrels of condensate, is operated by Shell Philippine Exploration (RDSa.L: Quote), Chevron Philippines and state-owned PNOC Exploration Corp.

In June 2011, the Philippines said it expected to award next year 15 contracts for oil and gas explorations requiring total investments of at least $7.5 billion, most of them in the Palawan and Sulu Sea areas. The Philippines claims it has the sovereign right to explore for oil and gas deposits on its own in the sea's Reed Bank section. The Philippine energy department has announced plans to auction off areas of the South China Sea for oil exploration, despite worsening territorial rows with China, which prefers bilateral talks on the disputes.

Ismael Ocampo, the department's director of energy resource development for the Philippines, told the Washington Post he'd like CNOOC to make a bid as that would mean Beijing acknowledges Philippine jurisdiction. But, with that unlikely to happen, he'd prefer a big American firm as "they have an armada of battleships" behind them.

The Filipino plan drew an angry response from China's official media, which accused the Philippines of violating a 2002 declaration between China and the Association of Southeast Asian Nations for self-restraint on the dispute. A China Daily editorial on Friday pointedly singled out the Philippines as it said the Chinese government would not allow its territory to be nibbled away. "There could well be a high price to pay for any misjudgment on the South China Sea issue by countries like the Philippines," it said.

CHINA-PHILIPPINES POLEMICS; US AND JAPANESE SUPPORT FOR MANILA

This reporting period featured repeated and widely publicized exchanges of accusations and charges between Chinese and Philippines officials over their South China Sea disputes that were reminiscent of the more protracted polemics in China's past disputes with Moscow, Washington, Taipei, Hanoi, and New Delhi. Also evident in Chinese media coverage was concern over the roles of the US and Japan in supporting the Philippines during its disputes with China.

China-Philippines Confrontation

The primary focus of attention was counter claims over the Second Thomas Shoal. Known as Ayungin in the Philippines and Ren'ai Reef in China, the shoal is 15 km long and 5 km wide and located near Reed Bank, an area claimed by both countries that is said to have important oil and natural gas deposits. On May 10, the Philippine government filed a protest with the Chinese Embassy in Manila against China's "provocative and illegal" deployment of a Chinese Navy ship and maritime surveillance ships near the shoal. About a week later, a local Philippines official told the media that a civilian boat carrying the official and 150 civilian passengers was chased by a Chinese warship as the Philippines boat passed near Second Thomas Shoal. At the end of May, the Chinese Foreign Ministry and Defence Ministry spokespersons joined the Chinese ambassador in Manila in condemning the Philippines for grounding an old warship on Second Thomas Shoal in 1999 and the continued deployment of a small contingent of marines there. The Foreign Ministry representative said that Beijing "has never tolerated Manila's illegal attempt to seize the reef and that Chinese government ships are entitled to patrol there."

The several back-and-forth exchanges between government officials in various forums over the summer even as the Philippines was able to resupply the Marines located on the abandoned ship without any obstruction from the Chinese vessels in the region.

The confrontation took another turn in late August when Philippine President Benigno Aquino cancelled a planned Sept. 3 trip to attend the annual China-ASEAN Trade and Business Expo in Nanning, China after China placed what Aquino described as "unacceptable conditions" on his attendance. China's Foreign Ministry told the media, without reference to the proposed presidential visit, that there were "difficulties" in relations and urged Manila to rectify them.

Roles of the United States and Japan

Senior Chinese officials tended to eschew mention of increased US and Japanese support for the Philippines military, for the Philippines seeking a UN tribunal's ruling on China's South China Sea claims, and for faster movement toward establishing a rules-based CoC in the South China Sea.

Chinese officials did not weigh in against strong remarks urging China to avoid intimidation and coercion in maritime disputes made by President Obama during a meeting with the

Chinese delegates to the annual US-China Strategic and Economic in July. They also demurred after similar statements that avoided direct reference to China by Secretary of Defence Hagel to the June Shangri-La Dialogue and by Secretary of State Kerry to the ASEAN Regional Forum in July.

Similarly, Chinese officials did not directly respond to Vice President Joe Biden pressing for faster movement on the South China Sea CoC during a visit to the region in July.

Nevertheless, lower level Chinese media commentary took aim at the United States and Japan for providing greater military support to the Philippines and at the US for conducting frequent ship visits and periodic military exercises with the Philippines government – steps seen as encouraging deeper security interaction with Washington and Tokyo in order to counter China. Official Chinese media responded promptly and negatively to the Philippine leaders' disclosure on July 31 that US spy planes were providing Manila with "crucial intelligence" about Chinese vessels in the South China Sea.

Chinese officials also strongly urged the US "to refrain from doing anything that could complicate matters" in the maritime disputes; the Chinese government also strongly opposed foreign efforts to expedite the process leading to a CoC in the South China Sea. The Chinese Foreign Ministry did formally condemn and protest a US Senate resolution in late July expressing concerns with Chinese actions regarding maritime disputes including those in the South China Sea.

BASIC CATEGORIES OF DISPUTES IN THE SOUTH CHINA SEA

There are three basic categories of disputes in the South China Sea, each with its own parties, rule sets, politics, and security concerns. These disputes have resulted in recurring flashes of tension and conflict for approximately forty years. Notable incidents over sovereignty include the Chinese attack on the forces of the Republic of Vietnam in the Paracel Islands in 1974, China's attack on Vietnamese forces near Fiery Cross

Reef in 1988, and China's military ouster of Philippines forces from Mischief Reef in 1995. The result of this series of incidents was the coalescence of a unified ASEAN political position in opposition to China's behaviour and, to decrease tensions with its neighbours, to China's acceptance of the 2002 ASEAN Declaration on the Conduct of Parties in the South China Sea, which included the agreement to "resolve their territorial and jurisdictional disputes by peaceful means, without resorting to the threat or use of force...." What followed was more than 15 years of relative regional calm as China pursued a policy of regional integration with its Southeast Asian neighbours with generous economic, commercial, infrastructure, and cultural programs. The United States repeatedly professed neutrality over the outcome of the sovereignty and jurisdictional disagreements as long as all parties continued to pursue peaceful means of dispute resolution.

This stability was shattered by a series of antagonistic Chinese actions. Recent flare-up in tensions in the South China Sea began when China pressured Vietnam and several oil companies over oil exploration and drilling off the Vietnamese coasts. As U.S. Deputy Assistant Secretary of State Scot Marciel testified before the Senate Foreign Relations Committee in July 2009, "Starting in the summer of 2007, China told a number of U.S. and foreign oil and gas firms to stop exploration work with Vietnamese partners in the South China Sea or face unspecified consequences in their business dealings with China." The Senate hearing was held in the wake of the March 2009 "Impeccable Incident," in which an American naval research vessel was aggressively harassed approximately 70 nautical miles off Hainan Island by Chinese 'fishermen' with the support of Chinese civilian and military vessels.

These Chinese actions resulted in a return to tensions in the region. In response to China's new strategy, U.S. Secretary of State Hilary Clinton stated at the ASEAN Regional Forum in July 2010,

The United States supports a collaborative, diplomatic process by all claimants for resolving the various territorial disputes without coercion. We encourage the parties to reach agreement on a full code of conduct. The United States, like every nation, has a national interest in freedom of navigation, open access to Asia's maritime commons and respect for international law in the South China Sea."

Until this time, the only common attribute of all South China Sea disputes was that they involved China as a party. However, China's turn in 2009 toward an assertive, even aggressive approach—especially in its efforts to control American naval activities in the South China Sea—resulted in new American attention to and interest in all three categories of disputes. In order to find a pathway to return to the desired state of regional stability, it is helpful to examine the attributes of each type of dispute.

Sovereignty. Disputes over sovereignty involve the question of which coastal state has the right to exercise sovereignty over the physical territory of the islands in the South China Sea. It involves China, Vietnam, Malaysia, the Philippines, Taiwan and perhaps Brunei. In 1992, China established its Law on the Territorial Sea and Contiguous Zone, which specifically claims sovereignty over each of the island groups in the South China Sea—the Pratas Islands (Dongsha), Paracel Islands (Xisha), Macclesfield Bank (Zhongsha), and the Spratly Islands (Nansha). In 1947 the government of the Republic of China began to publish maps with a U-shaped series of lines in the South China Sea to delineate its maritime boundaries.

The Chinese government repeated this cartographic feature after the Communist party came to power on the mainland in 1949 and today remains depicted on maps published in China or Taiwan. However, the nature of China's claim over the expanse of water and the numerous islands, shoals, rocks and islets contained within the nine dashes of the U-shaped line has never been specified. Among Chinese scholars and officials, there appear to be four dominant schools of thought as to the line's meaning, but the Chinese government maintains a studied policy of ambiguity about the meaning of the nine-dashed line

Sovereign Waters. Some Chinese policy analysts maintain that the waters within the U-shaped line should be considered sovereign Chinese waters, subject to the full measure of the government's authority, presumably as either internal waters or territorial seas. One group of senior Chinese defence analysts, for instance, describes Chinese offshore interests as "the area extending out from the Chinese mainland coastline between 200 nautical miles (to the east) and 1600 nautical miles (to the south)" or roughly to the 4 degrees northern latitude claimed in the 1935 report. They consider these "sea domains under Chinese jurisdiction ... [as] the overlaying area of China's national sovereignty."

Historic Waters. Some Chinese have suggested that the concept of 'historic waters' enables the government to legitimately claim broad control over the South China Sea. The concept is a variation on China's claim of sovereignty in the South China Sea and reflects the perspective held by many Chinese academics and policy-makers that the nine-dashed line represents a claim to historic waters, historic 'title,' or at least some kind of exclusive historic rights to administer the waters and territory within the line's boundaries. Perhaps the most authoritative statement of international law on the point was issued in 1951 by the International Couth of Justice in the *Fisheries Case,* in which the United Kingdom challenged before the International Court of Justice Norway's claim to sovereignty over waters along its craggy coast line beyond the traditional three-mile territorial sea limit at the time.

The Court considered three relevant factors: 1) the close geographical dependence of the territorial sea upon the land domain—the relevant portions of the Norwegian coastline are deeply indented with complex geographic features and an estimated 120,000 minor islands, islets, rocks and shoals; 2) sufficiently close links between the land formations and the sea space to make the region susceptible to a fully-sovereign regime of governance; and 3) unique economic interests belonging to the coastal state based on clear evidence of long usage. Based on its assessment of these factors, the court approved Norway's extension of sovereignty over the sea areas and the features contained within them based on its historic claims. The requirements laid out in the Fisheries Case for an extension of sovereignty over water space by a coastal state do not lend support to China's claim.

In particular, there is no close geographical dependence between the sea and the land in this region. Indeed, the land features are so insignificant that they have long been seen more as navigational hazards than as productive territory. Additionally, the islets themselves are relatively widely dispersed in comparison with the features along the Norwegian coastline. As such, the lack of sustainable land available to support an indigenous population and the sporadic presence of fishermen and traders strongly suggests that the region is not susceptible to a fully sovereign regime of governance.

Accordingly, China's claim of historic waters has weak support on these bases. Concerning the question of unique economic interests, China has had well-documented contacts with the islands of the South China Sea for many centuries by fishermen, traders and the occasional government official, but the historical record also reflects that Vietnam has had similar well-documented contacts with the islands and neither country has a record of sustained, exclusive use and reliance upon the resources of the South China Sea.

The people of the Philippines, Malaysia and Indonesia also maintained contacts with these islands in support of traditional fishing activities and in support of local trade. Thus, there is no evidence supporting any unique economic interests of China, or any single country, in and around the islands of the South China Sea.

Rather the evidence suggests the contrary—that the waters of the South China Sea and the sparse islands, islets, rocks, and reefs among them have for many centuries been the common fishing grounds and trading routes of all regional peoples. Indeed, this long-standing common usage suggests that rather than having been supervised as a zone of sovereignty, the South China Sea developed as a sort of commonly held regional zone in which all parties pursued their interests without fear of molestation by the authorities of other coastal states.

Island Claims the waters of the South China Sea

Some Chinese academics and policy-makers view the U-shaped line as asserting a claim of sovereignty over all the islands, rocks, sand bars, coral heads and other land features that pierce the waters of the South China Sea, and to whatever jurisdiction international law of the sea allows coastal states to claim based on sovereignty over these small bits of land.

On their face at least, China's claim to sovereignty over the islands and jurisdiction that is lawfully derived from it are legitimate in that the claims comply with the general provisions of UNCLOS and other aspects of law of the sea.

However, a series of fundamental problems undermine China's claims, including the fact that Vietnam, Malaysia, the Philippines, and Taiwan all maintain claims to sovereignty over some or all of the islands in the South China Sea. Since the 1995 Mischief Reef Incident between China and the Philippines there has been a static situation in which each of the claimants occupies some of the features.

China, of course, occupies and administers all of the Paracels, though Vietnam still maintains its claim to sovereignty over them. The Spratlys present a mixed case. Since 1996, Vietnam has occupied or controlled approximately 22 features, China 10 features, the Philippines 8 features, Malaysia 4 features, and Taiwan 1 feature.

In order to support a claim of sovereignty over an island, international law requires that a coastal state must demonstrate effective occupation or continuous administration and control. On this basis, China's claim to those of the Spratly Islands that it does not occupy or effectively administer and control is unsupported by international law. The same is true of the claims of any other parties that do not actually occupy a feature over which they claim sovereignty. Some observers wrongly conclude that the non-Chinese claims are based solely on European claims from the colonial era. In fact, the claims of

Southeast Asian states are at least in part an expression of the contacts all coastal peoples had with the South China Sea's islands and waters for many centuries and the national consciousness that international law should protect those interests.

Security Interests in South China Sea

Finally, a fourth Chinese perspective is that the U-shaped line reflects China's longstanding maritime security interests in the South China Sea and that these security interests should have legal protection.

The Chinese have long viewed the Bohai Gulf, the Yellow Sea, the East China Sea, and the South China Sea—the so-called 'near seas'—as regions of core geostrategic interest and part of a great defensive perimeter established on land and at sea to protect China's major population and economic centres along the coasts.

As one PLA Major General recently put it, the South China Sea comprises part of China's maritime "strategic stability belt." China's assertiveness about its claims in the waters of its 'near seas' has grown in tandem with the size of its navy and maritime services, and from these forces.

As one Chinese analyst put it, "The Navy is just one of the means of protecting our maritime rights and interests ... the primary means should be to rely on the law, on international law and internal legislation." To enforce these laws and our sovereign interests at sea, "in recent years we have started to carry out periodic patrols to safeguard our rights in the East and South China Seas."

Thus, some Chinese see international law in conjunction with their developing maritime power as a means to establish the long-desired maritime security buffer throughout the 'near seas,' including the South China Sea. That international law does not provide protection for a coastal state's security interests beyond the narrow territorial sea has not deterred Chinese proponents from seeking to change those norms.

Jurisdiction. A second category of disputes involves the delimitation of jurisdictional boundaries between neighbouring sea zones, including exclusive economic zones (EEZ) and continental shelves. China complicates these disputes through its ambiguous claims of authority over the water space within a nine-dashed line, but it is clear that the claim encompasses aspects of jurisdiction as well as aspects of sovereignty. Jurisdiction under international law is something less than full sovereignty in that it does not include the same degree of absolute and exclusive authority to govern all matters of interest to the state. Like sovereignty, jurisdiction is a reflection of *state power* within *specified boundaries*, but the concept of jurisdiction connotes the application of state authority only over *a limited, specified set of subject matters.* All of the disputants involved in the question of sovereignty are also involved in the jurisdictional disputes, plus Indonesia, which has an EEZ claim extending from Natuna Island that overlaps with China's nine-dashed line.

The two main sources of jurisdictional disputes in the South China Sea are the boundaries of the various national EEZ and continental shelf zones over which each state may exercise its authority. Within the geographic limits outlined in Article 76 (specified boundaries), coastal states are afforded exclusive authority (state power) to regulate the exploration and exploitation of the resources of the seabed, although the legal character of the water space above the continental shelf remains unchanged (a limited, specified set of subject matters). Thus, international law provides for limited coastal state jurisdiction within a specified zone known as the continental shelf.

Similarly, one of the key innovations of UNCLOS was that it specified coastal state authority in the water space beyond the territorial sea, a concept that had been steadily developing over the course of the 20th century. UNCLOS Part V established coastal state jurisdiction over a vast littoral swath of water space known as the EEZ, which may extend to 200 nautical miles from the coastal state's baselines (specified boundaries), in which the coastal state has "sovereign rights" to the resources plus related jurisdictional authorities (exclusive state power), for the purpose of managing those resources and (a limited, specified set of subject matters). Thus, UNCLOS completed the creation of jurisdictional regimes over resources in littoral waters. Accordingly, this second category of disputes is at its core disagreement over jurisdictional authority in the South China Sea to explore and exploit the resources on and under the Sea's continental shelf and in its water column.

China's Ambiguous Jurisdictional Claims

All states with a coastline that borders the South China Sea claim a continental shelf and an EEZ, however very little actual delimitation of the boundaries between coastal state zones has occurred. China's nine-dashed line claim in particular presents a major problem for resolving these disputes because in addition to relying on the line as a source of sovereignty, Chinese policymakers also refer to it as the basis for China's South China Sea jurisdictional claims.

Some Chinese scholars and policymakers assert that the concept of historic rights (as an alternative to, or in addition to, China's claim to historic waters in the South China Sea) applies as a basis for Chinese jurisdictional control over water space within the nine-dashed line. The concept of historic waters has only the briefest mention in UNCLOS, but exists in customary international law related to bays. It allows coastal states to claim extended jurisdiction over water space or islands when the coastal state's claim has been open and long-standing, exclusive, and widely accepted by other states. China's claim to a historic right to jurisdiction over the waters of South China Sea is seriously undermined by similar, overlapping claims maintained by the Philippines, Vietnam, Malaysia, Brunei and Indonesia, not to mention parallel claims made separately by Taiwan.

This demonstrates that however long-standing China's claims of jurisdiction in the South China Sea might be, clearly they are not exclusive or widely accepted by other states. Nonetheless, Chinese law asserts historic rights as a basis for jurisdiction over the South China Sea. The 1998 Law of the People's Republic of China on the Exclusive Economic Zone and Continental Shelf claims an exclusive economic zone emanating from all Chinese territory, which would logically include all relevant Chinese territory as specified in the 1992 Territorial Sea Law, which, specifically includes each of the island groups in the South China Sea. Thus, in combination, these two Chinese laws assert an EEZ and therefore jurisdictional control over nearly the entire South China Sea area within the U-shaped line.

In addition to its ambiguity and lack of specificity, there are many problems with China's approach to jurisdiction in the South China Sea. For instance, only a very few of the South China Sea's islands qualify under UNCLOS for more than the mere twelve nautical mile territorial sea. Another weakness of China's claim of jurisdiction over the South China Sea based on its assertion of sovereignty over the sea's rocks and sandbars is that China has objected to similar claims made by Japan to an exclusive economic zone and continental shelf rights around Okinotorishima, a small coral feature in the Pacific Ocean about 1,050 nautical miles south of Tokyo. International law prevents a state from claiming legal rights if it objects to the same type of claims by other states. As such, neither the provisions of UNCLOS nor historic rights are especially persuasive sources of law on which China can base its claims.

Jurisdictional Claims by Other States. In stark contrast to China's, the jurisdictional claims of Vietnam and Malaysia conform much more closely to international law. Vietnam, for instance, claims an exclusive economic zone that "is adjacent to the Vietnamese territorial sea and forms with it a 200-nautical-mile zone from the baseline used to measure the breadth of Viet Nam's territorial sea."

In addition to clarity about the boundaries of its claim, Vietnam also specifies the extent of its national jurisdiction. Vietnam's jurisdictional claims track nearly word-for-word with the requirements of UNCLOS articles 57 and 56 respectively, although it should be noted that Vietnam's baselines are considered to be excessive. Malaysia's Exclusive Economic Zone Act 1984 make similarly normative EEZ and continental shelf claims.

Additionally, the Joint Submission of Malaysia and Vietnam to the Commission on the Limits of the Continental Shelf makes a reasonable claim to an extended continental shelf beyond the 200-nautical-mile EEZ in accordance with UNCLOS article 76. The submission uses each coastal state's baselines as the starting point and measures 200 nautical miles without regard to any island features. Concerning the Spratly Islands, the legal approach taken by Vietnam and Malaysia, in contrast with the various Chinese approaches, complies with UNCLOS article 121 concerning the regime of islands and with recent case law.

Specifically, the Malaysia-Vietnam approach recognizes that the various islets, reefs and shoals in the southern part of the South China Sea are too small to form the basis of a claim to an EEZ or a continental shelf (or any other form of jurisdiction other than a territorial sea) of their own right. Another important aspect of Malaysia and Vietnam's claims is that they are specific and public. They represent a choice made by each government concerning how international law should be interpreted in regard to their jurisdiction over offshore zones. They provide a basis for discussion, negotiation, and even potentially litigation by other states that may have different perspectives. They do not rely on power—military or economic—to decide the issue. In these ways, the Malaysia-Vietnam approaches provide a basis for a stable resolution to any disputes.

The government of the Philippines established archipelagic baselines for its main islands in legislation completed in 2009 and filed on deposit with the UN. This legislation also claims a separate, non-specific regime of islands for its claims among the Spratly Islands, known as Kalayaan Islands, and its claim to the Scarborough Shoals. The Philippines also maintains an EEZ claim based on a 1978 Presidential Proclamation. The Philippines EEZ extends 200 nautical miles from its baselines, which were publicly established by the 2009 legislation. Thus, with regard to its main islands, the Philippines made a specific and public claim concerning the extent of its EEZ.

Concerning its continental shelf claim, the Philippines retains on file with the UN its Presidential Proclamation of 1968, which claims a continental shelf "to where the depth of the [Philippines] superjacent waters admits of the exploitation of such resources, including living organisms belonging to sedentary species." This outdated expression of the jurisdictional limits of the Philippines continental shelf claim stems from the definition that appeared in the 1958 Continental Shelf Convention, the provisions of which were updated by UNCLOS article 76. Additionally, the Philippines made a claim to an extended continental shelf in the Philippines Sea, but not in the South China Sea. The Philippines could improve the clarity of its jurisdictional claims to a continental shelf by bringing its proclamation into alignment with UNCLOS. Additionally, the government of the Philippines should publicly state what, if any, claims to jurisdiction over maritime zones it maintains, based on its claim of sovereignty over some of the Spratly Islands and Scarborough Reef. These steps would promote stability by removing sources of ambiguity and allowing for negotiations or arbitration in concert with international law.

In sum, the jurisdictional claims of Malaysia and Vietnam are fully public and stated with specificity. The claims of the Philippines are improving in clarity, but there continues to be room for improvement in that regard. The claims of Brunei should be made more publicly accessible by placing them on deposit with the UN. The jurisdictional claims of China in the South China Sea, however, remain ambiguous and non-public and therefore contribute to regional instability and present problems for all states whose vessels navigate the sea lanes of the South China Sea.

Control.The third category of disputes relates to control over the water space itself, and is fundamentally about the correct interpretation of international law concerning the balance of coastal state and international rights and obligations in the EEZ and other coastal state waters. This dispute primarily involves only China and the United States, but many other countries around the globe have an interest and a stake in its outcome since they involve China's attempts to alter international norms concerning freedom of navigation for military purposes and to roll back the balance of coastal state and international rights in coastal zones that were negotiated in the development of the provisions of UNCLOS.

This resulted in a series of confrontations between American and Chinese government vessels in the South China Sea between 2001 and 2009 that, although tension-producing, were manageable from a political and military perspective. China ended this mutual policy of 'managed friction' however on March 8, 2009 when it confronted the USNS *Impeccable* (T-AGOS 23) with five vessels—a PLA Navy intelligence ship, a government fisheries patrol vessel, a Maritime Surveillance Service Vessel of the State Oceanographic Administration, and two small fishing trawlers Under the observation of all three Chinese government vessels, the fishing trawlers maneuvered dangerously to a within 8 meters ahead of *Impeccable* and then abruptly stopped. This forced*Impeccable* to take emergency action to avoid a collision. Additionally, the Chinese aboard the fishing trawlers used a grappling hook to try to snag the Impeccable's towed cable. These Chinese actions violated international norms related to the duty to exercise due regard in navigation of vessels at sea and also constituted unlawful interference with the sovereign vessel of another state.

The Impeccable left the scene in order to reduce immediate tensions, but returned to the exact location several days later in the company of an American warship, the USS *Chung Hoon* (DDG). Thus, the Chinese escalation from past patterns raised the dispute over navigation issues from 'managed friction' to 'near conflict,' thereby initiating renewed American strategic attention to the waters of the South China Sea and to the international norms governing freedom of navigation for military purposes in the EEZ. The creation of the exclusive economic zone in 1982 by UNCLOS as a region extending beyond the territorial sea to a maximum of 200 nautical miles from a coastal state's shores was a carefully balanced compromise between the interests of coastal states in managing and protecting ocean resources and of maritime user states in ensuring high seas freedoms of navigation and over-flight, including for military purposes.

Thus, while in the exclusive economic zone the coastal state was granted sovereign rights to the resources and jurisdiction to make laws related to those resources, to ensure the participation of maritime powers high seas freedoms of navigation were specifically preserved for all states. Nonetheless, China has persistently attempted to shift this carefully balanced compromise by making more expansive claims of legal protection for its security interests, especially in the South China Sea. For instance, one statement by a Chinese military spokesman concerning international freedoms of navigation in the South China Sea is typical. Chinese Defence Ministry Spokesman, Senior Colonel Geng Yansheng, stated "We will, in accordance with the demands of international law, respect the freedom of the *passage* of ships or aircraft from relevant countries which are in compliance with international law."

When pressed to explain the distinction between 'passage' and 'navigation', other senior Chinese officials have stated that the Chinese government has not objected to U.S. Navy vessels that pass through the Chinese EEZ en route to another destination.

However, when such vessels conduct exercises, gather intelligence or other militarily useful data, or undertake activities other than mere passage, these officials argue that the vessels are in violation of international law and Chinese domestic law. U.S. Secretary of State Hilary Clinton, however, made clear at the ASEAN regional Forum in July 2010 that in the South China Sea, the United States will not accept China's limitations on freedoms of navigation for military purposes. She stated that the U.S., like all states, has "a national interest in freedom of navigation, open access to Asia's maritime commons, and respect for international law in the South China Sea."

9

Great Powers, Grand Strategies: The Fresh Game in the South China Sea

The South China Sea, notes Bernard Cole, a former US Navy captain who also taught maritime strategy at the National War College, covers four million square kilometers, has significant energy resources, and contains trade arteries through which one-third of the world's commerce transits. Its geographic location astride the Southeast Asian littoral makes it the maritime gateway between the Indian and Pacific Oceans. China's claim of sovereignty over the entire sea and conflicting claims by other countries in the region make the South China Sea a geopolitical flashpoint and potential scene of military conflict among regional and global powers.

Cole is one of twelve contributors to *Great Powers, Grand Strategies*, a new book published by the US Naval Institute Press that offers historical, regional, and global perspectives on the significance of the South China Sea to 21st century international politics.

The other contributors are a mix of retired US naval officers, university professors, think-tank scholars, and Asia experts, including one from Japan and one from Australia.

In separate but complementary essays, Bill Hayton, Ian Forsyth and James Fanell attempt to explain the motivations and strategies behind China's aggressive moves in the South China Sea. Some contemporary Chinese officials and scholars, including President Xi, claim that China's sovereignty over the area extends back to "ancient times", while others date Chinese rule to the Ming Dynasty in the 15th century and the voyages of Admiral Zheng He. Independent historians, Hayton notes, have "demolished" those narratives. "The evidence we have," Hayton writes, suggests that the South China Sea was an ungoverned space, a realm of semi-nomadic fisherfolk, sea gypsies, and pirates, until the beginning of the twentieth century.

In the 1930s and 1940s, the Republic of China (ROC) asserted various claims over reefs and islands in the South China Sea, including the Paracels and Spratlys. The ROC occupied and garrisoned Itu Aba in the Spratlys between 1946 and 1950, then reoccupied it six years later.

After the communists gained power on the mainland in October 1949, a new narrative was invented to justify expansion—the "Century of Humiliation" from the Opium War to the communist victory in the civil war was over. China would now reclaim its rightful place as the "middle kingdom", the center of the world.

Between 1988 and 1995, China occupied seven reefs in the Spratlys, but it only began to transform the reefs into islands capable of supporting military facilities in 2013. In 2009, it had issued the now famous map—U-shaped with nine dashes—to highlight its claim to sovereignty over virtually the entire sea.

While China constructed air and naval facilities on the new islands, it also repeatedly confronted rival claimants, especially Vietnam and the Philippines, at sea, and ignored or flouted international compacts and international law.

Ian Forsyth points out that if one of China's goals was to lessen US influence in the region, its aggressive moves in the South China Sea have produced the opposite effect. Several smaller powers in the region have out of necessity turned to the US to balance growing Chinese power.

Another consequence of China's assertiveness in the South China Sea, notes Leszek Buszynski, has been increased divisions within ASEAN. The individual ASEAN nations have reacted to China's moves based on their narrow self-interest. Some, like Vietnam, the Philippines, and Malaysia, have moved closer to the US and Japan. Others, like Laos and Cambodia, have sided with China.

Sean Liedman and Tongfi Kim, respectively, examine the evolution of US strategy in the South China Sea and the Obama administration's "pivot" or "rebalance" to Asia. US grand strategy toward China since the end of World War II, Liedman writes, has shifted from "containment" to "cooperative engagement" to "competition." With respect to the South China Sea, the US has sought to protect freedom of navigation and overflight by all countries, support its alliances and security commitments with other powers in the region, promote effective regional institutions such as ASEAN, and maintain the liberal international order—and America's leading role therein—that developed in the wake of the Second World War.

Professor Kim explores the Obama administration's diplomatic, economic, and military rebalancing toward Asia, which developments in the South China Sea accelerated. He notes that the economic importance of the Asia-Pacific, however, was the driving force behind the rebalance.

For its long-term economic growth, the United States needs to be a part of Asia-Pacific politics. This requires the United States to avoid disillusioning Asia-Pacific states about its strategic engagement, including the South China Sea disputes.

Here, as elsewhere, geopolitics influences the attitudes of other Asia-Pacific states. "[C]ountries that are closer to China and on mainland Asia," he writes, "are more cautious of embracing the U.S. strategy [whereas] [m]aritime states have more incentives to support the United States . . ."

Professor Takashi Inoguchi and *The Diplomat's* Ankit Panda provide an insightful essay on Japan's approach to the South China Sea. Japan has vital economic and energy security interests in assuring freedom of navigation through the South China Sea and East China Sea, and its overall security is linked to its alliance with the United States. Those are the two lodestars of its policy. China's aggressive moves have also drawn Japan closer to the Philippines, Vietnam, and other ASEAN countries, which have to some extent set aside "historical issues ... in favor of pragmatic cooperation."

China's bold actions in the South China Sea have also drawn policy responses from larger powers with interests in the region, including India, Russia, and the European Union (EU). Gordon Chang believes that China's expansionist policies have forced India to abandon non-alignment and closely cooperate with the United States to contain China. Stephen Blank describes a paradoxical Russian policy that initially sought an independent voice on East Asian issues but has settled for accommodating China, perhaps even as a junior Eurasian partner. Peter Solomon notes that the European Union has significant economic ties to China and the Asia-Pacific region as a whole, which gives it a "vital stake in the security of the South China Sea". But it lacks the military power projection capabilities to support an independent and effective counterweight to China.

SOUTH CHINA SEA ISLANDS

The South China Sea Islands consist of over 250 islands, atolls, cays, shoals, reefs, and sandbars in the South China Sea, most of which have no indigenous people, many of which are naturally under water at high tide, some of which are permanently submerged. The features are grouped into three archipelagos (listed by area size), Macclesfield Bank and Scarborough Shoal, which collectively comprise a land surface area of about 15 km^2 at low tide:

- The Spratly Islands, disputed between the People's Republic of China, the Republic of China, and Vietnam, with Malaysia, Brunei, and the Philippines claiming part of the archipelago

- The Paracel Islands, disputed between the People's Republic of China, the Republic of China, and Vietnam
- The Pratas Islands, disputed between the People's Republic of China and the Republic of China
- The Macclesfield Bank, disputed between the People's Republic of China, the Republic of China, the Philippines, and Vietnam.
- The Scarborough Shoal, disputed between the People's Republic of China, the Philippines, and the Republic of China

There are minerals, natural gas, and oil deposits on the islands and under their nearby seafloor, also an abundance of sealife, such as fish, animals and vegetation traditionally exploited as food by all the claimant nations for thousands of years - mostly without disputes that could risk war in the 20th Century, since the WW2 settlements failed to resolve ownership of such lesser areas of land, seas and islands, - and because of the economic, military, and transportational importance - their control, especially that of the Spratlys, has been in dispute between China and several Southeast Asian countries such as Vietnam from the mid-20th century onwards. True occupation and control are shared between the claimants.

History

The countries with the most extensive activity in the South China Sea Islands are China and Vietnam. In the 19th century, as a part of the occupation of Indochina, France claimed control of the Spratlys until the 1930s, exchanging a few with the British. During World War II, the Islands were annexed by Japan.

The People's Republic of China founded in 1949 claimed the islands as part of the province of Canton (Guangdong), and later of theHainan special administrative region.

Claims and Control

The Republic of China (ROC) named 132 of the South China Sea Islands in 1932 and 1935. In 1933, ROC government logged official protest to the French government after its occupation of Taiping Island. After World War II, ROC government occupied the islands earlier controlled by the Japanese. In 1947, the Ministry of Interior renamed 149 of the islands. Later in November, the Secretary Department of Guangdong Government was authorized to publish the Map of the South China Sea Islands.

The Japanese and the French renounced their claims as soon as their respective occupations/colonizations ended.

In 1958, the People's Republic of China (PRC) issued a declaration defining its territorial waters within what is known as the nine-dotted line which encompassed the Spratly Islands. North Vietnam's prime minister, sent a diplomatic note to Zhou Enlai, stating that "The Government of the Democratic Republic of Vietnam respects this decision." The diplomatic note was written on September 14 and was publicized on Nhan Dan newspaper (Vietnam) on September 22, 1958. Regarding this letter, there have been many arguments on its true meaning and the reason why Phim Van Đong decided to send it to Zhou Enlai. In an interview with BBC, Dr. Balazs Szalontai provided a detailed analysis of this issue:

The general context of the Chinese declaration was the United Nations Conference on the Law of the Sea, held in 1956, and the resulting treaties signed in 1958, such as the Convention on the Territorial Sea and Contiguous Zone. Understandably, the PRC government, though not being a member of the U.N., also wanted to have a say in how these issues were dealt with. Hence the Chinese declaration of September 1958. In these years, as I said before, North Vietnam could hardly afford to alienate China. The Soviet Union did not give any substantial support to Vietnamese reunification, and neither South Vietnamese leader Ngo Dinh Diem nor the U.S. government showed readiness to give consent to the holding of all-Vietnamese elections as stipulated by the Geneva Agreements. On the contrary, Diem did his best to suppress the Communist movement in the South. This is why Pham Van Dong felt it necessary to take sides with China, whose tough attitude toward the Àsian policies of the U.S. offered some hope. And yet he seems to have been cautious enough to make a statement that supported only the principle that China was entitled for 12-mile territorial seas along its territory but evaded the issue of defining this territory.

While the preceding Chinese statement was very specific, enumerating all the islands (including the Paracels and the Spratlys) for which the PRC laid claim, the DRV statement did not say a word about the concrete territories to which this rule was applicable. Still, it is true that in this bilateral territorial dispute between Chinese and Vietnamese interests, the DRV standpoint, more in a diplomatic than a legal sense, was incomparably closer to that of China than to that of South Vietnam.

It was also argued that, Pham Van Dong who represented North Vietnam at that time has no legal right to comment on a territorial part which belonged to the South Vietnam represented by Ngo Dinh Diem. Therefore, the letter has no legal value and is considered as a diplomatic document to show the support of the government of North Vietnam to the PRC at that time. In 1959, the islands were put under at the administrative level of banshichu *in 1959. In 1988, the* banshichu *were switched to the administration of the newly founded Hainan Province. The PRC strongly asserted its claims to the islands, but in the late 1990s, under the new security concept, the PRC put its claims less strongly. According to the Kyodo News, in March 2010 PRC officials told US officials that they consider the South China Sea a "core interest" on par with Taiwan, Tibet and Xinjiang In July 2010 the Communist Party-controlled Global Times stated that "China will never waive its right to protect its core interest with military means" and a Ministry of Defence spokesman said that "China has indisputable sovereignty of the South Sea and China has sufficient historical and legal backing" to underpin its claims.*

On the other hand, Vietnam claims that all the Spratly Islands belong to a district, first in 1973, of the Phuoc Tuy Province, then, of the Khanh Hoa Province.

Currently, Vietnam occupies twenty-nine islands or rocks, while the People's Republic of China occupies eight or nine.

In addition to the People's Republic of China and Vietnam, the Republic of China (Taiwan), Malaysia, Brunei, and the Philippines also claim and occupy some islands.

Taiwan claims all the Spratly Islands, but only occupies one island and one shelf including Taiping Island. Malaysia occupies three islands on its continental shelf. The Philippines claims most of the Spratlys and calls it the Kalayaan Group of Islands, and they form a distinct municipality in the province of Palawan.

The Philippines, however, only occupies eight islands. Brunei claims a relatively small area including islands on Louisa Reef. Indonesia's claims are not on any island, but on maritime rights.

Geography

The islands are located on a shallow continental shelf with an average depth of 200 metres. However, in the Spratlys, the sea floor drastically changes its depth, and near the Philippines, the Palawan Trough is more than 5,000 metres deep. Also, there are some parts that are so shallow that navigation becomes difficult, and prone to accidents.

The sea floor contains Paleozoic and Mesozoic granite and metamorphic rocks. Theabysses are caused by the formation of the Himalayas in the Cenozoic. Except one volcano-island, the islands are made of coral reefs of varying ages and formations.

Life

There are no known native animals, except boobies and seagulls, who are very common residents on the islands. Their faeces can build up to a layer from 10 mm to 1 m annually.

There are around 100–200 plant species on the Islands altogether. For example, the Paracels have 166 species, but later the Chinese and the Vietnamese introduced 47 more species, including peanut, sweet potato, and various vegetables.

RISK OF CONFLICT AND SOUTH CHINA SEA DISPUTES

The South China Sea has been the focus of several conflicting maritime claims by the littoral countries. The most prominent of these has concerned the Spratly Islands in the southern reaches of the South China Sea.

It is one of the most complicated territorial disputes in Asia, involving approximately 100 small islands, reefs, submerged banks, and rocks that total only a few square kilometres in an ocean area of several hundred thousand square kilometres. Five countries (China, Malaysia, the Philippines, Taiwan, and Vietnam) have standing claims to various portions of the South China Sea. These countries have occupied some of the Spratly locations with military outposts or civilian facilities over the past six decades. (Brunei is another claimant even though it does not physically occupy any of the disputed locations.)

Other potential South China Sea flashpoints include the Paracel Islands, which are occupied by China and also claimed by Vietnam. In addition, Scarborough Shoal, a desolate rock formation located north of the Spratlys in the Philippines' exclusive economic zone (EEZ), was the scene of a non-violent maritime showdown between China and the Philippines in April 2012. More recently, Manila declared that it has aerial images of concrete blocks on the shoal that indicate China is laying the foundations for building a facility.

Multiple factors drive the competing countries to aggressively defend their interests in the South China Sea. The sovereignty issue alone (i.e. states claiming ownership of various parts of the waters and island territories therein) accounts for the willingness to press their claims to the point of crisis and even armed clashes on occasion. Growing nationalism only complicates the situation by limiting diplomatic flexibility when these disputes periodically flare up. Security interests and regional competition for natural resources (fishing grounds and potential hydrocarbon resources) are also important complicating factors. Both fishing vessels and energy exploration ships have become pawns as the competing countries jockey for advantage to support their competing interests. Finally, the scramble for limited maritime resources is exacerbated by how some claimant countries choose to interpret the United Nations Convention on the Law of the Sea (UNCLOS). Most claimants use their continuous occupation of key locations among the Spratly Islands to support their national claims for an EEZ covering large portions of the South China Sea, although China relies on expansive claims concerning much of the South China Sea based on historical sovereignty considerations.

The competition among the claimant countries for sovereign control of the Spratlys appears to present less risk than a corresponding dispute between China and Japan in the East China Sea centered on the Diaoyu/Senkaku Islands, which flared up again in September 2012. However, the risk of unintended armed conflict from the persistent South China Sea disputes with wider international implications should not be underestimated, particularly given the interests of the claimant countries and several outside countries with strategic interests in the South China Sea, such as freedom of navigation. The complexity of the South China Sea disputes is increased by China's greater willingness to engage in coercive diplomacy to protect its interests along with the assertive role of the Philippines and Vietnam in confronting what they regard as Chinese encroachments on their maritime interests. The unexpected escalation of the protracted sovereignty disputes between Argentina and the United Kingdom over the Falkland Islands (or Malvinas) in 1982 is a prudent reminder that persistent territorial disputes sometimes erupt into unintended armed conflict with broader implications despite general expectations.

Although these disputes largely involve a war of words, they occasionally become violent. When the disputes move beyond diplomatic protests and charges, they can involve more provocative actions, sometimes resulting in the loss of lives, exacerbating regional tensions. About four decades ago, China forcibly displaced Vietnam from the Paracel Islands, which are located north of the Spratly Islands.

In 1988, China and Vietnam fought over the Fiery Cross Reef in the Spratlys with the resulting loss of three Vietnamese ships and an estimated 70 Vietnamese sailors killed or missing. In the mid-1990s, the Chinese substantially increased their presence by building "sea bastions" manned by troops at Mischief Reef, which is located in the heart of waters claimed by the Philippines. More recently, the South China Sea rivalry has taken the traditional form of sporadic incidents at sea as the claimant countries jockey to protect their interests. Sometimes these incidents turn deadly, usually when fishing boats are seized or sunk.

Along with the continuing skirmishes among the competing claimants, such incidents suggest the potential for such confrontations to escalate into deadly incident and military conflict. The persistent risk of armed conflict arising over the Spratly Islands is all the more dangerous because of its seemingly routine nature, which serves to conceal an underlying unpredictability. These territorial disputes, which mostly involve minor incidents and diplomatic exchanges, have the potential to escalate into armed conflict. Efforts to develop a Code of Conduct for the South China Sea have generally stalled within the Association of Southeast Asian Nations (ASEAN) forums. In at least one instance, however, a legal route is being undertaken: the Philippines has initiated an international arbitration process as part of UNCLOS, challenging Chinese claims to disputed South China Sea areas.

The risk of military conflict among the competing claimants has broader security implications even for non-claimant countries, including the United States, Japan, South Korea, Indonesia, Singapore, and Australia. One reason is the sheer volume of trade shipments that use the important maritime routes. For example, a substantial amount of Japan's energy resources are shipped along sea lanes that transit the South China Sea. The United States and other countries also have strong interests in maintaining the principle of freedom of navigation and overflight through the strategically located waters. Such activities occasionally result in confrontations.

For example, an incident occurred on April 2001 when a Chinese interceptor collided with a U.S. EP-3 reconnaissance aircraft operating in the South China Sea. The Chinese fighter crashed, killing the pilot, and the damaged U.S. aircraft made an emergency landing on China's Hainan Island. The crew and aircraft were held for several days before finally being released. The unexpected incident caused a short-lived but intense diplomatic showdown between Beijing and Washington.

The competing claims to the Spratly Islands might elicit relatively little concern among most non-claimant countries. But an armed conflict in the South China Sea, whether large or small, will create significant problems for certain neighbouring countries, particularly Japan, South Korea, Singapore, and Australia. Fighting in the South China Sea could threaten critical sea lanes and disrupt maritime trade flows, including energy supplies. The United States is likely to be placed in a difficult position of wanting to support American allies and friends while avoiding irreparable damage to U.S.-Chinese political and economic relations. It is preferable to mitigate the chances of armed conflict in the South China Sea than to deal with the consequences of a crisis or conflict being driven by actions of other countries.

THE SOUTH CHINA SEA MOMENT OF TRUTH IS ALMOST HERE

The Philippines' lawfare strategy in the South China Sea disputes is inching closer to a moment of truth. In coming weeks, an arbitral tribunal, formed under the aegis of the United Nations Convention on the Law of the Sea (UNCLOS), is set to pass a final judgment on the ongoing maritime spats between China and the Philippines. For the first time, a team of impartial, top-caliber legal experts will officially weigh on the validity of China's expansive claims and growing footprint across arguably the world's most important waterway. What is at stake is preventing China from fulfilling a Seldenian Closed Sea (*Mare clausum*) in favor of preserving a Grotian Free Sea (*Mare Liberum*) at the heart of the Western Pacific.

Astonishingly, Duterte has even expressed reservations concerning the wisdom ofongoing efforts to bolster the Philippines' minimum deterrence capability. "Fighter jets are good only for ceremonial flybys. I'm not in favor of building up external defense, I will not got to war with China," Duterte recently told reporters. Though known as often mercurial, he was actually consistent with his earlier stance during the campaign trail, when he dismissed the purchase of much-needed jet fighters as a "waste of money." For the incoming president, what matters is internal security operation, especially in light of the worrying resurgence of extremist groups, tied to Islamic State, in the southern island of Mindanao.

Duterte, meanwhile, has expressed growing interest in reviving long-frayed bilateral investment relations with China, even though this may come at the expense of a compromise on sovereignty disputes in the South China Sea. During his meeting with Chinese ambassador Zhao Jian, among the first dignitaries who met the president-elect shortly after the elections, Duterte and the Chinese envoy apparently went down to business right off the bat, discussing prospects for massive Chinese infrastructure investments in the Philippines. Obviously delighted by the cordial exchanges, with large-scale Chinese investments hanging in the balance, Duterte went so far as to praise Chinese President Xi Jinping as a "great" leader.

Duterte has also expressed doubts as to the utility of the Philippines' arbitration case against China, which has boycotted the proceedings and questioned the jurisdiction of the arbitral tribunal to oversee the South China Sea disputes. Encouraged by convivial exchanges with the incoming Philippine leadership, China recently reiterated its call on thePhilippines to entirely drop the arbitration case as a sign of goodwill. After all, the verdict is expected to be released a week after Duterte officially assumes power, so technically the case could still be dropped. And as Columbia University professor Matthew C. Waxman succinctlyexplains, much is also at stake for the whole international law regime, which may explain the curious timing of the expected release of the arbitration judgment.

The Trial of the Century

"For the UNCLOS system—as a body of rules and binding dispute settlement mechanisms—prominence and credibility are at stake," Waxman explains. The arbitration body faces the risk of "being ignored, derided and marginalized by the biggest player in the region."

Last October, the arbitral tribunal (formed under Article 287, Annex VIIof UNCLOS) decided that it would indeed exercise jurisdiction on almost half of the items in the Philippines' *memorial* (official complaint), with the remaining items subject to simultaneous examination in terms of both jurisdiction and merit. In a ten-page summary, the judges argued that the Philippine-initiated arbitration case "was properly constituted" and that the "act of initiating this arbitration did not constitute an abuse of process [as asserted by China]."

The judges reiterated that "China's non-appearance in these proceedings does not deprive the Tribunal of jurisdiction," and "international law does not require a State to continue negotiations when it concludes that the possibility of a negotiated solution has been exhausted." The Tribunal, which has no mandate to decide on questions of sovereignty, decided that it can nonetheless exercise jurisdiction on determination of the nature of disputed features, particularly the Mischief, Gaven, McKennan, Hughes, Johnson, Cuarteron and Fiery Cross Reefs, as well as Scarborough Shoal.

It can also exercise jurisdiction on allegedly aggressive maneuvers by China against Philippine vessels operating close to Scarborough Shoal, as well as the ecological impact of China's reclamation activities near Scarborough and Second Thomas shoals. But key items such as the validity of China's sweeping nine-dashed-line claims anddubious doctrine of "historical rights" were left for further deliberation. Meanwhile, China continuously ignored opportunities, in accordance to Article 5,

Annex VII, to formally participate in the proceedings. Thus, the arbitration body effectively demolished China's longstanding claim that (1) UNCLOS and arbitration bodies under its aegis have no mandate to arbitrate disputes concerning the South China Sea disputes; (2) the Philippines has yet to exhaust bilateral negotiations before resorting to compulsory arbitration; and (3) China, under Article 298, has exempted itself from such arbitration procedures.

This isn't just some legal hairsplitting. There are huge strategic implications. First of all, it means that not only the Philippines, but also other claimant countries could resort to a similar lawfare strategy to pressure and extract concessions from China. In effect, the Philippines' arbitration case could create a "lawfare multiplier." So far, Indonesia, which is inching closer to dropping its neutrality status in the South China Sea disputes, and Vietnam, which has ramped up defense ties with America, have threatened to go along the same path if China continues to press its advantage in adjacent waters. Secondly, and more importantly, the arbitration verdict could provide a perfection legal justification for not only America, but also other key naval powers such as Japan, to launch sustained, multilateral Freedom of Navigation Operations in the South China Sea. Coordinated and multinational FONOPs by America and its key allies hold the promise of creating just enough pressure to force China to recalibrate its posturing in disputed areas.

Hard Choices

What is clear is that the Duterte administration will not drop the arbitration case, which is in its final phase. This is just politically impossible, given the amount of domestic and international support the Philippines' lawfare has generated.

In fact, incoming foreign affairs secretary Perfecto Yasay made it clear that the Duterte administration will "not pursue any bilateral talks [with China] at this time until we hear, or wait for, the outcome of the decision of the arbitral tribunal to come out."

Of course, there is a possibility, albeit minimal, that the Philippines will lose on all key items in its arbitration case. For instance, the arbitral body may resort to indefinite legal semantics to avoid giving an impression of openly scolding China.

It could also shun exercising jurisdiction on key items like the validity of China's nine-dashed-line claims, while partially censuring China on other more minor items.

This would surely be a disaster for the Philippines and likeminded countries, which are eager to leverage international law against China, but still leaves Duterte the option of distancing himself from the potential debacle by dismissing it as nothing but a foolhardy maneuver of his predecessor.

BOUNDARIES IN THE SOUTH CHINA SEA

Determination of national jurisdiction in the South China Sea is a difficult problem that has been exacerbated by coastal states' interest in exploiting fisheries and controlling the region's potential energy resources. In recent years, competing claims to islands and rocks in the Spratley and Paracel Island groups, questionable claims that barren rocks meet UNCLOS' standard of human habitability (thereby gaining EEZs and the continental shelf, in addition to a 12-mile territorial sea), differing legal and historical claims for land jurisdiction, and a historical record of recourse to force have all combined to leave jurisdiction over islands (and maritime zones derived from the land) uncertain.

China continues to assert its claim of jurisdiction in the heart of the South China Sea, enclosed by China's "9-dash line," while Vietnam and the Philippines claim jurisdiction over specific islands in the Spratley and Paracel groups. China refuses to address jurisdiction through formal dispute settlement processes, and has so far resisted multilateral approaches to resolve the fate of the two island groups.

While armed confrontation linked to the Spratley and Paracel island groups had diminished during a period of cooperation between China and the ASEAN states, the potential for confrontation has once again increased, in part due to China's designation of the South China Sea as a "core interest" on the same level of strategic importance as Taiwan and Tibet.

There has also been continuing economic pressure throughout the region to exploit the continental shelf's energy resources. However, a new agreement between China and Vietnam to resolve their territorial disputes in accordance with international law suggests the use of force is again off the table—at least for the time being.

Claims in the southwest region of the South China Sea involving Indonesia, Singapore, Malaysia, and Brunei have been settled peacefully, but the claim indicated by China's "9 Dash Line" remains in conflict with these otherwise resolved boundaries.

If island and maritime claims in the South China Sea are not resolved in the near future, there exist four potential long-term outcomes. First, political uncertainty may discourage all commercial development of energy resources, and competing coast guards may deter significant fishing activities. Second, limited development activities may take place under state military protection. Third, the regional states may reach an agreement on an interim joint development regime while retaining their jurisdictional claims. Fourth, disputes may spiral into armed conflict.

Similarly, the establishment of sea lanes through archipelagos could become a source of friction or conflict if they are established without due consideration of the interests of maritime nations in shipping and aviation routes or paths for undersea cables.

Coastal State Threats to Maritime Freedoms

UNCLOS is a comprehensive document in terms of the issues it addresses, but it does not spell out every detail of how it is to be implemented. States that are party to the Convention are expected to implement its provisions in good faith, including respecting the rights of other parties. This is particularly true in the EEZ, where coastal states may establish laws and regulations pertaining to exploration and exploitation of natural resources, marine scientific research, and the marine environment, while taking into account rights of other states to exercise high seas freedoms. Warships and ships on government service are exempt from the provisions related to the marine environment, but are expected to honor their intent as much as possible.

Innocent passage. The right of innocent passage through the territorial sea is long standing, with the 1982 Convention simply providing greater clarity and limiting discretion by the coastal state over passage. Innocent passage never included a requirement for prior notification in customary law (and was not added by the 1982 Convention), but a number of states in the region—among them China, India, and Pakistan—now claim that foreign

flag vessels must give prior notification before exercising this right. Bangladesh requires advance notice for vessels entering its territorial sea with cargos containing "dangerous goods and chemicals, oil, noxious liquid, harmful substances, and radioactive material." These claims are challenged periodically under the US Navy's "Freedom of Navigation" program.

Transit passage. The right of transit passage derives from pre-Convention rights to pass through straits used in international navigation, with additional navigational freedoms defined in the Convention. Some strait states have claimed that the right of transit passage is available only to parties to the Convention, and that non-parties have only the more limited right to innocent passage through international straits.

As traffic through straits has increased, the financial and regulatory burdens on states bordering the straits has risen, as have the risks of catastrophic accidents, piracy, and armed robbery at sea. The UNCLOS regime leaves strait states responsible for providing for the safety of navigation and protection against crime, but it does not provide mechanisms for covering the domestic costs of supplying this international service. These costs can be quite high for a developing state, and to date, efforts to secure funding through voluntary contributions have fallen short. In the future, some international arrangements will be needed that provide for necessary services while respecting the sovereignty of the strait states and protecting the freedom of navigation for maritime states.

Limits on activities in the EEZ. In spite of provisions of the Convention that protect high seas navigation rights in the EEZ—and specifically protect rights of government ships, including warships—some states have sought to limit military activities within their EEZ. Most notable has been China's interference with military aircraft and government-owned ships engaged in survey and observation activities beyond the territorial sea. In 2001, the mid-air collision of a Chinese fighter and a US Navy EP3 reconnaissance aircraft (with the loss of the life of the Chinese pilot) demonstrated the seriousness of this effort to expand coastal-state jurisdiction at sea. Meanwhile, India claims the right to require prior consent for foreign military activities in its EEZ. The United States has protested all of these activities as unjustified restrictions on navigation rights.

Advanced notice of cable and pipeline maintenance in the EEZ. The right to lay and maintain cables and pipelines across the seabed of the EEZ is explicitly protected in UNCLOS. Despite the fact that undersea cables constitute the communication infrastructure for the Indian Ocean and South China Sea, some countries in the region have claimed the right to demand that firms submit advance notification and obtain prior permission before conducting cable-maintenance activities in their EEZs, in spite of the requirement that such activities not be impeded by the coastal state. While advance notice can facilitate managing uses of the ocean floor, it also allows bureaucratic inefficiency to delay essential maintenance operations. Submarine-cable companies must rely on their parent governments to challenge these requirements through diplomatic channels, with UNCLOS being a major source of leverage for action.

Monitoring, Regulation, and Enforcement

Parties to UNCLOS have the right to manage resource development, marine scientific research, and environmental protection in their EEZs, as well as the duty to combat piracy on the high seas. Without the capability to monitor activities and enforce regulations at sea, coastal states lack the ability to fulfil their responsibilities to combat illegal practices, and may suffer losses and damages as a result.

Piracy. As the most heavily travelled and high-value sea routes in the world, the points of confluence of sea lanes in the Indian Ocean and South China Sea have become attractive hunting grounds for pirates.

Small-scale piracy—based on the capture of ships and cargo over the past few years near the Horn of Africa and the Strait of Malacca—has been supplanted by capture and ransom activities against lightly crewed vessels with high-value cargoes traveling from the Persian Gulf and the Suez Canal, even as piracy in the eastern Indian Ocean has declined. (As of April 23, 2012, there were 151 acts against shipping worldwide, with 51 off the coast of Somalia. Of these, there were 13 hijackings, of which 11 were off the Somalia coast, while 158 of 173 hostages worldwide were taken off Somalia.

While piracy is an international crime to which all maritime nations must respond, many states have failed to provide domestic authority or resources to act against pirates. For example, local actions against Somalia-based pirates were impeded by the lack of a capable national government to act against pirates within national waters. Given that action by foreign states within a coastal state's territorial sea is normally a violation of international law, maritime states have had to seek and obtain a UN Security Council resolution to authorize states to pursue and capture pirates within Somalia's territorial sea. Since 2008, the UN Security Council has adopted 12 resolutions dealing with piracy, armed robbery at sea, and arms trafficking in maritime spaces. The Security Council has also endorsed operations of Combined Task Force 151 and other forces combating piracy off Somalia's shores. Illegal, unreported, and unregulated fishing on the high seas. The increasing sophistication of fishing systems has allowed modern fishing vessels and fleets to enter a fishery and quickly harvest available resources before moving on to other grounds. Many poor developing states have limited resources to invest in coast guards capable of patrolling their EEZ and enforcing fishery regulations. This situation has left these countries' offshore resources vulnerable to illegal, unreported, and unregulated (IUU) fishing, with major economic losses both to the state and to local fishing industries. IUU fishing has proven even more problematic for fisheries that straddle the EEZ and the high seas, or fisheries that migrate across national boundaries.

Somalia serves as a case in point regarding the loss of a national resource due to a lack of capacity for offshore management and regulation. While it would be an exaggeration to blame the rise of Somalia-based piracy solely on the decimation of the country's offshore fisheries and the subsequent displacement of fishermen to other livelihoods, the failure to protect and utilize Somalia's once-rich offshore fisheries is a major economic loss that undermines the development of a national government capable of regulating activities in its own EEZ.

The weakness of many littoral states notwithstanding, all of the coastal countries bordering the Indian Ocean and South China Sea belong to one or more regional fishery bodies and most belong to a regional seas program. Increasingly, they may turn to inter-governmental and non-governmental organizations for assistance in developing management plans for their EEZs.

In the years ahead, heightened demand for fish for domestic consumption and international trade will increase pressure on high seas– and straddling fish stocks. If coastal states and flag states prove unable to both monitor fishing in the EEZ and enforce regulations in port and at sea, then IUU fishing will likely increase, to the detriment of coastal state fishing interests and consumers.

Protection of the Marine Environment

Ship breaking. Dismantling ships to salvage equipment and recycle metals is highly labour intensive. This is one of the primary reasons the ship-dismantling industry has moved to India and other nations with large, low-cost labour forces. Instead of dismantling vessels in a dock, ships are often simply run up on shore, where they are broken apart. Over their working life, ships accumulate significant petroleum-related residues. Dismantling ships releases these hazardous materials into coastal waters to the detriment of the environment, local populations, and marine ecosystems.

Under UNCLOS, states are responsible for enacting and enforcing laws to prevent pollution of the marine environment, but by itself, this responsibility is not enforceable at the international level. The Convention encourages the development of regional and global agreements that lay out specific rules addressing pollution from land or continental shelf activities.

Climate change and sea level rise. Rising sea levels driven by global climate change have potentially serious implications for coastal cities and infrastructure. There are also significant implications for maritime jurisdiction, since rising sea levels can move maritime baselines inward, taking with them the territorial seas and EEZs that are drawn from those baselines. More critical is the threat that rising seas pose to small island nations, where in some cases the highest points of land sit only meters above current ocean levels. Rising sea levels could eventually submerge these island states' land territory, and with it all of their claims to EEZs and continental shelves.

Migration driven by rising seas has already occurred with the submergence of Bangladesh's Bhola Island in 1995. The loss of Bhola Island, which was located inside Bangladesh's coastal baselines, had no effect on the country's maritime jurisdiction, however. Looking forward, the Maldives—where 80 percent of the country's territory has an elevation of one meter or less above sea level—may be similarly submerged. This would force the Maldivian population off the archipelago and eliminate the Maldives' EEZ, with parts of its continental shelf likely being transferred to India and the British Indian Ocean Territories.

CHINA'S CURRENT SECURITY POLICY

In response to the attacks in Africa during the last five years, China has confronted the problem of nontraditional security threats in several ways. The PRC's initial reaction is to work with local governments. "China will cooperate closely with immigration departments of African countries in tackling the problem of illegal migration, improve exchange of immigration control information, and set up an unimpeded and efficient channel for intelligence and information exchange," China's 2006 *Africa Policy* stated.

"In order to enhance the ability of both sides to address nontraditional security threats, it is necessary to increase intelligence exchange, explore more effective ways and means for closer cooperation in combating terrorism, small-arms smuggling, drug trafficking, transnational economic crimes, etc." Beijing has instructed its embassies in Africa to keep a close watch on local security. The swift and successful evacuation of Chinese citizens from Chad also demonstrated that China has developed operational scenarios to deal with these emergencies. The Chinese government has also started issuing travel advisories.

In Sudan and Kenya, state-owned companies receive protection from local armed forces against attacks by rebels. Beijing has signed an agreement with South Africa to prevent the Chinese diaspora from turning into a target for armed gangs. Such measures are designed to help Chinese citizens and companies avoid some of the risks related to operating in Africa, but they do not provide any guarantee for safeguarding China's economic activities if the situation keeps deteriorating. In the case of Sudan, China learned the hard way that prodding instable governments can have drastic consequences. If problems start to occur at the regional level, supporting these emerging states might prove even riskier.

Nor does this narrow security response address China's uncertainty about the military capability of African nations. The dilemma reverts back to the realistic supposition of self-help. Is the PRC trying to safeguard its interests by building up its own military presence in Africa?

Bilateral military exchanges are a first indicator to test whether this assumption holds true. According to the Chinese government, interaction with other armed forces expanded significantly, with 174 high-level visits in 2001 and more than 210 in 2006. This upward trend was not maintained in Africa, however, where such bilateral exchanges have remained stable at an annual average of 26. Beijing has established a permanent military dialogue only with South Africa. Interviews with European diplomats in ten randomly chosen African countries also reveal that the number of accredited military officers in Chinese embassies, i.e., military attachés and their support staff, has barely or not expanded at all in the last few years. In fact, only in 15 countries are Chinese military attachés assigned on a permanent basis. China's military diplomacy in Africa remains modest, and it has not kept up with the impressive number of Chinese trade officials posted in African nations to strengthen economic ties in the last few years. Military aid is another indicator. Providing military hardware to partner nations can serve various objectives. In a context of competition, it helps to thwart defence cooperation with other states or to prevent other powers' attempts to alter the regional military balance. Defence aid might help a privileged political partner to safeguard economic interests. Whereas these three objectives are motivated by security issues and long-term economic interests, defence aid may well be the result of more short-sighted aspirations. There is no evidence that China's military aid successfully counterbalances other powers, such as the United States.

Apart from Sudan and Zimbabwe, most countries that have received Chinese military aid in the last few years are also supplied by Washington. In 2007, Beijing temporarily froze the supply of heavy arms to Khartoum after pressure from the

West. When Nigeria's Vice President, Atiku Abubakar, announced that his nation would turn to China instead of the United States for arms, Beijing's response was reluctant, and no major supply operations materialized. China's military aid programs should not be considered as support for its forays into the mining industry. For instance, between 2004 and 2008, resource-rich Nigeria received only half as much military aid as Ghana or Uganda. During this period, China provided more military assistance to Angola than to Sudan, even though the security challenges in the latter were much greater.

Although violence in Somalia has threatened China's oil exploration activities in both Ethiopia and Kenya, China only made a commitment to Kenya to help in protecting its border. China has, at times, provided military aid, but such assistance does not seem to be part of any coherent strategy related to protecting its security interests.

Finally, self-help would imply the deployment of military forces whenever China's interests are threatened, possibly in an attempt to train friendly armed forces and dissuade any challengers. Yet, such a Chinese military presence is negligible. China has no bases in Africa, as does the United States and France, nor has it trained African soldiers to counter threats to its national interests.

In Sudan, Zimbabwe, Cameroon, and Gabon, China has employed teams of three to ten instructors, but they are assisting in the maintenance of equipment, rather than providing training for combat missions. In Zambia and Algeria, similar examples of cooperation exist but are limited to medical activities. Other major powers deployed naval vessels in an effort to combat piracy and to maintain the maritime supply lines surrounding Africa. During such operations, the Chinese Navy has rarely shown its flag.

In 2000, China sent its newest *Luhai*-class guided missile destroyer and a supply ship to Tanzania and South Africa. A 2002 fleet composed of a guided missile destroyer, the *Qingdao*, and a supply ship, the *Taicang*, visited Egypt. These voyages were gestures of courtesy rather than a reaction to security challenges. They were limited in duration, and no actions were attempted against pirates or poachers. In December 2008, however, the Chinese government did deploy two destroyers and a replenishment ship in the Gulf of Aden to participate in the United Nations-backed mission against piracy. A mission that was only undertaken after receiving a positive signal from US Pacific Command chief Admiral Timothy Keating.

Instead of dealing with security threats unilaterally, China has resorted to bandwagoning. Although in the 1980s and early 1990s, Beijing opposed attempts by the international community to intervene in African security issues, nowadays it tends to join them. Beijing is increasingly recognizing the United Nations' role in resolving the numerous conflicts and safeguarding the sovereignty of developing nations. In the 1990s, China began supporting United Nations (UN) missions designed to implement peace agreements between rivalling parties, on the condition that a well-defined and restricted mandate was included. Traditional peacekeeping operations such as those in Somalia (UNSOM I), Mozambique, Rwanda, and Sierra Leone all were supported. When the UN Security Council decided to dispatch forces to Liberia in 2003, China offered to support the mission and gradually increased the number of its peacekeepers to 1,300 in 2007. At the same time, however, failed states and national governments that had actively participated in atrocities challenged the efficacy of many of the traditional UN operations. China's focus on the primacy of sovereignty, requiring at a minimum the state's consent, collided with the willingness of other nations to intervene aggressively under the UN Charter's Chapter VII mandate.

Beijing loudly opposed the move by European countries to push for Operation Turquoise in Rwanda, Washington's call to broaden the UNSOM mandate, or France's demand for a troop increase in the 2004 UN operation in Ivory Coast. Despite its strong concerns, China did not veto these interventions at the UN Security Council, but rather abstained and remained aloof from implementation. Sudan was the first instance where China actively lobbied an African government to permit a UN mission on its soil. Via active brokering and indirect pressure, China succeeded in neutralizing the incompatibility between its economic interests and the principle of noninterference on the one hand, and western appeals for intervening in Darfur and the need for long-term stability on the other.

That Beijing recognizes the importance of collective security became apparent in 2006, when China was the first nation to ask the UN Security Council for a peacekeeping mission in Somalia. In June that year, at a Security Council meeting in Addis Ababa, China's Permanent Representative to the UN, Wang Guangya, scolded other diplomats for neglecting Somalia and urged them to support the deployment of peacekeepers. "I was reluctant to take on this role," said Wang, explaining that African governments had been pushing China to raise the issue in the Council, "but there was a lack of interest by the other major powers." Initially, the proposal was tentatively received by Great Britain and the United States, but after various talks in New York, Beijing and Washington jointly sponsored a resolution for the deployment of a UN mission. In 2007, in early consultations with France, China supported a French draft resolution on Chad calling for the dispatch of mainly European peacekeepers under the auspices of Chapter VII. It was significant that China approved the "close liaising" with the Hybrid Operation in Darfur (UNAMID), where earlier it had objected to the development of links between UNAMID and UN missions. "Our support for the resolution on Chad shows that we are prepared to cooperate to tackle security issues at a regional level and that our awareness on the increasing complexity of violent conflicts in Africa grows," a Chinese diplomat explained.

China is also turning to African regional organizations to collaborate on security issues. In the China-Africa Action Plan, approved in November 2006, Beijing vowed "to support Africa in the areas of logistics" as well as "to continue its active participation in the peacekeeping operations and demining process in Africa and provide, within the limits of its capabilities, financial and material assistance as well as relevant training to the Peace and Security Council of the African Union." In June 2006, the Chinese government granted the African Union's Mission in Sudan $3.5 million in budgetary support and humanitarian aid. Earlier, it provided financial and technical support to the Association for West African States.

Slowly but surely, China is showing itself ready to participate in international efforts to prevent conflicts, fueled by the easy availability of small arms and illegally exported natural resources. In 2002, for instance, Beijing revised its regulation on the control of military products for export and published the "Military Products Export Control List" supplying guidelines for the export of military-related products. In the same year, it signed the "Protocol Against the Illicit Manufacturing of and Trafficking in Firearms," which committed the People's Republic to control the manufacturing, marking, import, and export of firearms, and to confiscate and destroy all illicit firearms. In 2005, the government launched a national information management system for the production, possession, and trade of light arms, and it introduced a system to monitor end-users of Chinese-made weapons to prevent the arms from finding their way to "sensitive regions" around the world via third parties. In 2006, China supported a draft UN resolution on the illicit trade of small arms and light weapons, in contrast to the United States. In 2002, China joined the Kimberley Process, a joint government, international diamond industry, and civil initiative designed to stem the flow of conflict diamonds originating from Africa. In 2005, China allowed a voluntary peer review of its support for the Kimberly Process. Although these actions still have many flaws, they seem to prove that China wishes to do more than just put "boots on the ground" in response to Africa's internal conflicts.

Despite the strategic importance of Africa, China does not try to safeguard its foothold in the region by unilaterally projecting military power. In Africa, its military diplomacy remains limited when compared with defence initiatives in other regions. If the PRC does pursue bilateral cooperation programs, these are more likely to be a part of its diplomatic charm offensive, rather than addressing threats to China's economic and security interests. Instead of relying on a military presence to counterbalance other powers, the PRC tends to join collective security efforts within the framework of the United Nations and African regional organizations. Over the past few years, this strategy of joint ventures has evolved from passive support to active cooperation. Beijing has softened its devotion to noninterference. While maintaining the primacy of sovereignty, it has become willing to support interventions whenever regional stability is at stake.

Although China has become a revisionist power in terms of its economic aspirations on the continent, it is acting as a status-quo power in terms of security objectives. There are several explanations for this stance. First, China only recently began its economic focus on the African continent. For the past two decades, China concentrated on curbing the military and diplomatic influence of Taiwan; the focus on "economization" of its Africa policy only began in the late 1990s.

Hence, the security challenges it is facing now are a recent phenomena, and solutions to these challenges are just starting to be explored. The PRC is going through the early stage of resecuritization of its Africa strategy, and joining with other nations in an allied strategy can be considered the easiest immediate response. Second, and related to this point, China has not developed sufficient means to back up its security policy with military power. This is a matter of budgetary constraints. Building an independent and sustained military presence is a costly affair and would, at present, overstretch the PLA's capabilities, while Asia remains its primary focus. The PLA does not possess the logistical capacity to support sustained region wide deployment in Africa. Its long-range airlift and sealift, as well as its intelligence and command capabilities, are not up to the task. Third, the Chinese government wants to avoid the People's Republic being perceived as a hegemonic power.

In the initial stage of its economic charm offensive, the PRC tried to pursue a business-as-usual approach, maintaining a low profile and steering clear of political entanglements. That approach is no longer possible now that China stands at the forefront of Africa's political scene, actively altering the economic balance of power. Beijing is well aware of the dichotomy between its weak and strong identities and is reluctant to demonstrate any independent military capacity. Such a show of strength might reduce its diplomatic maneuverability, increase resistance from African nations-just as Washington is now experiencing-and raise suspicions elsewhere regarding Chinese intentions. Yet, as interests, perceptions, and capacities are susceptible to change, the question remains whether China will stay on this track of cooperative security.

China's interests in Africa have changed over the past decades and will undoubtedly continue to evolve. The concept for its security policy in the region will depend on the role that Africa plays as a supplier of natural resources. Africa currently supplies approximately 30 percent of China's oil imports. Beijing and its African partners announced that they are preparing to increase bilateral trade to $100 billion by the year 2010. Most of this increase will come from the import of raw commodities. In recent years, Chinese companies have laid the foundation for a substantial increase in the production of resource industries. Exploration in the Gulf of Guinea, Angola, and the Horn of Africa have the potential for an increase in oil exports to China of more than 80 percent in the next ten years. Chinese companies are just starting to tap the large mines that were recently acquired in Gabon, the Democratic Republic of Congo, Namibia, and elsewhere on the continent. Given the fact that other emerging markets such as India and Brazil are shifting the use of their raw materials from export to domestic consumption, the economic relevance of Africa to China cannot be overstated.

How necessary it is to back up these Chinese economic ventures with more overt security measures is yet to be seen. The incidents described in the first section of this article, the persistent instability in nations, as well as the weak position of amicable political leaders will undoubtedly position Africa higher on Beijing's foreign security agenda and require a more complete approach. The question again arises whether it is in China's best interest to apply its African policy independently or in synergy with other nations.

The short-term costs of any unilateral action would certainly exceed those of collective action, but long-term uncertainty about the intentions of other major players might influence any concerns related to cost-effectiveness.

If Washington or Delhi decides to change course and contain China's expanding influence in Africa by pursing a strategy of counterbalancing and sea denial, the repercussions for the People's Republic will be dramatic.

The concerns of the national security establishments in India and the United States and their expanding military presence in Africa are not unnoticed in China, and they highlight the necessity for the PRC to build a legitimate capacity to deal with crises unilaterally.

China's diplomatic identity will help shape policy decisions in support of a more active and autonomous security strategy. Beijing is realizing that the comfortable cloak of frailty it previously presented to the world no longer fits. African partners do not attach much value to China's diplomatic schizophrenia and the complex image of an economic giant, political dwarf, and minor military player it projects. When mayhem erupts, China automatically ends up on the frontline, finding itself hounded by African governments asking it to exercise its leverage.

The cases of Chad and Somalia are not the only examples of this. South Africa has accosted China regarding illegal immigrants from Zimbabwe. Central Africa has carefully examined the violent incursions from Sudan. The African Union has called upon China several times to play a more active role in promoting security. The possibility exists that individual countries may be compelled to form a closer alliance with China in order to reduce their current reliance on the European Union and United States for security. Nigeria's announcement that it would rely on China instead of the United States for military support hints at this direction. The ability of the PRC to keep a low military profile is diminishing.

On the other hand, China's self-perception is also in transition. The "Century of Humiliation" is far behind and is being replaced by a national attitude of confidence and assertiveness. Chinese leaders have built on the success of their policy of good neighbour diplomacy that resulted in fewer frictions and more influence in Asia. The People's Republic has drawn confidence from the successful launch of a number of new defence systems. As China sees its diplomatic leverage expanding geographically from the Strait of Formosa, via Asia to the rest of the developing world, its ability to deal with emerging security issues is likely to follow suit.

Finally, there is the factor of capacity. China is gearing its military for a greater deployment capability. Its large immobile army is gradually being converted into a highly specialized and flexible organization. Simultaneously, the PLA is launching new military systems that will enhance its capacity to transport these forces. In 2007, the Chinese government approved the development of large passenger jets, including military transport variants similar to the American C-17 Globemaster III. Beijing has also ordered several new ships in an effort to enhance its naval transport capacity. In 2006, the hull of the first T-071 vessel was laid. This landing-platform dock has a range that goes far beyond Taiwan, with the aim of providing sea-based support to operations on land, humanitarian aid, and assisting in evacuations and disaster management. These vessels will be supported by a new generation of large replenishment ships and could be escorted by advanced frigates and destroyers. The Chinese flotilla that was sent to Somalia demonstrates China's new blue-water capacity. The type 052C *Lanzhou*, for instance, is a showcase of the advanced detection capacity for China's Navy. Its multifunction, active phased-array radar has a detection range of 450 kilometers and is complemented with a long-range, two-dimensional air search radar that has a 350-kilometer range and three additional systems to detect incoming missiles and aircraft. China is advancing its ability to pursue a more confident and independent security policy in Africa.

Will all this newfound military activity be sufficient to offset the antagonistic response it is likely to provoke? Probably not. If China decides to go solo and to pursue a more aggressive security policy in Africa, it is improbable that it will be able to overcome countermoves by India and the United States. It will be difficult for China to safeguard maritime trade with Africa if India exercises its naval dominance in the Indian Ocean. The sheer geographical divide between the PRC and the African continent makes it extremely difficult to support military activities if the United States or India opposes them. Contrary to China's revolutionary phase of the 1950s and 1960s when trade and economic interests only played a small part, China's increasing reliance on Africa renders it highly vulnerable to sea denial operations or a *guerre de course*. The fragile Cold War balance between the United States and the Soviet Union that allowed Mao to meddle with America's interests in Africa without having to fear political or economic reprisals can no longer be counted on. These days China has much to lose if it provokes Washington or Delhi.

PEACEFUL DISPUTE RESOLUTION IDEAS

The International Forum on Marine Peace and Sustainability hosted by the Democratic Pacific Union, National Taiwan Ocean University and several other organizations was held in Keelung on Oct. 20 and Oct. 21. Twelve papers by experts from Taiwan, Japan, China, the US, Australia, France and Indonesia were presented at the forum, which was also well attended by members of Taiwan's diplomatic community. The two-day conference covered many important and timely topics, and the participants analysed and debated the issues and solutions from theoretical, historical, legal, economic and strategic perspectives.

In A Comprehensive Mapping of Conflicts in the South and East China Seas: Implications for Conflict Resolution and Regional Stability, Dennis Sandole of George Mason University provided a theoretical overview of the conflicts and the approaches to conflict resolution.

In Maritime-Dispute Resolution: Examples of Success and Failure by Australian David Falvey and Cases of International Settlement on Disputed Islands by Wong Ming-hsien of Tamkang University, the speakers used cases of maritime dispute resolution as examples of both success and failure to explain requisite factors and conditions essential for successful and peaceful settlement.

Why are China and Japan sliding toward armed conflict over the Diaoyutai Islands — known as the Senkakus in Japan — five small, uninhabited islands, which are also claimed by Taiwan?

Ironically, Chiang Kai-shek turned down then-US president Franklin Roosevelt's offer at the 1943 Cairo Conference to return the islands to China's control after the end of World War II.

When Japan proposed to amicably settle the dispute with Beijing in 1972 and 1978, on both occasions then-Chinese leaders Zhou Enlai and Deng Xiaoping said that they preferred to put the dispute aside and let the leaders of future generations deal with the matter.

However, history does not remain stationary. China's perspective changed in the wake of the discovery of gas and oil, and the strategic importance of the islands has also been transformed along with China's rise in economic and military power, as Beijing pursues maritime expansion and acquires new geo-strategic interests.

Japan's domestic political dynamics are intertwined with its dispute with China. In September last year, the Japanese government nationalized three of the Diaoyutais in an effort to mitigate Chinaese anger and protests over then-Tokyo governor Shintaro Ishihara's ploy to buy them.

The move backfired and provoked violent protests throughout China, which heightened tensions between the two countries. Since then, Chinese coast guard vessels have sailed into the waters around the Diaoyutais dozens of times and Chinese military planes have flown toward the islands almost daily to challenge Japan's claim of sovereignty.

The escalation of the Sino-Japanese dispute risks involving the US, Japan's key ally. Washington says that the US is neutral on the issue of sovereignty, but in reality it sides with Japan. On many occasions, US officials have emphasized that the US-Japan Defence Treaty covers the islands. Furthermore, several joint US-Japan maritime exercises in Guam and the waters around Okinawa demonstrate the determination of the allies to stop China from changing the "status quo" in the East China Sea.

Not surprisingly, Japanese Prime Minister Shinzo Abe says that the Senkakus are Japan's sovereign territory and it cannot tolerate any challenge now or in the future.

In his paper Senkaku Island Issues and Japan-China Relationship, Sadaharu Kataoka of Waseda University in Japan predicted that "a speedy resolution of the long-standing dispute" over the islands is unlikely.

Lee Chao-shing from National Taiwan Ocean University stated in his paper Is it Possible to Solve the Disputes in the Diaoyutai/Senkaku Peacefully? that Taiwan has the best claim to the islands, with the most geological, geographical, historical and cultural evidence in support. However, the nation has recently become pragmatic in dealing with Japan over the Diaoyutais. Former vice president Annette Lu, founder of Democratic Pacific Union, said in her opening speech at the forum that Taiwan decided to put aside the matter of sovereignty and on April 10 signed a fisheries agreement with Japan. This is a new tack; it protects and enhances the rights of Taiwanese fishermen operating within a designated zone and extends their fishing area by 4,350km^2.

In the spirit of problem-solving and peace, Lu also cited the 1959 Antarctic Treaty and called for demilitarization and the creation of marine preservation zones in the region. Beijing is not pleased with the Taiwan-Japanese modus vivendi, nor does it welcome Lu's proposal, as China has for years urged President Ma Ying-jeou to join it in opposing Japan. Ma was compelled to say no to Beijing and emboldened to support the interests of Taiwanese fishermen, apparently due to US intervention.

It stands to reason that Beijing strongly dislikes the US meddling in its disputes with Japan and Southeast Asian states. Beijing sees the US as an outsider and a nonparty to these regional disputes, and has sought to exclude the US from participating in the conflict resolution process, but in vain. The US insists that freedom of navigation and overflight in the Asia-Pacific is vital to its national interests, and that China and its neighbours should resolve their territorial and maritime disputes peacefully without resorting to force or coercion.

US President Barack Obama's last-minute cancelation of his trips to the APEC meeting in Indonesia and the East Asia summit in Brunei last month may have undermined the credibility of the US "pivot to Asia" to some extent. However, it is doubtful that Chinese leaders made much progress in winning the trust and goodwill of ASEAN leaders in Obama's absence.

Chinese Premier Li Keqiang was uncompromising on Beijing's extensive territorial claims in the South China Sea as he reiterated in Bali the "indisputable rights" of China within the nine-dash line. Moreover, Li was audacious in warning countries not directly involved, including the US, Japan, Australia and India, to stay out of the disputes.

Most ASEAN members welcome the presence of external players, especially the US' rebalancing, to offset China's hegemony and to protect their own interests. Could and would ASEAN play a more active and stronger role to shape regional norms and help resolve the disputes in the South China Sea?

Hasjim Djalal, from Indonesia, made an interesting proposal in his paper The South China Sea in Legal Perspective. He suggested that the six ASEAN non-claimants to sovereignty in the South China Sea, including Indonesia and Singapore, act as "facilitators" to invite the four ASEAN claimants, including

Philippines and Vietnam, to sit down and negotiate the matter with the two non-ASEAN claimants; Taiwan and China. Djalal called on the ASEAN chairman to take the initiative to put the "6+4+2 formula" into action.

For some reason, some ASEAN states question if Taiwan is a legitimate South China Sea participant to the regional dialogue process. Taiwan possesses and controls Itu Aba Island, the largest of the Spratly Islands. Moreover, during 2006 and 2007, the Democratic Progressive Party government took several measures, including the extension of Taiping Island's airport runway, to strengthen its garrison and bolster its claim of sovereignty.

Can Taiwan play a more active role in the South China Sea and participate more effectively in the regional dialogue process? In The South China Sea Dispute: Taiwan's Response and Challenge it Faces, Song Yann-huei of Academia Sinica attributed the nation's problems in the South China Sea to the Ma government's adherence to the "one China" principle and making almost identical absurd territorial claims as China has done.

For Taiwan to be a serious player and participate meaningfully in the regional dialogue, it must redefine its identity and its national interests in the South China Sea and toward ASEAN.

Taiwan should not allow China to pre-empt its participation in East and Southeast Asia issues. The two are separate international actors and their national interests are not identical. Taiwan's territorial claim in the South China Sea should be based on facts and international law, and not on history alone. As a member of the community of democracies, Taiwan should work with other democratic nations to achieve a peaceful solution to the disputes in the East and South China seas.

10

Dispute and Objectives of the South China Sea

There are three severable categories of disputes, each with its own parties, rule sets, and politics. Unfortunately, the region's states are currently pursuing win-lose solutions to these three disputes based on competing claims of exclusive sovereignty and jurisdiction. A careful analysis of the nature of each dispute reveals opportunities for more productive pathways to dispute resolution based on a return to Asia's history of win-win problem solving based on mutual interests.

The recent heightening of the competition between China and its neighbours over sovereignty, resources, and security in the South China Sea has drawn the attention of U.S. diplomatic and military leaders who seek to promote stability and security in these globally important waters. As American leaders discuss policies and strategies in support of regional stability, some have described the complex disputes in the South China Sea as essentially a single tangled knot of intractable challenges. In fact there are three severable categories of disputes, each with its own parties, rule sets, and politics. Unfortunately, the region's states are currently pursuing win-lose solutions to these three disputes based on competing claims of exclusive sovereignty and jurisdiction. A careful analysis of the nature of each dispute reveals opportunities for more productive pathways to dispute resolution based on a return to Asia's history of win-win problem solving based on mutual interests.

THE DISPUTE AFFECT TRADE ROUTES IN THE SEA

As much as 50 percent of global oil tanker shipments (GlobalSecurity) pass through the South China Sea, which sees three times more tanker traffic than the Suez Canal and over five times that of the Panama Canal, making the waters one of the world's busiest international sea lanes.

More than half of the world's top ten shipping ports are also located in and around the South China Sea, according to the International Association of Ports and Harbors.

As intra-ASEAN trade has markedly increased—from 29 percent of total ASEAN trade in 1980 to 41 percent in 2009—maintaining freedom of navigation has become of paramount importance for the region.

"This is a very important issue, and has become the main concern of Japan, the United States and even right now the European Union," said Dr. Yann-Huei Song, a fellow at Academia Sinica in Taiwan. However, Yann-Huei says China is unlikely to instigate an interruption in traffic because its business, exploration, and importation rely entirely on freedom of navigation as well. Experts argue that the mutual benefits from regional economic integration provide an extremely compelling incentive for cooperation on resources, conservation, and security movements, according to a Harvard Quarterly paper.

What are the Military Stakes?

*The region has also seen increased militarization in response to China's burgeoning power, raising the stakes of a potential armed conflict and making disputes more difficult to resolve. Vietnam and Malaysia have led regional military buildups and increased arms trade with countries like Russia and India, while the Philippines doubled its defence budget in 2011 and pledged five-year joint military exercises (*TheDiplomat*) with the United States. The Philippines also embarked on a modernization program costing roughly $1 billion that will rely heavily on U.S. sales of cutters and potentially fighter jets.*

"Behind it all, it's essentially the industrial revolution of Asia. And the South China Sea has become the hub of that." — David Rosenberg, professor of political science at Middlebury College

Ships are commonly involved in naval disputes, as exhibited in the Scarborough Shoal incident in April when the Philippines said its largest warship—acquired from the United States—had a standoff (Guardian)*with Chinese surveillance vessels after the ship attempted to arrest Chinese fishermen but was blocked by the surveillance craft. The involvement of the navy made political compromise more difficult, says the ICG.*

"There's nothing like NATO in Asia, and that's what's worrisome," Rosenberg said. "Unlike the U.S. and EU, which are engaged in other regions of the world, the Southeast Asian countries are compelled to spend more protecting their most immediate interests. It's not the Cold War by any means, but they're still not very open with each other about military modernization."

What is Being done to Resolve the Disputes?

One of the largest impasses to a resolution is China's insistence on conducting most of itsdiplomacy on a bilateral basis, writes CFR's Stewart Patrick. Nationalism has also fueled many of these stalemates. International tribunals, like the International Tribunal for the Law of the Sea, are available, but nations use it selectively in light of the potential domesticpolitical ramifications of appearing conciliatory. China also has repeatedly rejected the mechanisms (GlobalNation) *for arbitration provided by the UN.*

A July 2012 ASEAN summit attempted to address ways to mitigate the conflict but ended without producing any communiqué (CNA), which some experts say highlights the difficulties the region of multilateral approaches. ASEAN's six-point statement in Julymade no reference to specific incidents, and only outlined an agreement (Reuters) to draft and implement a regional code of conduct, respect international law, and exercise self-restraint. CFR's Josh Kurlantzick said in August 2012 that while ASEAN was an appropriate venue to mediate this dispute, the organization still has not yet found its footing in transitioning to a "more forceful, integrated organization that can provide leadership." In a November 2012 IIGG working paper, Kurlantzick looks at how ASEAN can strengthen its role in the region to meet challenges such as the South China Sea.

Consequently, joint management of resources has been widely proposed by experts as the best way to ease current tensions, according to the ICG. China and Vietnam have managed to cooperate on a common fishery zone in the Tonkin Gulf, where the two countries have delineated claims and regulated fishing. However, oil development has remained a highly contentious issue, as both Vietnam and the Philippines have gone ahead with gas exploration projects (PDF) with foreign companies in disputed areas.

What does this mean for the United States' pivot to Asia?

The U.S. pivot to the area, coupled with the region's myriad conflicts, raises concerns about the future of U.S. interests in Southeast Asia. The Obama administration has not only worked to strengthen ties with ASEAN, but has also forged tighter relations with individual countries like Myanmar, where it has developed a new focus and strategy of engagement. The U.S. has also ramped up security cooperation with Vietnam, while Malaysia and Singapore have also signaled desire for increased security cooperation.

A 2012 Johns Hopkins paper notes that Southeast Asia has transformed in the last two decades to an area where Chinese power and strategic ambition confront an established U.S. military presence, and where a Chinese perception of the status of the South China Sea-isfundamentally at odds with a long-settled consensus among major maritime states.

Experts say that the United States faces a dilemma and tough balancing act in the region, as some countries in ASEAN would like it to play a more forceful role to counter what they see as a greater Chinese assertiveness, while others want to see less U.S. involvement. The priority on all sides should be to avoid military conflict, according to Bonnie Glaser of the Centre for Strategic and International Studies in this Contingency Planning Memorandum; even as China spars with its Southeast Asian neighbours, it is becoming the largest trading partner and one of the biggest direct investors of most Southeast Asian states since an ASEAN-China free trade area came into effect.

SPRATLY ISLANDS DISPUTE

The Spratly Islands dispute is a territorial dispute over the ownership of the Spratly Islands, a group of islands located in the South China Sea. States staking claims to various islands are: Brunei, China (People's Republic of China), Malaysia, the Philippines,Taiwan (Republic of China), and Vietnam. All except Brunei occupy some of the islands.

The Spratly Islands are important for a number of reasons: the Spratly area holds significant reserves of oil and natural gas, it is a productive area for world fishing and commercial shipping, and coastal countries would get an extended continental shelf. But only some states, such as China (PRC), Taiwan (ROC), and Vietnam have made claims based on historical sovereignty of the islands. The Philippines, however, claims it as its territory under UNCLOS, an agreement which all competing countries have ratified.

Reasons for the Dispute

Hydrocarbons

There are multiple reasons why the neighbouring nations would be interested in the Spratly Islands. In 1968, oil was discovered in the region. The Geology and Mineral Resources Ministry of the People's Republic of China (PRC) has estimated that the Spratly area holds oil and natural gas reserves of 17.7 billion tons (1.60×10^{10} kg), as compared to the 13 billion tons (1.17×10^{10} kg) held by Kuwait, placing it as the fourth largest reserve bed in the world. These large reserves assisted in intensifying the situation and propelled the territorial claims of the neighbouring countries.

In 1968, the Philippines started to take their claims more seriously and stationed troops on three islands which had been claimed by the adventurer Tomas Cloma as part of Freedomland. In 1973 Vietnamese troops were stationed on five islands.

On 11 March 1976, the first major Philippine oil discovery occurred off the coast of Palawan, near the Spratly Islands territory. As of 2010, these oil fields accounted for fifteen percent of all petroleum consumed in the Philippines. In 1992, the PRC and Vietnam granted oil exploration contracts to U.S. oil companies that covered overlapping areas in the Spratlys. In May 1992, the China National Offshore Oil Corporation (CNOOC) and Crestone Energy (a U.S. company based in Denver, Colorado) signed a cooperation contract for the joint exploration of the *Wan'an Bei-21* block, a 25,155 square kilometres (9,712 sq mi) section of the southwestern South China Sea that includes Spratly Island areas. Part of the Crestone's contract covered Vietnam's blocks 133 and 134, where PetroVietnam, PetroStar Energy(USA) and ConocoPhillips Vietnam Exploration & Production, a unit of ConocoPhillips, agreed to evaluate prospects in April 1992. This led to a confrontation between China and Vietnam, with each demanding that the other cancel its contract.

Commercial Fishing

An additional motive is the region's role as one of the world's most productive areas for commercial fishing. In 1988, for example, the South China Sea accounted for eight percent of the total world catch, a figure which rose to 35 percent in 2010. The PRC has predicted that the South China Sea holds combined fishing and oil and gas resources worth one trillion dollars. There have already been numerous clashes between the PRC, the Philippines and other nations over "foreign" fishing vessels in its Exclusive Economic Zone(EEZ) and the media regularly report the arrest of Chinese fishermen. In 1984,

Brunei established an exclusive fishing zone encompassing Louisa Reef in the southeastern Spratly Islands.

Commercial Shipping

The region is also one of the busiest shipping lanes in the world. During the 1980s, at least two hundred and seventy ships passed through the Spratly Islands region each day, and currently more than half of the world's supertanker traffic, by tonnage, passes through the region's waters every year. Tanker traffic through the South China Sea is over three times greater than through the Suez Canal and five times more than through the Panama Canal; twenty five percent of the world's crude oil passes through the South China Sea.

Confrontations and other Incidents

There have been occasional naval clashes over the Spratly Islands. In 1988, China and Vietnam clashed at sea over possession of Johnson Reef in the Spratlys. Chinese gunboats sank Vietnamese transport ships supporting a landing party of Vietnamese soldiers. 64 Vietnamese soldiers were killed.

On May 23, 2011, Philippine President Benigno Aquino III warned the Chinese defence minister of a possible arms race in the region if tensions worsened over disputes in the South China Sea. Aquino said he told visiting Chinese Defence Minister Liang Guanglie in their meeting that such an arms race could result if there were more encounters in the disputed and potentially oil-rich Spratly islands. The Philippines warned China that it might increase its military capabilities. The Philippines has already filed a formal protest unter the International Tribunal on the Laws of the Sea (ITLOS)

Extended Continental Shelf Claims

The United Nations Convention on the Law of the Sea (UNCLOS) procedure for countries with coastlines to submit claims for theircontinental shelf to be extended beyond 200 nautical miles of their shores brought the spotlight back to the South China Sea and Spratly Islands in May 2009. Two such submissions were made - one by Vietnam for a claim over the northern portion of the sea which included the Paracel Islands, and another jointly by Vietnam and Malaysia for a joint claim over a "defined area" in the middle of the sea between the two countries which included part of the Spratly Islands. Brunei, a potential claimant, has not submitted such a claim but had provided preliminary information to the United Nations notifying it of its intention to claim a continental shelf beyond 200 nautical miles from its shores.

China immediately issued protests over the two submissions and called on the United Nations not to consider them. It also issued a stern warning to countries not to claim the islands which it said were its sovereign territory.

Moves Towards Resolution

Diplomatic Moves

Following a 1995 dispute between China and the Philippines, an ASEAN-brokered agreement was reached between the PRC and ASEAN member nations whereby one country would inform the other of any military movement within the disputed territory and that there would be no further construction. The agreement was promptly violated by China and Malaysia. Claiming storm damage, seven Chinese naval vessels entered the area to repair "fishing shelters" in Panganiban Reef. Malaysia erected a structure on Investigator Shoal and landed at Rizal Reef. In response the Philippines lodged formal protests, demanded the removal of the structures, increased naval patrols in Kalayaan and issued invitations to American politicians to inspect the PRC bases by plane. The Philippine senate also debated to send troops and navy forces to attempt the invasion in the islands.

In the early 21st century, the situation is improving. China recently held talks with ASEAN countries aimed at realizing a proposal for a free trade area between the ten countries involved. China and ASEAN have also been engaged in talks to create a code of conduct aimed at easing tensions in the disputed islands. In November 2002, a Declaration on the Conduct of Parties in the South China Sea was signed. The parties explicitly undertook in this declaration, "to resolve their territorial and jurisdictional disputes by peaceful means, without resorting to the threat or use of force, through friendly consultations and negotiations by sovereign states directly concerned,". The declaration eases tensions, but falls short of a legally binding code of conduct. In July 2012, China announced that it is open to launching discussions on the Code of Conduct in the South China Sea, but calls for all parties to exercise self-restraint in keeping with the spirit of previous declarations and United Nation conventions.

Declaration on the Conduct of Parties in the South China Sea 2002

This declaration was signed by the 10 foreign ministers of ASEAN countries and China on 4 November 2002 in Phnom Penh where the signatory countries pledged to resolve their sovereignty disputes in a peaceful manner, without resorting to the use of force and through direct negotiations among the countries concerned. The parties also undertook to exercise self-restraint with activities that would complicate or escalate disputes and affect peace and stability, including refraining from inhabiting on the presently uninhabited islands, reefs, shoals, cays, and other features.

In the interim, the parties pledged to carry out confidence building measures, such as by holding dialogues and exchange of views as appropriate between their defence and military officials; ensuring just and humane treatment of all persons who are in danger or distress; notifying on a voluntary basis other Parties concerned of any impending joint/combined military exercise; and exchanging, on a voluntary basis, relevant information.

The Partics may also explore or undertake cooperative activities such as marine environmental protection; marine scientific research; safety of navigation and communication at sea; search and rescue operation; and combating transnational crime, including but not limited to trafficking in illicit drugs, piracy and armed robbery at sea, and illegal traffic in arms.

United States Reaction

On 2 August 2012, the United States Senate unanimously passed a resolution declaring that China's recent actions to unilaterally assert control of disputed territories in the South China Sea "are contrary to agreed upon principles with regard to resolving disputes and impede a peaceful resolution."

In a statement released on 3 August 2012, United States Department of State deputy spokesman Patrick Ventrell said that the US has a "national interest in the maintenance of peace and stability, respect for international law, freedom of navigation, and unimpeded lawful commerce in the South China Sea."

He added that the US does not take a position on competing territorial claims and that it urges all involved parties to clarify and pursue their territorial and maritime claims in accordance with international law.

He further said the US is urging all parties to take steps to lower tensions in keeping with the 1992 ASEAN Declaration on the South China Sea and the 2002 ASEAN-China Declaration on the Conduct of Parties in the South China Sea.

The United States has supported the Philippines and Vietnam by expanding military ties.

Various Claims

Brunei

Brunei claims the part of the South China Seas nearest to it as part of its continental shelfand Exclusive Economic Zone (EEZ).

In 1984, Brunei declared an EEZ encompassing the above-water islets it claims in Louisa Reef. Brunei does not practice military control in the area.

Basis of Brunei's Claim

Brunei's claims to the reef are based on the Law of the Sea. It states that the southern part of the Spratly Chain is actually a part of its continental shelf and therefore a part of its territory and resources.

Malaysia

Malaysia has militarily occupied three islands that it considers to be within its continental shelf. Swallow Reef (*Layang Layang*) has been turned into an island through land reclamation and hosts a dive resort.

The Malaysian military currently occupies Ardasier Reef (*Terumbu Ubi*), Mariveles Reef (*Terumbu Mantanani*) and Swallow Reef(*Terumbu Layang* or *Pulau Layang Layang*).

Basis of Malaysia's Claim

Malaysia's claims are based upon the continental shelf principle, and have clearly defined coordinates. This argument still requires that the islands were *res nullius*, though.

People's Republic of China and Republic of China (Taiwan)

The People's Republic of China (PRC) claim all of the Spratly Islands as part of China and had a historical naval presence. Recently, they have had a profound military impact on the area.

The Republic of China (ROC), which ruled mainland China before 1949 and has been confined to Taiwan since 1949, also claims all of the Spratly Islands. Today, the People's Liberation Army and the Republic of China Armed Forces are both stationed in several islands, including the largest, Taiping Island - occupied by ROC.

From 1932 to 1935, the ROC continued to include the territory in its administrative area through the Map Compilation Committee. When France claimed nine islands of the territory in 1933, it immediately encountered a revolt from Chinese fishermen and a protest from the Republic of China government in Nanking. Although China continued to claim the islands, theSecond Sino-Japanese war drew its attention for the meantime from 1937 onwards. After the second world war,

China reclaimed sovereignty over the islands through post World War II arrangements based on various treaties of the Allied Powers and China built a stone marker on the island.

In 1947, the ROC government renamed 159 islands in the area and published the *Map of the South China Sea Islands*. The ROC was the first government to establish a physical presence in the Spratly Islands. It has occupied Taiping Island, the largest island in the Spratlys, constantly since 1956.

In 1958, the People's Republic of China, having taken over mainland China and having left the Republic of China with control over Taiwan, Penghu, Kinmen, Matsu, and some outlying islands, issued a declaration of a 12 nautical mile limit territorial waters that encompassed the Spratly Islands. North Vietnam's prime minister, sent a formal note to PRC's Premier Zhou Enlai to recognize these claims; and stated that the Government of the Democratic Republic of Vietnam (North Vietnam) respects the decision on the 12 nautical mile limit territorial waters, although South Vietnam continued to claim sovereignty over the islands.

Basis for PRC's and ROC's Claims

China claims to have discovered the islands in the Han Dynasty in 2 BC. The islands were claimed to have been marked on maps compiled during the time of Eastern Han Dynasty andEastern Wu (one of the Three Kingdoms).

Since the Yuan Dynasty in the 12th century, several islands that may be the Spratlys have been labeled as Chinese territory, followed by the Ming Dynasty and the Qing Dynasty from the 13th to 19th Century. In 1755, archaeological surveys the remains of Chinese pottery and coins have been found in the islands and are cited as proof for the PRC claim.

The Philippines

The Philippines base their claims of sovereignty over the Spratlys on the issues of *Res nullius* and geography. The Philippines contend their claim was *Res nullius* as there was no effective sovereignty over the islands until the 1930s when France and then Japan acquired the islands. When Japan renounced their sovereignty over the islands according to the San Francisco Treaty, there was a relinquishment of the right to the islands without any special beneficiary. Therefore, argue the Philippines, the islands became *Res nullius* and available for annexation.

In 1956, a private Filipino citizen, Tomas Cloma, unilaterally declared a state on 53 features in the South China Sea, calling it "Freedomland". As the Republic of Chinamoved to occupy the main island in response, Cloma sold his claim to the Philippine government, which annexed (*de jure*) the islands in 1978, calling them Kalayaan. On June 11, 1978, President Ferdinand Marcos of the Philippines issued Presidential decree No. 1596, declaring the Spratly Islands (referred to therein as the Kalayaan Island Group) as Philippine territory.

The Philippine claim to Kalayaan on a geographical basis can be summarized using the assertion that Kalayaan is distinct from other island groups in the South China Sea, because of the size of the biggest island in the Kalayaan group. A second argument used by the Philippines regarding their geographical claim over the Spratlys is that all the islands claimed by the Philippines lie within its 200-mileExclusive Economic Zone according to the 1982 United Nations Convention on the Law of the Sea. This argument still requires that the islands were *res nullius*, though. The Philippines also argue, under maritime law that the People's Republic of China can not extend its baseline claims to the Spratlys because the PRC is not an archipelagic state.

Vietnam

Vietnam's response to China's claim is that Chinese records on Qianli Changsha and Wanli Shitang are in fact records about non-Chinese territories. For example, Qianli Changsha and Wanli Shitang were referred to in the ancient Chinese texts Ling Wai Dai Da and Zhu Fan Zhi as being in the Sea of Jiaozhi, Jiaozhi being the old name for a Chinese province in modern-day northern Vietnam, or as writings on foreign countries.

Vietnam's view is that the Chinese records do not constitute the declaration and exercise of sovereignty and that China did not declare sovereignty over the Spratlys until after World War II. On the other hand, Vietnam claims the Spratlys based on international law on declaring and exercising sovereignty.

Vietnamese claims that it has occupied the Spratley and the Paracel islands at least since the 17th century, when they were not under the sovereignty of any state, and that they exercised sovereignty over the two archipelagos continuously and peacefully until they were invaded by Chinese armed forces.

The Cairo Declaration, drafted by the Allies and China towards the end of World War II, listed the territories that the Allies intended to strip from Japan and return to China. Despite China being among the authors of the declaration, this list did not include the Spratlys. Vietnam's response to China's claim that the Cairo Declaration somehow recognized the latter's sovereignty over the Spratlys is that this claim has no basis in fact.

At the San Francisco Conference on the peace treaty with Japan, the Soviet Union proposed that the Paracels and Spratlys be recognized as belonging to China. This proposal was rejected by an overwhelming majority of the delegates. On July 7, 1951, Tran Van Huu, head of the Government's (State of Vietnam) delegation to the conference declared that the Paracels and Spratlys were part of Vietnamese territory. This declaration met with no challenge from the 51 representatives at the conference.

The text of the Treaty of San Francisco listed the Spratlys as not part of the list of territories to be returned to China.

After the French left, the government of the Republic of Vietnam (RVN) exercised sovereignty over the islands, by placing border markers on the Spratlys to indicate South Vietnamese sovereignty over the archipelago. Up to the end of the Vietnam War the Republic of Vietnam Navy held military control over the majority of the Spratly Islands until 1975, when North Vietnamese troops attacked South Vietnamese troops and occupied the islands. After the Vietnam War, the unified Vietnam SRV (Socialist Republic of Vietnam) continued to claim the Spratly islands as an indisputably integral part of Vietnam, accordingly the Phan Van Dong DRV notice to the PRC in 1958 had not ceded the RVN and consequently the SRV claims, hence that Notice became of no effect on the RVN/SRV rights.

Vietnam currently occupies 31 islands. They are organized as a district of Khanh Hoa Province. At the 12th National Assembly Election held early in TrýÝng Sa, the people and soldiers also voted for their local district government for the first time. For the first time, is organized like a normal inland district, with a township and two communes. Forty nine people were elected to the communes' people's councils.

In July 2012 the national assembly of Vietnam passed a law demarcating Vietnamese sea borders to include the Spratly and Paracel Islands.

CHINA IN SOUTH CHINA SEA DISPUTES - A CHINESE PERSPECTIVE

By Zhang Zhexin - Tensions between China and some Southeast Asian states over territorial claims in the South China Sea (SCS) appear to have eased with the agreement reached in Bali on July 20 between China's Foreign Minister and his ASEAN counterparts. The ministers reiterated their countries' commitment to exercise self-restraint and agreed to guidelines for voluntarily implementing a non-binding Declaration on Conduct of Parties (DOC) in the SCS signed by China and ASEAN states in 2002.

Many observers see the agreement as a direct consequence of the US's strong diplomatic and quasi-military efforts that implicitly took sides with Vietnam and the Philippines to deter China's otherwise more hardline actions-another successful example of the US role as an "off-shore balancer." However, such engagment should not be regarded as a model for the US's long-term strategy in the region, because it is rooted in four long-held misperceptions of China's objectives and approaches concerning the SCS disputes.

The first misperception is that China alone should be held responsible for recent tensions on the SCS for its violation of the DOC. Yes, Beijing has sent more patrol boats and fighter jets to waters around disputed islands or reefs in recent years. However, this was only because some Southeast Asian states have been unilaterally accelerating their surveying and exploitation of natural resources in disputed waters, and expanding military and civilian facilities on disputed islands currently under their occupation-both violate the guiding spirit of the DOC. Thus, the image of a rising Titan bullying its small neighbours comes more from a natural sympathy for the weaker parties than from a balanced appreciation of the situation.

The second misperception is that China claims most of the SCS as its internal waters. It is true that Beijing needs to provide a detailed official explanation for the controversial Nine-dashed Line-its historical and legal standing, as well as specific territorial boundaries and rights. Yet it has never declared the vast SCS waters to be its territorial sea, but rather more legally-vague "historic waters." Beijing's official position has remained that "China has indisputable sovereignty over the SCS islands (within the Nine-dashed Line) and their surrounding waters." China has often reiterated-especially over the past decade-the importance of maintaining secure and free navigation in the SCS. For example, a whole chapter in the DOC was written to specify rights and rules concerning straits used for international navigation, mainly in accordance with the UN Convention on the Law of the Sea (UNCLOS) signed in 1982.

Some may argue that China keeps infringing on other states' free navigation rights, as examplified by its consistent efforts to deny access of the US's military surveillance ships into its claimed Exclusive Economic Zones (EEZs). It is worth noting, however, that while Washington maintains that

UNCLOS did not clearly define and, therefore, did not change the rights of military vessels to conduct non-threatening activities in others' EEZs, "peaceful uses" has been acknowledged as an overarching principle for all ocean activities under the treaty that the US has yet to ratify. Therefore, many Chinese scholars argue that the US should respect this principle and stop conducting military-related activities in others' EEZs.

The third misperception is that China has pursued a "divide and defeat" strategy towards claimant ASEAN states, and thus resisted a multilateral approach. Beijing did oppose multilateral negotiation or even discussion of the SCS disputes in such forums as the East Asian Summit (EAS) and ASEAN Regional Forum (ARF), but it did so in large part because the disputes are only between China and four ASEAN states, the latter also having many overlapping claims of their own. Given the fact that there are already many bilateral channels (though not always effective) to address territorial disputes and that most non-claimant ASEAN states feel reluctant to choose sides, a multilateral approach towards the final solution of SCS disputes very likely would impair the rapidly developing China-ASEAN strategic partnership and pose new challenges to ASEAN unity.

The final misperception is that China aims to dominate the SCS as a key step to monopolize Southeast Asia, a "Monroe Doctrine for maritime Asia" as some put it. China's rapid military buildup in recent years further fuels such concerns. Undoubtedly, Beijing should do more in explaining to the world how it intends to use its emerging capabilities and try its best to match its actions with words, yet in overstating China's ambition in the SCS, one might overlook crucial facts regarding Beijing's long-term goals and concerns.

According to the *Whitebook on Peaceful Development of China* published by the State Council Information Office on September 6, the first official document to specify China's core interests and strategic goals in a descriptive manner, the trajectory of China's rising power has been-and will remain in the decades to come-by and large internally focused, i.e., preoccupied with maintaining domestic stability and economic growth, as well as promoting an equitable distribution of wealth among its people. Despite a hunger for natural resources, seeking to dominate Southeast Asia while risking acute conflicts with other major powers simply goes against China's domestic blueprint.

With regard to the often ambiguous and even discordant messages sent by China in SCS disputes over the past years, the above-mentioned four misperceptions are not totally groundless. If they continue to dominate American political thinking, then the US is very likely to carry on with its current power-balancing strategy in the SCS. However, such a strategy is intrinsically problematic, as its two major objectives-to forestall potential military clashes and balance China's rising power-may well conflict with each other. By even seeming to align with claimant ASEAN states to balance China, the US is actually encouraging them to take adventurous actions which, in turn, will not only increase the possibility of acute conflicts on the SCS but also push China towards stronger determination to override the US in the region.

A power-balancing strategy may seem to be the easiest option for the US, and one which may appear to be working now. In the long run, the US can better protect its interests by joining hands with China to improve mutual strategic trust and help construct a stable cooperation framework in the region. China, likewise, should not lose sight of its own limits and the mixed historical memories of its neighbours. From this positive perspective the SCS disputes provide a new opportunity to test the understanding, wisdom and patience of all relevant parties.

SOUTH CHINA SEA DISPUTE: THE FARCE OF CHINESE MULTILATERALISM

In the most dangerous turn of events in the South China Sea, on July 23, China's military body, the Central Military Commission approved the deployment of the People's Liberation Army to guard the islands claimed by it. Earlier in June, China's State Council had raised the administrative status of the seas to the level of a city, which it calls Sansha and which is located in the disputed Paracel Islands. These two moves indicate Beijing's growing aggressiveness and unilateralism, which clearly go against the spirit of the 2002 DOC (Declaration of Conduct of parties), a multilateral political document agreed upon by the ASEAN and China that calls for resolution of 'territorial and jurisdictional disputes by peaceful means, without resorting to the threat of force.'

The main hindrance to the resolution of the South China Sea dispute is, of course, China's aversion to any multilateral solution to what is in effect a multilateral dispute arising out of the competing territorial claims of China, Taiwan, Philippines, Malaysia, Vietnam and Brunei. From the beginning China has insisted on bilateral negotiations with individual Southeast Asian countries. In fact, the Chinese government held that 'major regional security issues related to territorial dispute is best handled by bilateral negotiations rather than by multilateral means'. Although Beijing accords multilateralism a more central place in Chinese foreign policy, it however subordinates it to the principle of sovereignty. This was palpable during the 1995 Second ASEAN Regional Forum (ARF) Ministerial Meeting, which laid out three stages of development of regional security cooperation: confidence building; preventive diplomacy; and, conflict resolution strategies. While adhering to the first stage, the PRC has displayed serious reservations about the second and third stages since the preventive diplomacy and conflict resolution processes conflicted with China's sovereignty issues. Needless to point out, the bilateral mechanism allows China to keep the multiple claimants divided and confused about the territorial resolution and offers Beijing greater manoeuvrability in the negotiating process. In other words, resolution of the South China Sea dispute has been crippled from the beginning on account of China's limited and pretentious multilateralism and its strong emphasis on the principle of national sovereignty. To add to the present crisis, China has unilaterally gone ahead and laid claim to almost the whole of the South China Sea. This has clearly rendered China's multilateralism as a completely farcical foreign policy formulation.

Indeed, China's aggressive moves in the South China Sea have rendered multilateralism a mere sham. Multilateralism, in the Chinese understanding, emerged essentially as a strategic tool to oppose US hegemonic and unilateralist policies. It was also meant to achieve an equitable international political and economic order by allowing Beijing a larger share in the decision making process. Further, it was also aimed at diminishing the 'China threat theory' and building an image of a responsible China among the Southeast Asian countries. But by going unilateral on the South China Sea, China has, in effect, acted not any differently from the United States.

Beijing's unilateralism in the South China Sea also invalidates its theoretical proposition of the New Security Concept (NSC), out of which evolved China's own understanding of multilateralism. Ironically, the NSC was explained at the ASEAN's 30th anniversary in December 1997 by the then Chinese Foreign Minister Qian Qichen as China's cooperative security model opposed to the US hegemonic unilateral model. It set out the principles of international relations based on mutual trust, mutual benefit, equality and coordination. NSC also claimed to offer "an alternative system for managing relations between countries which differ in their social systems, values and developmental levels." In the subsequent period, riding on the principles of the NSC, the formulation of peaceful rise was made, which now lies shattered under the impact of China's unilateral measures in the South China Sea and which are threatening to push the region into a war-like scenario.

China's motivation of national aggrandizement couched in the peaceful altruistic notion of the NSC is in reality not an alternative model of international relations. When the Chinese leadership speaks of 'setting aside dispute and pursuing joint development' in the South China Sea, it means four things:

"the sovereignty of the territories concerned belong to China; when conditions are not ripe to bring about a territorial solution, discussion on sovereignty may be postponed; the territories under dispute may be developed in a joint way; and, the purpose of joint development is to enhance mutual understanding through cooperation and create conditions for the eventual resolution of territorial ownership."

Embedded in this Chinese perspective on resolution of disputed territories are two issues: First, China's retention of the sovereignty prerogative despite the competing claims; and second, its aversion to multilateralism in conflict resolution. Clearly, China's ideas of multilateralism and sovereignty are based on the Westphalian model of state building and do not in any manner offer an alternative system.

Thus, multilateralism is basically a farce in Chinese foreign policy. For China, the South China Sea dispute is merely a sovereignty issue in which it brooks no interference of external forces. It opts to settle the issue on its own terms rousing nationalism, constructing false historiography and displaying military muscle. Paradoxically, on the one hand it upholds 'joint development' of disputed areas, but on the other it criticizes the US for upholding freedom of navigation in the South China Sea and for displaying a 'Cold War mentality'. In the ultimate analysis, on territorial and sovereignty related issues, China is likely to increasingly display unilateral tendencies. This is commensurate not only with China's growing power but also with the relative decline of the United States.

TERRITORIAL DISPUTES IN THE SOUTH CHINA SEA

The South China Sea disputes involve both island and maritime claims among several sovereign states within the region, namely the Nation of Brunei, the People's Republic of China, the Republic of China (Taiwan),Malaysia, the Republic of the Philippines, and the Socialist Republic of Vietnam. Non-claimants want the South China Sea to remain as international waters, with the United States of America conducting "freedom of navigation" operations.

There are disputes concerning both the Spratly and the Paracel islands, as well as maritime, areas near to sea, boundaries in the Gulf of Tonkin and elsewhere. There is a further dispute in the waters near the Indonesian Natuna Islands. The interests of different nations include acquiring fishing areas around the two archipelagos; the potential exploitation of crude oil and natural gas under the waters of various parts of the South China Sea, and the strategic control of important shipping lanes.

The Shangri-La Dialogue serves as the "Track One" exchange forum on security issues surrounding the Asia-Pacific region, includingterritorial disputes in the South China Sea. The Council for Security Cooperation in the Asia Pacific is the "Track Two" forum for dialogue on security issues.

In February 2016, President Obama initiated the U.S.-ASEAN Summit atSunnylands for closer engagement with the Association of Southeast Asian Nations. Territorial disputes in the South China Sea were a major topic, but its joint statement, the "Sunnylands Declaration", did not name the South China Sea, instead calling for "respect of each nation's sovereignty and for international law". Analysts believe it indicates divisions within the group on how to respond to China's maritime strategy.

In July 2016, an arbitral tribunal consitituted under Annex VII of theUnited Nations Convention on the Law of the Sea ruled against China's territorial claims in *Philippines v. China*. Although it is not enforceable China does not acknowledge the tribunal nor abide by its ruling, insisting that any resolution should be through bilateral negotiations with other claimants.

Specific disputes

The disputes involve both maritime boundaries and islands. There are several disputes, each of which involved a different collection of countries:

1. The nine-dash line area claimed by the Republic of China, later People's Republic of China which covers most of the South China sea and overlapsExclusive Economic Zone claims of Brunei, Indonesia, Malaysia,

the Philippines, Taiwan, and Vietnam. Singapore has reiterated that it is not a claimant state in the South China Sea dispute and therefore allows Singapore to play a neutral role in being a constructive conduit for dialogue among the claimant states.

2. Maritime boundary along the Vietnamese coast between Brunei, Cambodia, China, Malaysia, the Philippines, Taiwan, and Vietnam.
3. Maritime boundary north of Borneo between Brunei, China, Malaysia, Philippines, Taiwan, and Vietnam.
4. Islands in the South China Sea, including the Paracels Islands, the Pratas Islands, Scarborough Shoal and theSpratly Islands between Brunei, China, Malaysia, the Philippines, Taiwan, and Vietnam.
5. Maritime boundary in the waters north of the Natuna Islands between Cambodia, China, Indonesia, Malaysia, Taiwan, and Vietnam.
6. Maritime boundary off the coast of Palawan and Luzon between Brunei, China, Malaysia, the Philippines, Taiwan, and Vietnam.
7. Maritime boundary, land territory, and the islands of Sabah, including Ambalat, between Indonesia, Malaysia, and the Philippines.
8. Maritime boundary and islands in the Luzon Strait between the China, the Philippines, and Taiwan.
9. Maritime boundary and islands in the Pedra Branca (and Middle Rocks) between Singapore and Malaysia.

Background

The area may be rich in oil and natural gas deposits; however, the estimates are highly varied. The Ministry of Geological Resources and Mining of the People's Republic of China estimate that the South China Sea may contain 17.7 billion tons of crude oil (compared to Kuwait with 13 billion tons). In the years following the announcement by the ministry, the claims regarding the South China Sea islands intensified. However, other sources claim that the proven reserve of oil in the South China Sea may only be 7.5 billion barrels, or about 1.1 billion tons. According to the US Energy Information Administration (EIA)'s profile of the South China Sea region, a US Geological Survey estimate puts the region's discovered and undiscovered oil reserves at 11 billion barrels, as opposed to a Chinese figure of 125 billion barrels. The same EIA report also points to the wide variety of natural gas resource estimations, ranging from 190 trillion cubic feet to 500 trillion cubic feet, likely located in the contested Reed Bank".

The South China Sea is dubbed by China as the "second Persian Sea." The state-owned China Offshore Exploration Corp. planned to spend 200 billion RMB (US$30 billion) in the next 20 years to exploit oil in the region, with the estimated production of 25 million metric tons of crude oil and natural gas per annum, at a depth of 2000 meters within the next five years.

The Philippines began exploring the areas west of Palawan for oil in 1970. Exploration in the area began in Reed Bank/ Tablemount. in 1976, gas was discovered following the drilling of a well. However, China's complaints halted the exploration.

On 27 March 1984, the first Philippine oil company discovered an oil field off Palawan, which is an island province bordering the South China Sea and the Sulu Sea. These oil fields supply 15% of annual oil consumption in the Philippines.

The nine-dotted line was originally an "eleven-dotted-line," first indicated by the then Kuomintang government of the Republic of China in 1947, for its claims to the South China Sea. After, the Communist Party of China took over mainland China and formed the People's Republic of China in 1949. The line was adopted and revised to nine as endorsed by Zhou Enlai.

The legacy of the nine-dotted line is viewed by some Chinese government officials, and by the Chinese military, as providing historical support for their claims to the South China Sea.

In the 1970s, however, the Philippines, Malaysia and other countries began referring to the Spratly Islands as included in their own territory. On 11 June 1978, President Ferdinand Marcos of the Philippines issued Presidential decree No. 1596, declaring the Spratly Islands (referred to therein as the Kalayaan Island Group) as Philippine territory.

The abundant fishing opportunities within the region are another motivation for the claim. In 1988, the South China Sea is believed to have accounted for 8% of world fishing catches, a figure that has grown since then. There have been many clashes in the Philippines with foreign fishing vessels (including China) in disputed areas. China believes that the value in fishing and oil from the sea has risen to a trillion dollars.

The area is also one of the busiest shipping routes in the world. In the 1980s, at least 270 merchant ships used the route each day. Currently, more than half the tonnage of oil transported by sea passes through it, a figure rising steadily with the growth of Chinese consumption of oil. This traffic is three times greater than that passing through the Suez Canal and five times more than the Panama Canal.

As of 1996, Vietnam, the Philippines, Brunei, Malaysia and other countries asserted claims within the Chinese nine-dotted line The United Nations Convention on the Law of the Sea, which came into effect on 16 November 1994, resulted in more intense territorial disputes between the parties.

As of 2012, all of the Paracel Islands are under Chinese control. Eight of the Spratly Islands are under Chinese control; Vietnamese troops control the greatest number of Spratly islands, 29. Eight islands are controlled by the Philippines, five by Malaysia, two by Brunei and one by Taiwan. In 2012 the Indian Ambassador to Vietnam, while expressing concern over rising tension in the area, said that 50 per cent of its trade passes through the area and called for peaceful resolution of the disputes in accordance with international law.

On March 17, 2016, in accordance with Memorandum Circular No. 94 s. 2016, President Aquino created the National Task Force for the West Philippine Sea, to secure the State's sovereignty and national territory and preserve marine wealth in its waters and exclusive economic zone, reserving use and enjoyment of the West Philippine Sea exclusively for Filipino citizens.

Incidents

Foreign ships which illegally fished in Indonesian waters were destroyed by the Indonesian government, many of them were Vietnamese ships. The Vietnamese government objected to the destruction of its own ships. 660 Vietnamese were apprehended in 2015 by Indonesia. Indonesian waters were violated by Filipino fishermen.

On 19 March 2016, China coast guards prevented Indonesian authorities from detaining a Chinese fishing boat near the Natunas, although China accepts that the Natuna islands and seas around them belong to Indonesia. The crew were detained by Indonesia earlier, but their fishing boat was rammed free by a Chinese guards vessel while been towed. Indonesia summoned the Chinese ambassador in protest and China in turn demanded the release of the crew as they were in "traditional Chinese fishing grounds". However, Indonesia refused to release the crew and accused China of sharply raising tensions in the region.

After they breached waters belonging to Thailand Vietnamese ships were snatched by Thailand. Chinese and Vietnamese ships were detained by the Philippines. For breaching waters of Malaysia, a Vietnamese ship was snatched by Malaysia. Papua province waters belonging to Indonesia were breached by Vietnamese and Filipino fishermen who were arrested. In Riau's vicinity in Indonesian waters Vietnamese ships were snatched by Indonesia.

2011 agreement

On 20 July 2011, the PRC, Brunei, Malaysia, the Philippines and Vietnam agreed to a set of preliminary guidelines which would help resolve the dispute. The agreement was described by the PRC's assistant foreign minister, Zhenmin, as "an important milestone document for cooperation among China and ASEAN countries". Some of the early drafts acknowledged aspects such as "marine environmental protection, scientific research, safety of navigation and communication, search and rescue and combating transnational crime," although the issue of oil and natural gas drilling remains unresolved.

Chinese objection to Indian naval presence and oil exploration

On 22 July 2011, the INS Airavat, an Indian amphibious assault vessel on a friendly visit to Vietnam, was reportedly contacted 45 nautical miles from the Vietnamese coast in the disputed South China Sea by a party identifying itself as the Chinese Navy and stating that the ship was entering Chinese waters. A spokesperson for the Indian Navy explained that as no ship or aircraft was visible, the INS Airavat proceeded on her onward journey as scheduled.

The Indian Navy further clarified that "[t]here was no confrontation involving the INS Airavat. India supports freedom of navigation in international waters, including in the South China Sea, and the right of passage in accordance with accepted principles of international law. These principles should be respected by all."

In September 2011, shortly after China and Vietnam signed an agreement seeking to contain a dispute over the South China Sea, India's state-run explorer, Oil and Natural Gas Corporation (ONGC) said that its overseas investment arm, ONGC Videsh Limited, had signed a three-year agreement with PetroVietnam for developing long-term co-operation in the oil sector, and that it had accepted Vietnam's offer of exploration in certain specified blocks in the South China Sea In response, Chinese Foreign Ministry spokesperson Jiang Yu, without referring to India by name, stated as follows:

"China enjoys indisputable sovereignty over the South China Sea and the island. China's stand is based on historical facts and international law. China's sovereign rights and positions are formed in the course of history and this position has been held by Chinese Government for long. On the basis of this China is ready to engage in peaceful negotiations and friendly consultations to peacefully solve the disputes over territorial sovereignty and maritime rights so as to positively contribute to peace and tranquillity in the South China Sea area. We hope that the relevant countries respect China's position and refrain from taking unilateral action to complicate and expand the issue. We hope they will respect and support countries in the region to solve the bilateral disputes through bilateral channels. As for oil and gas exploration activities, our consistent position is that we are opposed to any country engaging in oil and gas exploration and development activities in waters under China's jurisdiction. We hope the foreign countries do not get involved in South China Sea dispute."

An Indian foreign ministry spokesman responded, "The Chinese had concerns, but we are going by what the Vietnamese authorities have told us and [we] have conveyed this to the Chinese." The Indo-Vietnamese deal was also denounced by the Chinese state-run newspaper *Global Times*.

Retrenchment

In Spring 2010, Chinese officials reportedly communicated to US officials that the South China Sea is "an area of 'core interest' that is as non-negotiable" and on par with Taiwan and Tibet on the national agenda. but may have backed away from that assertion in 2011.

In October 2011, China's *Global Times* newspaper, published by the Communist Party, *People's Daily*, editorialised on South China Sea territorial disputes under the banner "Don't take peaceful approach for granted". The article referenced recent incidents involving Philippines and South Korea detaining Chinese fishing boats in the region:

"If these countries don't want to change their ways with China, they will need to prepare for the sounds of cannons. We need to be ready for that, as it may be the only way for the disputes in the sea to be resolved." Global Times (China), 25 October 2011 Responding to questions about whether this reflected official policy, a Chinese Foreign Ministryspokeswoman stated the country's commitment "to resolving the maritime dispute through peaceful means."

Alan Dupont of the University of New South Wales has said that the Chinese government appears to be directing its fishing fleet into disputed waters as a matter of policy.

Oil development

Vietnam and Japan reached an agreement early in 1978 on the development of oil in the South China Sea. As of 2012, Vietnam had concluded some 60 oil and gas exploration and production contracts with various foreign companies. In 1986, the "White Tiger" oil field in the South China Sea came into operation, producing over 2,000 tons of crude oil per year, followed by the "The Bear" and "Dragon" oil fields. As of 2011, Vietnam was the sixth-largest oil producer in the Asia-Pacific region although the country is now a net oil importer; in 2009 while petroleum accounted for 14 percent of government income, this was down from 24 percent in 2004.

China's first independently designed and constructed oil drilling platform in the South China Sea is the *Ocean Oil 981*. The major shareholders are J.P. Morgan Chase & Co. (19%), Commonwealth Bank of Australia (14%), T. Rowe Price Associates, Inc. and affiliates (6%), and BlackRock, Inc. (5%). It began operation on 9 May 2012 in the South China Sea, 320 kilometres (200 mi) southeast of Hong Kong, at a depth of 1,500 m and employing 160 people. On 2 May 2014, the platform was moved near to the Paracel islands, a move Vietnam stated violated their territorial claims whileChinese officials said was legal as it falls within surrounding waters of the Paracel Islands which China militarily controls.

Non-claimant views

United States

The United States and China are currently in disagreement over the South China Sea. This disagreement is exacerbated by the fact that the US is not a member of the United Nations Convention on the Law of the Sea (UNCLOS). Nevertheless, the US has stood by its manoeuvres, claiming that "peaceful surveillance activities and other military activities without permission in a country's Exclusive Economic Zone (EEZ)," is allowed under the convention. Additionally, a South China Sea free to access is in the US's economic and geopolitical interests. In relation to the dispute, Secretary Clinton voiced her support for fair access by reiterating that freedom of navigation and respect of international law is a matter of national interest to the United States. Her comments were countered by China's Foreign Minister Yang Jiechi as "in effect an attack on China," who warned the United States against making the South China Sea an international issue or multilateral issue.

Clinton testified in support of congressional approval of the Law of the Sea Convention, which would strengthen US ability to support countries that oppose Chinese claims to certain islands in the area. On 29 May 2012, a spokesman for the Chinese Foreign Ministry expressed concern over this development, stating that "non-claimant Association of South East Asian Nations countries and countries outside the region have adopted a position of not getting involved into territorial disputes." In July 2012, the United States Senate passed resolution 524, initially sponsored by Senator John Kerry, stating (among other things) the United States' strong support for the 2002 declaration of conduct of parties in the South China Sea, reaffirms the United States' commitment to assist the nations of Southeast Asia to remain strong and independent, and supports enhanced operations by the United States armed forces in the Western Pacific.

Bibliography

Acharya, Amitav: *Constructing a Security Community in Southeast Asia. ASEAN and the problem of regional order.* London: Routledge, 2001.

Austin, Greg: *China's Ocean Frontier: International Law, Military Force and National Development.* St. Leonards: Allen & Unwin, 1998.

Barua, Pradeep: *Gentlemen of the Raj: The Indian Army Officer Corps, 1817–1949,* 2003.

Dino Patti: *The Geopolitics of Indonesia's Maritime Territorial Policy.* Jakarta: Centre for Strategic and International Studies, 1996.

Djalal, Dino Patti: *The Geopolitics of Indonesia's Maritime Territorial Policy.* Jakarta: Centre for Strategic and International Studies, 1996.

Epsey Cooke: *The Socialist Republic of Vietnam and the Law of the Sea.* The Hague: Martinus Nijhoff, 1998.

Farrell, Epsey Cooke: *The Socialist Republic of Vietnam and the Law of the Sea.* The Hague: Martinus Nijhoff, 1998.

Felix K. Chang: *'China's Naval Rise and the South China Sea: An Operational Assessment.'* 2012.

Galdorise, George V. and Kevin R. Vienna: *Beyond the Law of the Sea.* New York: Praeger, 1997.

Garver, John W.: *Face Off: China, the United States, and Taiwan's Democratization.* Seattle: University of Washington Press, 1997.

Gerald H.: *The Peaceful Management of Transboundary Resources.* London: Graham & Trotman, 1995.

Greenfield, Jeanette: *China's Practice in the Law of the Sea.* Oxford: Clarendon Press, 1992.

Greg, Austin: *China's Ocean Frontier: International Law, Military Force and National Development.* St. Leonards: Allen & Unwin, 1998.

Hagström, Linus: *Japan's China Policy: A Relational Power Analysis,* London and New York: Routledge, 2005.

Harrison, Selig: *China, Oil and Asia: Conflict Ahead.* New York: Columbia University Press, 1992.

Heathcote, T. A.: *Indian Ocean – The Garrison of British Imperial India, 1822–1922.* David & Charles. Newton Abbot, Devon. 1974.

Heimanson, Rudolph: *Dictionary of Political Science and Law,* N.Y.: Oceana Publications, 1967.

Jagannath P. Panda: *China's Path to Power : Party, Military and the Politics of State Transition,* Pentagon, Delhi, 2010.

James Manicom: *Bridging Troubled Waters: China, Japan, and Maritime Order in the East China Sea,* Georgetown University Press; 2014.

James R Blaker: *Transforming Military Force : The Legacy of Arthur Cebrowski and Network Centric Warfare,* Pentagon Press, Delhi, 2008.

Jones, W.H.: *The Government and Politics of Indian Military,* London, Hutchinson, 1971.

Joon Ahn: *The Rise of China and the Future of East Asian Integration,* Asia-Pacific Review, London, Carfax Publishing Company, 2004.

Kansakar, V. B. S.: *"International Migration and Citizenship in Nepal".* Kathmandu: Central Bureau of Statistics/UNFPA, 2003.

Kevin R. Vienna: *Beyond the Law of the Sea.* New York: Praeger, 1997.

Leena Parmar: *Military Sociology : Global Perspectives,* Rawat, Delhi, 1999.

Lewis, John Wilson & Xue Litai: *China's Strategic Seapower. The Politics of Force Modernization in the Nuclear Age.* Stanford Cal.: Stanford University Press, 1994.

Lowe, A.V.: *The Law of the Sea.* Manchester: Manchester University Press, 1983.

Major Donovan: *Air Defence Power.* Sampson Low. London, 1940.

Neil Frank R.: *The Philippines and the South China Sea Islands: Overview and Documents.* Metro Manila: Foreign Service Institute, 1993.

Park Hee Kwon: *The Law of the Sea and Northeast Asia.* The Hague: Kluwer, 2000.

Peter G. Tsouras: *Dictionary of Military Quotations,* Manas, Delhi, 2006.

Prabir De: *India and China in an Era of Globalisation : Essays on Economic Cooperation,* Bookwell, Delhi, 2005.

Radhakrishna: *Military Ethics: Guidelines for Peace and War*, Sumit Enterprises, Delhi, 2009.

Raj Kumar: *Weapons and Military Technology*, Sumit Enterprises, Delhi, 2009.

Randall Forsberg: *The Arms Production Dilemma: Contraction and Restraint in the World Combat Aircraft Industry,* Cambridge, Massachusetts: MIT Press, 1994.

Robert M Cassidy: *Counterinsurgency and the Global War on Terror : Military Culture and Irregular War*, Pentagon Press, Delhi, 2008.

Rosen, P.: *Societies and Military Power: India and its Armies*, Ithaca, Cornell University Press, 1996.

Sam Bateman: *Maritime Change: Issues for Asia*. St. Leonards: Allen & Unwin, 1993.

Samuel P. Huntington: *The Soldier and the State : The Theory and Politics of Civil-Military Relations*, Natraj Pub, Delhi, 2005.

Samuels, Marwyn: *Contest for the South China Sea*. New York: Methuen, 1982.

Shaun Narine, *Explaining ASEAN: Regionalism in Southeast Asia*, Boulder, CO: Lynne Rienner Publishers, 2002.

Singh Jadoan: *Military Geography of South East Asia*, Anmol, Delhi, 2001.

Stephen Bates : *Calming the Waters. Initiatives for Asia Pacific Maritime Cooperation*. Canberra Papers on Strategy and Defence, 1996.

Suresh Goel: *International Encyclopaedia of Military, Security and Intelligence Agencies*, MD Publications, Delhi, 2009.

Sutton, J., *Technology and Defence Market Structure*, MIT Press, Delhi, 1998.

Thapa, Deepak : *Understanding the Maoist Movement of Nepal*, Centre for Social Research and Development, Delhi, 2003.

Valencia, Mark J.: *Malaysia and the Law of the Sea*. Kuala Lumpur: Institute of Strategic and International Studies Malaysia (ISIS), 1991.

Wakamiya Yoshibumi, *The Postwar Conservative View of Asia,* Tokyo: LTCB International Library Foundation, 1999.

Zou, Keyuan: *Law of the Sea in East Asia: Issues and Prospects,* Routledge; 2005.

Index

A

Arms Race Commences, 165.
Asian Polarisation, 54, 56.

B

Blame Game, 115.

C

China Sea Contentious, 16.
China Sea Islands, 231, 232, 233, 276.
Chinese Policy, 214.
Chinese Sovereignty, 25, 86, 181.
Code of Conduct, 14, 25, 29, 32, 35, 75, 93, 94, 95, 96, 97, 99, 101, 102, 106, 120, 137, 141, 144, 152, 239, 273.
Cold War, 142, 162, 165.
Commercial Shipping, 61, 181, 269.
Competing Rivalries, 10.
Comprehensive Policy, 3.

D

Developments, 20, 36, 44, 45, 51, 54, 106, 107, 110, 112, 114, 119, 137, 141, 153, 154, 164, 169, 230.
Diplomacy, 11, 34, 36, 53, 61, 92, 118, 122, 141, 151, 161, 175, 186, 203, 208, 214, 237, 251, 255, 259, 283, 286.
Diplomatic Developments, 137.
Dispute Resolution, 67, 70, 90, 123, 215, 261, 265.

E

East China Sea, 166.
Economic Power, 79, 164.
Eliminate Terrorism, 155.
External Environment, 203, 204, 205, 209.

F

Financial Agreements, 153.
Freedom, 12, 16, 21, 23, 28, 31, 37, 40, 41, 45, 51, 52, 53, 57, 71, 96, 98, 110, 111, 113, 139, 151, 156, 159, 161, 163, 167, 174, 179, 184, 185, 193, 194, 204, 205, 216, 226, 227, 230, 231, 237, 238, 242, 245, 246, 247, 248, 263, 266, 274, 285, 291, 294.
Fresh Game, 228.

G

Global Flashpoint, 88, 168, 172.

Global Strategic Implications, 53.
Governments, 21, 70, 182, 183, 246, 250, 253, 254, 258.
Great Powers, 228.

I

Indian Ocean, 212, 244, 246.
Internal Environment, 203, 209.
International Cooperation, 247.
International Law, 243.
International Security, 201.
Islands Dispute, 269.

L

Landmark Ruling, 64.
Leading Flashpoint, 78.

M

Marine Environment, 60, 66, 129, 133, 245, 249.
Maritime Forces, 165.
Maritime Freedoms, 244.
Maritime Pollution, 244.
Maritime Safety, 244, 246, 247.
Maritime Security, 161, 162, 214, 243, 245, 247.
Maritime Silk Road, 202, 209.
Military Ambitions, 2.
Military Balance, 211.
Military Law, 168.
Military Modernization, 165.
Military Power, 3, 38, 54, 57, 88, 166, 172, 175, 208, 231, 255, 256, 261.
Military Stakes, 266.

N

New Tensions, 7.

O

Opportunity, 32, 41, 85, 86, 104, 124, 140, 143, 144, 146, 162, 174, 202, 204, 207, 210, 282.
Organizations, 161.

P

Philippines Claims, 57, 211, 235.
Policy, 3, 5, 11, 30, 31, 32, 40, 42, 45, 51, 60, 72, 80, 84, 88, 96, 141, 143, 161, 164, 171, 174, 180, 183, 184, 186, 189, 194, 196, 203, 206, 207, 208, 215, 216, 217, 219, 226, 231, 244, 246, 250, 256, 257, 258, 259, 260, 283, 284, 285, 292, 293.
Policy Approach, 244, 246.
Political Conflict, 158, 163.
Potential Flashpoint, 14.
Powers, 28, 30, 31, 33, 35, 36, 37, 55, 61, 78, 79, 80, 81, 105, 152, 153, 165, 177, 183, 203, 204, 227, 228, 229, 230, 231, 242, 251, 252, 254, 256, 276, 282.
Projects, 25, 49, 96, 101, 109, 211, 258, 268.

R

Regional Strategic Implications, 55.

S

Security, 6, 14, 15, 24, 28, 30, 31, 32, 33, 43, 45, 46, 47, 51, 54, 55, 56,

57, 58, 67, 78, 79, 82, 101, 103, 104, 105, 106, 111, 118, 120, 121, 124, 126, 128, 134, 140, 141, 146, 153, 155, 156, 157, 158, 160, 164, 165, 166, 167, 173, 174, 177, 179, 180, 182, 183, 184, 186, 189, 190, 193, 197, 199, 200, 201, 203, 209, 210, 213, 214, 218, 220, 223, 227, 230, 231, 234, 236, 238, 240, 243, 244, 245, 246, 247, 250, 251, 252, 253, 254, 255, 256, 257, 258, 259, 260, 265, 266, 268, 283, 284, 286.

Security Policy, 256, 257, 260.

Silk Road, 202, 209.

South China Sea, 160, 162, 163, 164, 165, 166, 167, 210, 214.

South China Sea Disputes, 15, 29, 32, 34, 53, 54, 55, 77, 141, 193, 208, 212, 216, 230, 237, 239, 240, 242, 285.

South China Sea Issue, 211.

South China Sea Moment, 239.

Specific Disputes, 286.

State of Crisis, 123.

State Threats, 244.

T

Territorial Disputes, 7, 15, 16, 33, 36, 41, 44, 82, 90, 91, 105, 108, 109, 161, 166, 194, 200, 215, 236, 237, 238, 244, 281, 286, 289, 292, 294.

Terrorism, 160, 163.

Trade Routes, 144, 148.

Troubled Waters, 77, 151.

W

Water Wars, 71.

❑❑❑